T0186401

The Insider's Guide
to Outsourcing Risks
and Rewards

OTHER AUERBACH PUBLICATIONS

Agent-Based Manufacturing and Control Systems: New Agile Manufacturing Solutions for Achieving Peak Performance
Massimo Paolucci and Roberto Sacile
ISBN: 1574443364

Curing the Patch Management Headache
Felicia M. Nicastro
ISBN: 0849328543

Cyber Crime Investigator's Field Guide, Second Edition
Bruce Middleton
ISBN: 0849327687

Disassembly Modeling for Assembly, Maintenance, Reuse and Recycling
A. J. D. Lambert and Surendra M. Gupta
ISBN: 1574443348

The Ethical Hack: A Framework for Business Value Penetration Testing
James S. Tiller
ISBN: 084931609X

Fundamentals of DSL Technology
Philip Golden, Herve Dedieu,
and Krista Jacobsen
ISBN: 0849319137

The HIPAA Program Reference Handbook
Ross Leo
ISBN: 0849322111

Implementing the IT Balanced Scorecard: Aligning IT with Corporate Strategy
Jessica Keyes
ISBN: 0849326214

Information Security Fundamentals
Thomas R. Peltier, Justin Peltier,
and John A. Blackley
ISBN: 0849319579

Information Security Management Handbook, Fifth Edition, Volume 2
Harold F. Tipton and Micki Krause
ISBN: 0849332109

Introduction to Management of Reverse Logistics and Closed Loop Supply Chain Processes
Donald F. Blumberg
ISBN: 1574443607

Maximizing ROI on Software Development
Vijay Sikka

Mobile Computing Handbook
Imad Mahgoub and Mohammad Ilyas
ISBN: 0849319714

MPLS for Metropolitan Area Networks
Nam-Kee Tan
ISBN: 084932212X

Multimedia Security Handbook
Borko Furht and Darko Kirovski
ISBN: 0849327733

Network Design: Management and Technical Perspectives, Second Edition
Teresa C. Piliouras
ISBN: 0849316081

Network Security Technologies, Second Edition
Kwok T. Fung
ISBN: 0849330270

Outsourcing Software Development Offshore: Making It Work
Tandy Gold
ISBN: 0849319439

Quality Management Systems: A Handbook for Product Development Organizations
Vivek Nanda
ISBN: 1574443526

A Practical Guide to Security Assessments
Sudhanshu Kairab
ISBN: 0849317061

The Real-Time Enterprise
Dimitris N. Chorafas
ISBN: 0849327776

Software Testing and Continuous Quality Improvement, Second Edition
William E. Lewis
ISBN: 0849325242

Supply Chain Architecture: A Blueprint for Networking the Flow of Material, Information, and Cash
William T. Walker
ISBN: 1574443577

The Windows Serial Port Programming Handbook

The Insider's Guide
to Outsourcing Risks
and Rewards

Johann Rost

CRC Press
Taylor & Francis Group
Boca Raton London New York

CRC Press is an imprint of the
Taylor & Francis Group, an **informa** business
AN AUERBACH BOOK

AU7017_Discl.fm Page 1 Tuesday, March 7, 2006 1:07 PM

First published 2006 by Aurbach Publications

Published 2019 by CRC Press
Taylor & Francis Group
6000 Broken Sound Parkway NW, Suite 300
Boca Raton, FL 33487-2742

© 2006 by Taylor & Francis Group, LLC
CRC Press is an imprint of Taylor & Francis Group, an Informa business

First issued in paperback 2019

No claim to original U.S. Government works

ISBN 13: 978-0-367-45364-0 (pbk)
ISBN 13: 978-0-8493-7017-5 (hbk)

This book contains information obtained from authentic and highly regarded sources. Reasonable efforts have been made to publish reliable data and information, but the author and publisher cannot assume responsibility for the validity of all materials or the consequences of their use. The authors and publishers have attempted to trace the copyright holders of all material reproduced in this publication and apologize to copyright holders if permission to publish in this form has not been obtained. If any copyright material has not been acknowledged please write and let us know so we may rectify in any future reprint.

Except as permitted under U.S. Copyright Law, no part of this book may be reprinted, reproduced, transmitted, or utilized in any form by any electronic, mechanical, or other means, now known or hereafter invented, including photocopying, microfilming, and recording, or in any information storage or retrieval system, without written permission from the publishers.

For permission to photocopy or use material electronically from this work, please access www.copyright.com (http://www.copyright.com/) or contact the Copyright Clearance Center, Inc. (CCC), 222 Rosewood Drive, Danvers, MA 01923, 978-750-8400. CCC is a not-for-profit organization that provides licenses and registration for a variety of users. For organizations that have been granted a photocopy license by the CCC, a separate system of payment has been arranged.

Trademark Notice: Product or corporate names may be trademarks or registered trademarks, and are used only for identification and explanation without intent to infringe.

**Visit the Taylor & Francis Web site at
http://www.taylorandfrancis.com**

**and the CRC Press Web site at
http://www.crcpress.com**

Library of Congress Cataloging-in-Publication Data

Rost, Johann.
   The insider's guide to outsourcing risks and rewards / Johann Rost.
       p. cm.
   Includes bibliographical references and index.
   ISBN 0-8493-7017-5 (alk. paper)
   1. Offshore outsourcing. I. Title.

CONTENTS

ANNOTATED CONTENTS

This introductory chapter includes sections about best practices, myths, and risks, along with a checklist and a glossary. It provides many entry points and references to other chapters of the book where specific issues are analyzed in more detail.

First-timers in offshore business have much to learn. This section lists some myths that are commonly believed by inexperienced buyers and that have even appeared in some published articles.

Some best practices have been successful in a number of projects and according to the experience of the author. Notice, however, that best practices are guidelines — not a panacea. More important than understanding the "how-to-do-it" is understanding the "what-can-go-wrong" when dealing with best practices.

Many hazards exist in offshore outsourcing. That is what the entire book is about: making responsible managers aware of what can go wrong and what steps could be considered to mitigate these risks. This section highlights some particularly frequent challenges and references the reader to the chapters and sections where the issues are analyzed in more detail.

The following checklist provides a number of questions that can

*At the time when this book was written, widely accepted hard
numbers were difficult to find. Many organizations that submitted such numbers had vested interests to influence the public
opinion about global sourcing in one or the other direction. This
might explain why even numbers submitted by governmental
statistical institutions exhibited huge differences, depending on
which government controlled the respective institution.*

*Another reason for not including extensive surveys and stud-
ies in this book is that the numbers from these studies become
outdated rather quickly. In particular, "expert prognoses" that
refer to the future are prone to require "corrections" soon after
they are published. Thus, only a few selected numbers and expert
opinions that are currently under discussion are presented here.*

*Offshore outsourcing has developed its own vocabulary. This
section provides a concise overview of the terms used and includes
references to the chapters where these concepts are explained in
more detail.*

2   Drivers 19

The potential cost reduction is a compelling argument in favor
of offshore scenarios for many companies. Due to its dominant
role in a considerable a number of offshore projects, an entire
chapter of this book, Chapter 3, is dedicated to cost aspects.

In addition to the obvious financial motivation of cost reduction, commercial (strategic) or technological issues might be
taken into consideration, such as:

- Efforts to acquire and maintain IT know-how
- Access to scarce talent
- Additional flexibility
- Focus on core activities

*Gaining access to leading-edge technology may be an important
reason for considering an outsourcing scenario. In many cases
the customer wants to outsource the IT-specific know-how,
although the domain expertise and business know-how should
remain in house. A technologically strong vendor specialized in*

An advantage of outsourcing is that the buyer gains a certain degree of flexibility: staff must be paid only as long as needed. To some extent fixed costs are turned into variable costs. The validity of this outsourcing advantage must be questioned, how-ever, and assessed in the particular scenario at hand; the cus-tomer is frequently keen on staff stability on the vendor's side. Continuity of staff in the context of cost efficiency requires a certain degree of continuity of orders.

The outsourcing relationship allows the customer to focus on its core activities. The other side of the coin is a higher dependency on the external vendor providing crucial IT services.

Many of the published success stories of offshore outsourcing refer to rather large organizations — say, those with at least 50 in-house IT staff. Small organizations have access to offshore outsourcing as well, but they need more creative solutions.

Technological, commercial, or financial drivers may play a role when designing offshore plans. Depending on the degree of pri-ority assigned to each of these factors, the outsourcing scenario will look completely different. For this reason it is of foremost importance that the customer fully understand its motivations and establish its priorities.

American and Western European companies receive offers for software development from emerging countries such as China, India, and Eastern European nations almost every day. Some-times the prices put forward are as low as 25 percent of the price offered by onshore providers for the same services — in extreme cases, even below this rate. These numbers suggest that cost reductions of at least three quarters should be expected if software projects are outsourced to offshore vendors. Never-theless, most case studies report savings of only 15 to 30 percent. Even these considerably smaller savings are achieved only after the offshore relationship has been established and the cooperation has found its rhythm; the first few projects frequently involve no savings at all and sometimes entail even higher costs than in the case of onshore workers. This raises

communication costs led to reduced communication and consequently to compromised management quality.

can have a serious impact on the customer's business continuity. Some countries are more prone to political instabilities or disasters and others are less vulnerable. If emergency situations are likely to occur, the customer might want to establish a disaster recovery plan.

Partners from at least two countries contribute to the offshore scenario. The responsible managers should have some basic knowledge about these countries. This information has to come from reliable sources; otherwise, it is useless or even harmful. The governments of the developing country or institutions closely related to the government are not necessarily the best sources in this instance because they are likely to make biased statements; most governments throughout the world are vying for foreign investors because such investors are highly attractive for their countries' economy. For obvious reasons, a government might be tempted to paint its country's image in exaggeratedly bright colors. Thus it might be better to enlist the help and common-sense expertise of independent sources. Foreigners who have who have worked in the country's software industry could be reliable advisers. Organizations that provide ratings of the investment climate in various countries are another source of information.

This chapter provides a checklist of what should be known about the countries and companies involved. Some items might not be answered, but others might have limited relevance for the offshore scenario at hand. Some of the questions could have an obvious answer for some managers but not for other members of the offshore relationship. The questions offer some guidance for further investigation and may help prospective participants in an offshore relationship avoid potentially costly information deficiencies. The checklist identifies items that may qualify as truisms in industrialized countries but are not to be taken for granted when it comes to developing nations — e.g., continuous supply of electricity, telecommunication, and Internet access.

4.1   Importance of Background Information about the Contributing

about their future partners. This background information is necessary to cross-check the calculation made on an offer. It helps executives anticipate risks that might arise in future projects and find possible mitigations. It may even provide some essential information that might lead to the cancellation of future cooperation before it has actually started. One reason for canceling the cooperation might be that there is no acceptable solution for the anticipated risks: sometimes it is better not to start cooperation at all rather than to have it end in a fiasco.

The political situation in the offshore country can greatly influence the long-term success of the offshore scenario. Political instability or territorial conflicts might lead to war, which makes business virtually impossible. Potential natural disasters are other reasons for an emergency plan. There are huge differences in the way foreign managers perceive the level of security in everyday life in emerging countries. If personal freedom or human rights are overly restricted, a smooth work flow may become impossible.

Cost efficiency is a prime issue in most offshore scenarios. This is why potential investors should know some basic economic facts about the emerging country, including average income, cost of living, and prices for office space and other real estate. Taxes are important, and the prognosis for labor cost influences the long-term feasibility of the offshore relationship.

The executives of all contributing companies need a basic understanding of the legal systems in the other countries involved. There are huge differences in the practical aspects of legal systems in emerging countries and in industrialized countries. In practice, the differences are even larger than the study of the published laws may suggest.

It's all about relationships in outsourcing business. The first decisions for the emerging relationship are already made before its actual onset at the time when the customer selects a vendor and the two parties negotiate the outsourcing contract. This

establishing the relationship. The customer's first step is defining
the vendor selection criteria and clarifying the motivations for
the outsourcing decision: financial, technical, or commercial.
After both sides have elicited reliable information, the exact
stipulations of the contract can be negotiated. Once the outsourcing scenario is established, the customer must manage the
vendor and oversee the work of the offshore team. When the
cooperation gains speed, it is quite likely that sooner or later
disputes about technical or contractual issues will appear. Litigation is almost always the worst solution. Therefore, many
outsourcing contracts include a dispute resolution procedure,
which usually starts with forwarding the conflict in a predefined
way to higher management. If the issue remains unsolved, the
partner can apply mediation or arbitration in an attempt to find
a mutually acceptable settlement before taking the ultimate step
of going to court.

One widely applied method of government and vendor
management is benchmark audits; an independent third party
provider of benchmarking services helps to analyze the relationship and evaluates the vendor's performance by comparing
it to that of peer companies. The benchmark study should
determine whether the service level still matches the state of
the art and whether the prices are appropriate and the contractual provisions are fair. The benchmark report may conclude
that the vendor has to solve any identified problems within a
reasonable time period or that the fees need adaptation. Benchmark clauses are adopted in many outsourcing contracts. For
the customer, they are a way to keep the vendor honest. A
successful benchmark audit can increase customer satisfaction
and thus improve the customer–vendor relationship.

In scenarios where the customer works with a single provider, this vendor can gain undue influence because of its
monopoly position. Some customers try to avoid these problems
by working with more than one vendor in parallel. Such so-
called "multisourcing" scenarios can have a number of advantages because they introduce a competitive element. However,
coordinating multiple vendors who are competitors on the
market creates other challenges and requires advanced skills in

*Vendor selection and negotiation of the outsourcing contract are
major items on the list of costs in the process of establishing the
outsourcing relationship. However, it is possible to save costs by
applying a well-defined, carefully considered, and structured
process evolving from the first informal discussion to the signed
contract in a systematic way.*

*Any outsourcing relationship (not only offshore) is based on trust.
Before the customer can enter this relationship, it has to do some
due diligence and collect some basic data about the future partner:*

■ *Cost reductions are a strong motivation in many offshore
  scenarios. If the vendor is overly cheap, this may be a indication of economic instability, which is against the best interests of the customer.*
■ *Because the vendor's team is part of the customer's extended
  enterprise, the buyer has to validate the qualifications of the
  offshore workers. A particular problem of teams in emerging
  software industries is the worryingly high attrition numbers.*
■ *Many customers ask for references from the vendor to evaluate its reputation in the market. However, reading and
  interpreting recommendations requires experience and a
  good deal of skepticism.*
■ *Most offshore scenarios are designed for long periods of time.
  For this reason, many analysts suggest that synergy of strategic goals is necessary.*
■ *Security is a particularly important issue in offshore scenarios. The customer needs to ensure that the future partner's
  security measures reach the necessary standards.*

*In many scenarios it can prove difficult to elicit reliable and
complete information regarding the listed items. The vendors
might have good reasons to disclose only part of the required
information or give misleading or even false information.*

*Like customers, vendors need information about their prospective
partners. The offshore team should have a profound understanding of the client's business culture and the values promoted by
the buyer's organization — i.e., how things are done at the
customer's site. The differences in labor costs are a key motivation*

The buyer is well advised to implement strong and cautious management, carried out by people who fully understand the content and strategic goal of the outsourcing deal, oversee the work of the offshore team, and manage the relationship. This steering committee constitutes an interface to the offshore team, facilitates dispute resolution, and serves as an internal advocate of the offshore scenario.

In many practical cases, it turns out that overseeing the work of an offshore team is no easier than developing the software in house. The customer's team usually needs additional training to deal with the challenges of remote project management.

During the long term of an offshore cooperation, it is quite likely that disputes about technical and contractual issues will appear. Frequently, litigation is the last and least desirable option. For this reason, many offshore contracts provide for a set of procedures for conflict resolution that defines a way in which the partners can express their concerns and search for a mutually accepted solution without resorting to costly litigation. This so-called escalation procedure includes alternative dispute resolution (ADR) and a reasonable number of preliminary levels before the ultimate step of legal action.

During a benchmark study the service levels and prices of the deal are compared to the conditions of the vendor's peer companies. Usually an independent third party, the benchmark provider, carries out the audit. A successful benchmark requires careful preparation, which starts with defining the scope of the audit and eliciting the necessary raw data during a monitoring period. Some contracts provide an automatic adaptation of the prices as a consequence of the audit. In other relationships, the results are used as a basis for discussion without immediate legally binding consequences.

Not all analysts agree on the methodological reliability of a benchmark audit. Some object that most IT projects are unique and not really amenable to a like-to-like comparison. Another objection is that the quality of the relationship can hardly be measured by means of normalized comparison.

are important. However, other viewpoints should be considered as well, including those of:

- The developers in the emerging country — who are working for relatively low pay
- Onshore technical staff — many of whom will probably lose their jobs
- Offshore managers and entrepreneurs — who might face conflicting interests
- Envoys of Western companies — who have to work temporarily or permanently in emerging countries
- Offshore liaisons — who are visiting the customer's office in the industrialized country

All these groups have a say in and an important contribution to the success of the offshore cooperation. These stakeholders can have secret plans for the future, which may not necessarily be in line with the contract. Only rarely do the other parties involved consider these plans "fair."

experience have many options both in the emerging country and abroad.

Some offshore business models require that managers and technical staff temporarily or permanently relocate to the developing country — e.g., as customer's representatives. These so-called envoys take an important role in the communication mechanisms of the offshore relationship.

In developing countries, costs of living are usually lower. However, if the envoy wants to keep up Western living standards, the cost of living might be even higher than in industrialized countries. As compared to the low per capita income in the developing country, the envoy is considered rather well-off; such individuals are attractive targets for crimes with economic motivations.

Liaisons are employees of the offshore vendor who work for a certain time at the customer's site (see also Section 7.4). In many offshore scenarios, liaisons facilitate international communication and narrow cultural gaps. The liaison usually bears a lot of responsibility within the project. For this reason, these people are very qualified and carefully selected — which makes them particularly attractive to headhunters.

A possible conflict of interest arises if the offshore worker wants to use the liaison role as a base for starting a software business.

Due to the liaison's large influence in the project, the customer might be tempted to corrupt the liaison to gain undue advantages, apart from the "officially" negotiated ones.

Establishing an offshore scenario requires much background information about the contributing countries and about IT outsourcing management. Some specialized consulting companies offer this know-how and can help the customer find a qualified vendor and establish the relationship

Some offshore scenarios enlist the help of specialized companies consisting of offshore professionals to establish the cooperation. The advisers working for these companies are experts in the offshore outsourcing of IT projects. They are well acquainted with the state of affairs in both countries, they are sufficiently knowledgeable on software technology and contracts, and they maintain

Analysis of offshore scenarios has shown that only a limited number of business architectures turn out to be successful in practice. Some business models that are successful on domestic markets may fail in an offshore scenario. Two aspects should be considered when establishing which business model is reasonable in a given offshore scenario: the projects' characteristics and the consequential damages if the project fails.

Costs for communication can be high in offshore scenarios, and management quality can seriously suffer as a consequence of lack of quality communication. Many analysts consider these facts among the prime reasons for failing offshore scenarios. For this reason, the business architecture has to address communication cost from the very onset. Following is a Business Models Overview.

Another factor that influences the business model is the size of the contributing units: although most published case studies refer to large customers, small clients often have to find more creative solutions.

Important business models that are frequently applied in off-shore outsourcing are onsite offshoring, body leasing, agencies, and subcontracting (daisy chains). The so-called follow-the-sun model is used in help desk management where 24/7 availability is required.

Some specific factors have to be considered when designing the business architecture of an offshore scenario. The business architecture should take into account the high startup cost of the offshore relationship and the precious know-how that needs protection. Some business models, such as foreign subsidiaries, require much information on the countries involved and professional background on software projects. For the customer, it is wise to carefully analyze whether this know-how is available in its organization.

A major challenge for offshore software projects is the unavoidable long-distance communication. If this problem is not solved in a satisfactory manner, the communication costs are likely to take up most of the potential cost savings. For this reason the business architecture should be designed so that communication is minimized. (See Section 3.3.)

In general it is more cost efficient to outsource an entire project — not parts of a project, i.e., modules. In addition outsourcing only some phases (like implementation or test) causes higher costs than outsourcing the entire life cycle of the project. The staff at the offshore site should have enough competence and ownership to assume responsibility for the entire product — i.e., for the final result. Otherwise, the project may fail because noone is truly responsible for the outcome, i.e., for the success of the project in its entirety. A rule of thumb says: Outsource entire things (not parts) for their entire life span and make the offshore site accountable for the overall result. In many offshore scenarios this rule leads to acceptable costs of communication.

The following tactical approaches can help reduce the cost of communication as well as the cultural distance.

*sourcing. In this way the unduly strong monopoly position of the
sole vendor is broken, and competition can put the outsourcing
scenario in motion. Multi-sourcing, however, requires advanced
skills in both management of the multiple vendors and IT politics.*

Certain types of projects can be transferred offshore more easily
than others can. For this reason, the selection of suitable projects
is a crucial success factor for an offshore scenario. The category
of projects that can be outsourced advantageously includes short
projects and routine work–based projects. In projects that
require very specific know-how, outsourcing can lead to considerable advantages. It is generally easier to outsource entire
projects than parts. Highly iterative processes such as "eXtreme
Programming" require specific business architectures to be
accessible for offshore outsourcing. More obstacles have been
reported within projects that fall into one of these categories:

- Projects with high risks of consequential damages in case
  of failure
- Projects that include confidential intellectual property or
  technologies that are covered by export restrictions —
  e.g., military projects
- Innovative products that require much interaction
  between the software team and domain experts or management
- Projects that require a high degree of security

*Less challenging projects, routine work, and short projects are
easily accessible to offshore outsourcing. Thus, these projects are
a frequent entry point into an offshore relationship.*

*Some specific technical problems can be very easy to solve for
someone who already did this work but extremely time-consuming for someone who is green in the field and has who must first
learn the technology. Therefore, outsourcing the solution to specific technological problems can be a major advantage.*

The contracts used in outsourcing business can be roughly grouped in three categories.

1. *Fixed-price contracts.* An estimate of the workload is prepared in advance, and the contract partners agree on a fixed amount of money for the entire project.
2. *Unit-price contracts.* The contract sets a certain sum to be paid per hour of actual working time.
3. *Service agreements.* The provider substitutes for the cus-tomer's internal IT department for a certain period of time. The contract specifies the vendor's duties and the monthly fees

is followed by a guarantee period during which reported failures must be repaired without additional payment.

Requirements are usually developed in several steps that provide an increasing level of detail: the Product Vision Statement, the Concept of Operations (CONOPS), and one or more detailed Software Requirements Specifications (SRS). Before the CONOPS is agreed upon, the project is considered to be in the "brainstorming phase." In this phase many projects are likely to undergo fundamental changes regarding the feature set and the volume of investments. Quite a number of projects are cancelled before they reach the phase of detailed specification.

Frequently, the vendor has to contribute in one way or another to the requirements phase. In some outsourcing scenarios, the partners start discussing technical aspects even before the contract is completely negotiated and signed. This practice raises two important issues:

1. How is the vendor's precontractual investment protected?
2. How is the confidentiality of the requirements ensured?

In a fixed-price contract, the partners agree in advance on a certain price for a specified project. The requirements must be rather well specified in advance and in written form because they form the basis of cost estimation. For customers, the fixed-price contract has the advantage that it provides prior information on how much the project will cost. In practice, however, this apparently firm base of calculation must be questioned because most software projects require changes and extensions even before the first version is delivered. These changes add to the price. In extreme cases the final price can be double the initially agreed-on fixed price — or even higher.

The "acceptance" is an important milestone in the life cycle of a software project because it triggers the start of the guarantee period. In addition, the payment for the project must be made at this stage — at least a significant part of it.

A specific problem that might arise in fixed-price contracts is cancellation. Unless the contract includes a carefully drafted clause, the customer can only cancel the project with high losses.

does not limit the budget for the contract. Because a limited project budget is of vital importance for most buyers, unit-price contracts frequently include upper limits, ensuring that the project will be finished within this budget.

Unless the contract provides something else, the maintenance of a unit-price project is paid for separately. This is at the very least a nuisance for the customer because it has to pay the vendor for repairing its own faults. In some cases the maintenance can significantly increase the costs of the project.

Because the customer has to pay for each working hour, it has an interest in making sure that the reported hours have really been used for its project. Verification of the reported hours is a particular issue if the vendor is offshore.

The purpose of the guarantee period is to provide the customer with the right to free-of-charge repair of defects discovered after the project has been delivered. Although the guarantee period is an important part of most contracts, some issues require further in-depth consideration.

There will usually be a delay between the error report and the corrected version. The customer would like to obtain the corrections as fast as possible. In practice, however, this is not always possible.

Some defects require that a service engineer come to the user's site and analyze the problem there. The costs for travel are usually much higher than the few working hours spent correcting the error. If this is an issue, the contract should provide how such costs are handled.

Repairing reported faults is much more efficient if the failure is reproducible on the developer's computer— i.e., if the developer has a known procedure that always shows the reported wrong behavior. Mature defect reports, however, require additional efforts on the side of the user. A particularly challenging class of defects is "transient defects" — i.e. failures that occur only sporadically, even if the same sequence of operations is performed on the same computer. Resolving defects of this class can be very costly. Thus, the contract should include stipulations in case the project is prone to this class of errors.

In some cases it may be debatable whether a reported behavior is in fact a failure or if it is a desirable feature. Many of these potential disputes are clarified in style guides, which specify in

> *Repairing the defect is only one step. Delivery of the corrected version causes additional costs. In general, not each fixed problem justifies a new version.*
>
> *Software does not wear out over time. All failures that are identified afterwards are already present in the software at the time of delivery. In some countries, legislation does not cover this case adequately, and it might be necessary to make clear that these are not "latent defects" — otherwise, the guarantee period for software would never end.*

> *In many software projects the responsibility for source code (in jargon called "ownership") is transferred during the life cycle of a software project. Prior to a certain date, a certain team "owns" the source code; after that date, another team is responsible for it. Notice that in this context "ownership" is equivalent to responsibility and does not hint at the notion of ownership in a legal sense.*
>
> *One example where transfer of ownership is necessary is the guarantee period: before the guarantee period ends, the vendor is accountable; afterward the customer is responsible (unless the contract provides otherwise). Transfer of ownership can entail difficult defect responsibility issues.*

> *A service level agreement usually includes the following parts (among others):*
>
> ■ *Contract terms — How long is the contract valid?*
> ■ *Scope of services. What exactly are the vendor's duties?*
> ■ *Service Level Agreement (SLA). A detailed specification of the quality of provider services (e.g., response time).*

10 Industrial Espionage 213

Confidential assets benefit from little legal protection in emerging countries. In this chapter, an introductory case study shows how easy it was for a Pakistani clerical worker to threaten a prestigious American hospital with publishing their confidential patient files on the Internet. Ultimately, the Pakistani worker could not even be sentenced for what she had done.

Potential targets of industrial espionage include data, source

of the vendor, professional industrial spies, criminal attacks against the vendor (e.g., forced entry into the office building), and vendors who are also working for the customer's competitors.

Protection against espionage includes tight monitoring of human resources and understanding of the legal systems of the countries involved — to provide the necessary deterrence of adequate punishment in case the attacker is caught. Despite all precautions, watertight protection of confidential material in developing countries has been difficult, at least so far. For this reason, the customer has to assess carefully which risks its organization can afford and whether the cost advantage justifies the risk.

■ *The protected data is placed on a server that can be accessed by offshore staff, either foreign engineers who gain access to the server password in an unauthorized way or developers*

■ *Workers in emerging countries are rather poor and thus more tempted to take up unserious offers. Although many customers have some lines of defense in place against external attacks, the defense against attacks from inside is frequently rather poor. Throughout the offshore cooperation, foreign staff can gain the status of insiders. In this case it may be ridiculously easy for the offshore developer to break the lines of defense that were supposed to protect against "attacks from inside."*

■ *Some offshore vendors subcontract part of the work to other countries where the salaries are even lower — and so is the reliability of workers.*

■ *Another category of unreliable workers is spies in software teams who get employed from the very beginning for the main purpose of stealing confidential information.*

■ *A special kind of espionage strategy is that of "intentional security vulnerabilities" — fragments of code that are included in legitimate software allowing unauthorized access to classified information (e.g., "backdoors" and "Trojan horses").*

■ *Security in emerging countries frequently fails to meet the standards of industrialized nations. Unless the vendor's office building is under permanent surveillance, it is quite likely that sooner or later forced entries will be reported. Other potential security gaps include the vendor's networks.*

■ *Vendors who are also working for competitors constitute a particular danger for confidential information. In extreme cases, the competitor could even buy the vendor's organization.*

Careful preparation of lines of defense and tight monitoring of human resources can greatly improve the security of confidential material. Another important solution is severe punishment if the attacker is captured. Nevertheless, the protection of confidential material in emerging countries does not reach the high standards level that it does in industrialized countries. For this reason, the customer has to assess carefully which risks to take.

Only a few outsourcing scenarios continue indefinitely. All others end sooner or later; they are limited to one or more projects, or they are designed for a certain period of coopera-

important, of course. Experience shows, however, that contractual provisions alone are not enough to meet the requirement of business continuity after finishing the outsourcing relationship. The exit plan must also include careful management of in-house know-how and practical business decisions, e.g., maintaining leadership in essential business relationships.

These conditions seem obvious; nevertheless, they cannot always be taken for granted in practice. In many outsourcing relationships, the customer's dependency on the vendor constantly grows until it reaches an extent where the customer cannot go on anymore without the vendor. In this case the customer cannot easily escape this binding relationship — even if it is not necessarily legally binding and the contract includes provisions for termination of the cooperation.

If the buyer is not really in a position to end the relationship, this vulnerability might turn to its disadvantage in time; the vendor might change its pricing strategy or decrease its service level.

A recent poll shows that it is anything but rare that IT services have to be brought back in house (see Figure 11.1).

11.1 Contractual Stipulations 252

Most contracts allow termination due to breach of material obligation. Termination for convenience allows the customer to end the contract without any reason whatsoever, paying a fee agreed upon in advance. Some contracts include other reasons for termination — e.g., in case of insolvency or if the vendor leaves the business. Contractual provisions are important if the customer wants to terminate the contract. Additional practical preparations, however, are necessary to provide business continuity.

11.2 Vendors Forestall the Departure of a Customer 256

The vendor has good reasons to build up a strong position with the customer and thus increase the customer's dependency on its services:

■ *The vendor wants to receive additional orders from that customer in the future.*
■ *The vendor tries to keep the client away from potential competitors. During the time of the contract, the vendor will take*

from one vendor to a competitor. These obstacles help the provider consolidate its position with this client.

A customer who wants to switch from one vendor to another will encounter a transition problem that includes:

- *The necessary transfer of know-how from the old vendor's staff to the new vendor's staff*
- *Access to technical documentation, intellectual property, source code, and other deliverables*
- *Leadership in business relationships*
- *The posttermination assistance might turn out to be inefficient because the relationship is strained and the vendor is uncooperative.*

PREFACE

HOW TO READ THIS BOOK

The chapters and sections of this book are independent and can be read in any sequence. The Annotated Contents provides an entry point. Readers who cannot afford the time to read cover to cover may want to skim through the introductory abstracts and then read more details in particular chapters and sections.

Other such entry points are the sections on myths, best practices, and risks and the checklist. These sections contain lists of short statements and references to where these statements are analyzed in more detail.

I have included numerous anecdotes in the text, most of which are based on actual projects. However, details have been modified to avoid the possibility of tracing them back to real persons and organizations. The names in the anecdotes are taken from my imagination. If a name matches an existing person or organization, it is pure coincidence, not intention.

At the beginning of each chapter and each chapter section, there are introductory abstracts meant to summarize the main statements. The index should be used to look up keywords with a rather narrow or "crisp" meaning — such as "stalking horse" or "RFP." It is not recommended to search the index for broad keywords like "relation" or "cost" — because the entire book is about relations or costs. Searching for such broad topics is better done in the Annotated Contents or in the sections of Chapter 1, which contain many cross-references. These sections are organized according to the logical relationship between the respective issues, not just according to alphabetical order. I have tried to include only statements that can be backed up by my own experience. This approach bears the

Many topics discussed in this book are valid for onshore consulting firms as well, not just for offshore scenarios.

I am writing observations from my own experience. The book does not provide tax or legal advice.

HOW I DECIDED TO WRITE THIS BOOK

A German company considered starting an offshore scenario. I had known the customer previously — my company had developed a few fixed-price projects for them. This time, however, was different; the entrepreneur asked for consultation regarding the envisioned offshore scenario.

The company did not share many details before the consultation meetings — so I could not prepare very much in advance. With empty hands, I came to the meetings with the entrepreneur (alone). He asked a number of questions and I told him my honest opinion about how things are done in this business over there. One second I thought I was dreaming: the chief executive officer (CEO) was sitting at the desk like a student, listening carefully and taking many notes. Hours!

On the flight back I reviewed my experience, asking myself what just happened? After all, this entrepreneur is an important man. His software department alone employs more than 100 engineers. If my experiences are so interesting to this influential man, it is quite likely that they are worthwhile reading for others as well — when they are well arranged in chapters and sections.

Johann Rost

ACKNOWLEDGMENTS

The author wishes to thank Robert L. Glass, Karl Jessenk, Thomas Ondrak, and Alina C. Pohrib for their helpful remarks on an earlier version of the manuscript.

ABOUT THE AUTHOR

Johann Rost, Ph.D. has worked in the software industry as a consultant, software developer, technical leader, software manager, and entrepreneur for 18 years. He spent about half of this time offshore in Romania. He received his doctorate in computer science from the University at Paderborn, Germany. Currently he is teaching information systems at the University Politehnica in Bucharest, Romania and providing consultancy for software projects, both onshore and offshore. Contact him at johann_rost@yahoo.com.

1

INTRODUCTION

ABSTRACT

This introductory chapter includes sections about best practices, myths, and risks, along with a checklist and a section with a definition of terms. It provides many entry points and references to other chapters of the book where specific issues are analyzed in more detail.

1.1 MYTHS ABOUT OFFSHORE OUTSOURCING

First-timers in offshore business have much to learn. This section lists some myths that are commonly believed by inexperienced buyers and that have even appeared in some published articles.

Myth: Outsourcing leads to immediate cost savings.

Reality: The first offshore project carried through by an inexperienced buyer rarely leads to any cost savings at all; in most instances, it leads to higher cost instead. (See Chapter 3, in particular Section 3.2.)

Myth: The cost savings at the beginning of the contract are valid for the entire term.

Reality: Some vendors offer "back-loaded" contracts that lead to unrealistically high savings at the beginning of the contract. The savings are balanced by rather high costs towards the end of the term. This kind of financial engineering allows the responsible manager on the customer's side to report immediate high savings. The so-called cost

2 ■ The Insider's Guide to Outsourcing Risks and Rewards

Myth: If the salaries in a developing country are 80 percent lower than in an industrialized country, one should expect cost savings of 80 percent.
Reality: Only a few case studies report cost reductions higher than about 15 to 30 percent. (See Chapter 3, in particular Section 3.1.)

Myth: "Best practices" are the best you can do in offshore projects.
Reality: More important than understanding the "how-to-do-it" is understanding the "what-can-go-wrong." (See Section 1.2 and Section 1.3.)

Myth: Following "best practices" leads to cost savings.
Reality: Most so-called best practices have been successfully applied in certain types of offshore scenarios but have failed in others. (See Section 1.2.)

Myth: The customer is the stronger party in an offshore scenario.
Reality: Large vendors have carried out hundreds of projects, and their experience includes tens of thousands of hours at the negotiation table. Many of their customers are first-timers in that field. Thus, the vendor usually has a much clearer vision of how the relationship will develop. (See Section 5.1.)

Myth: An offshore deal is a turn-key agreement.
Reality: Businesspeople who have been involved in successful offshore deals report that governing the ongoing offshore project entails more investments than starting the offshore scenario does. (See Section 5.4.)

Myth: Fixed-price projects have a fixed price.
Reality: Most projects require changes and extensions even before the first version is installed. These changes involve extra payment. The extensions often constitute a significant fraction of the initial price — in some cases even more. (See Section 9.2.)

Myth: Top-tier providers in India are the only options.
Reality: Local wages will increase as the country progresses. The provider might have a secret pricing strategy for the future; some of the most mature offshore vendors have already started asking why the

Reality: It is very difficult to end a relationship with an outsourcer once the vendor is involved in projects of strategic importance for the buyer. This can be thought of as the "Golden Rule of Outsourcing." Some providers are aware of this fact and incorporate it into their pricing strategy: they start rather cheap — with "price-to-win." When the relationship reaches the point at which the buyer cannot get out easily, they increase the margins. That is why the rule is called "Golden." (See Chapter 11.)

Myth: Offshore outsourcing is a win–win situation.

Reality: In many respects buyer and vendor have conflicting interests, preventing the scenario from being a win–win game. (See Section 6.2.)

1.2 BEST PRACTICES

Some best practices have been successful in a number of projects and according to the experience of the author. Notice, however, that best practices are guidelines — not a panacea. More important than understanding the "how-to-do-it" is understanding the "what-can-go-wrong" when dealing with best practices.

1.2.1 Fixed-Price Contracts

Many customers prefer fixed-price contracts because the client knows in advance how much the project will cost. Fixed-price contracts need detailed specification of requirements before the implementation starts; otherwise, no reasonable cost estimation is possible. However, even if fixed-price contracts provide more control of the cost than other contract types do, the price is nowhere near as "fixed" as the customer would like it to be. (See Section 9.2.)

1.2.2 Cost Estimation

Realistic estimation of cost includes cost for transferring the information technology (IT) offshore, cost for additional communication, risk reserve, and budget for terminating the contract with the vendor. Costs in offshore countries are changing over time. Salaries have been steadily increasing in recent years, and further growth can be expected. (See Chapter 3 and Chapter 11.)

and envoys. Outsource entire entities for their entire lifespan. (See Section 3.3.)

1.2.4 Changed Business Requirements

Changed business requirements may demand much decreased or radically changed IT services. In this case another vendor might offer more advantages. For this reason savvy buyers take into consideration that the relationship might end one day. (See Chapter 11.)

1.2.5 Plan for Divorce

It is difficult to terminate a relationship with an outsourcer once the provider is involved in projects of strategic importance for the customer. Prepare for a plan of terminating the offshore scenario if necessary and how business continuity will be provided for after the relationship has been terminated. (See Chapter 11.)

1.2.6 Assess Your Demand for Information

First-time customers have a great deal to learn about offshore business. Find out what you know, what you do not know, and what you ought to know. Find out whether what you know is correct or incorrect. (See Chapter 4 and Section 1.4, Section 5.1, and Section 5.2.)

1.2.7 Start an Offshore Scenario Slowly and Be Risk Sensitive

Use pilot projects. If it is not necessary to make a decision then it is necessary to make no decision.

1.2.8 Governance Is More Important than Vendor Selection

Implement a steering committee that oversees the work of the vendor. Provide enough resources for governance. The size of the in-house steering committee should be about 10 percent of the outsourced project size. (See Section 5.4.)

1.2.9 Internal Communication and Backlash

AU7017_book.fm Page 5 Thursday, March 16, 2006 5:07 PM

of communication is convincing only if it is combined with realistic career paths. (See Section 6.5.)

1.2.10 Outsource Entire Projects for Their Entire Life Cycle and Make the Offshore Site Accountable for the Overall Result

Outsourcing only parts of a project (e.g., some modules or only specific phases) causes much higher communication costs. (See Section 8.3 and Section 8.4.)

1.2.11 Look for Ways to Keep the Vendor Honest in the Long Run

One of the strongest management instruments in the hands of the buyer is a well-drafted "termination on convenience" clause — if it is connected with a reasonable early termination fee. (Section 11.1.) However, this provision is not usually included in fixed-price contracts, so the customer has to find another way to keep the vendor honest.

1.2.12 Carefully Select an Offshore Adviser

An offshore adviser can save the customer a lot of money, time, and sleepless nights. Especially for first-time buyers and for companies that want to start an offshore subsidiary (not just buying from an independent vendor), the fees for the consultant may turn out to be a great investment.

Not all consultants are equally suited for this task, however. Some advisers are closely related to a certain offshore provider. They are in fact marketing departments, and their main purpose is to find customers and provide for a steady ingress of orders. These "offshore advisers" are not suitable if the customer is still undecided about the choice of vendor, the best business model, or whether to go offshore at all because the consultant's advice is biased towards a specific vendor and its business model. And the decision "offshore — yes or no" should be beyond discussion in any event. Discussing this decision with an offshore adviser is like going to a TV shop and trying to discuss with the salesclerk whether it is good for a family to have a TV in the home.

Offshore consultancy is a good business to be in right now, and it attracts many would-be experts who do not have adequate experience. For this reason buyers are well advised to carefully assess their consultancy

customers. Others have experience only in relation to specific roles — e.g., as consultants; they participate at the beginning of the project for a couple of weeks, hold discussions with top executives, write a document titled "business plan," and then leave the project. Perhaps they come back after a year or two asking for a questionnaire to be filled in about how things turned out.

Even certain book authors have never worked in an offshore project. Instead they read mailing lists, articles, and other books; compile this information; and rewrite it using a pleasant and convincing writing style. That is how myths can come into existence. (See Section 1.1.) Such journalistic activity is not necessarily undesirable. On the contrary, it is important work that helps the reader get an overview of the general issues. However, the customer has to decide whether these individuals are the ideal consultants when starting an offshore scenario. (See also Section 6.9 and Section 6.10.)

1.2.13 Before You Start Applying "Best Practices"

There is no shortage of advice and "best practices" in offshore business. Notice, however, that best practices are anything but similar to Pythagoras' Formula — something that can be applied with or without understanding it because it will always deliver a correct result. "Best practices" are different: most suggestions have been successfully applied in some projects but have failed in others. Only a few "best practices" can be applied to all kinds of offshore scenarios. Some "best practices" even contradict others.

Thus, it is necessary to validate so-called best practices by using reliable sources that testify that the suggested practice has been applied in projects of similar size and profile. The reliability of the sources is particularly important in cases where the inventor of the best practice has an economic interest in its actual implementation.

Understanding the background of the best practice is very important: why is this practice expected to work? Even more important is to understand what can go wrong.

1.3 RISKS AND HAZARDS

Many hazards exist in offshore outsourcing. That is what the

AU7017_book.fm Page 7 Thursday, March 16, 2006 5:07 PM

The sequence of the listed items does not imply any priority: in some projects one of these risks may constitute the dominant problem, although the same risk is completely insignificant in other offshore scenarios.

1.3.1 Underestimation of Communication Costs

The long distance and higher expenses for communication when working with offshore vendors require a completely new set of management techniques. (See Section 3.3 and Section 7.4.)

1.3.2 Inadequate Governance

The buyer needs an in-house steering committee to oversee the work of the vendor. The size of the steering committee should be about 4 to 10 percent of the entire project team, and its members require specific qualifications. (See Section 5.4.)

1.3.3 Loss of Control over Key Information, Crucial Knowledge, and Technical Staff

The technical staff, their know-how, and the documentation they produce are controlled by an independent vendor that has its own balance sheet and its own interest — which might be different than the buyer's interests. (See Section 2.1 and Section 11.2.)

1.3.4 Loss of Leadership in Business Relations

Outsourcing relations have the tendency to expand. The vendor might take over leadership in the buyer's business relations; in time some of these relations may be managed by the vendor, and the communication will pass its desk. (See Section 11.3.)

1.3.5 Buyer's Business Continuity

The buyer's dependency on the vendor might grow in time. How will the buyer continue its business — in particular after switching to another vendor or bringing the services back in house? (See Chapter 11.)

influence on the success or failure of the envisioned outsourcing scenario. However, they are very aware that many of them will lose their jobs after the offshore relationship is established. (See Section 6.5.)

1.3.7 Dynamic of Costs

Salaries in developing countries have been growing steadily, and further increases can be anticipated. In addition, the vendor might change its pricing strategy. (See Section 3.2.)

1.3.8 International Litigation May Turn Challenging

Litigation with developing countries can be challenging. If something goes wrong, it might be difficult to obtain adequate compensation.

1.3.9 Outsourcing of Unsuitable Projects

Some kinds of projects can be outsourced much more easily than other kinds can. (See Section 8.5.)

1.3.10 Sly and Unfair Providers

The provider might turn out to be unexpectedly clever and sly and could abuse its superior experience in outsourcing projects to the disadvantage of the customer. Thus, the cooperation might end in a very unpleasant way that could be surprising for the inexperienced buyer. (See Section 6.2.)

1.3.11 Vendors Working for Competitors

In time the vendor might work also for competitors of the customer. In this way business know-how that has been trustfully transferred to the vendor at the onset of the relationship might be used competitively against the customer who provided the know-how. (See Section 5.2 and Section 10.2.)

1.3.12 How to Prevent the Vendor from Becoming a Competitor

The customer has to transfer the business know-how to the vendor at the beginning of the relationship. The vendor controls the technical staff and

headhunt a few of the customer's best staff and start a little business over there." (See Section 5.2 and Section 10.2.)

1.3.13 Risk of Failed Projects

The customer might suffer high consequential damages when a project fails or is not delivered on time. This makes the customer vulnerable. In extreme cases unfair developers on the vendor's side could exploit this vulnerability and blackmail the project by saying that either they get much more money or they will quit immediately. (Section 6.3 includes such an anecdote.)

1.3.14 Distribution of Risks between Buyer and Vendor

The vendor is required to deliver according the outsourcing contract. Discontented customers can resort to litigation, which may or may not be successful. This is one side of the coin. The other is that if the customer does not get the needed IT services, the fate of its entire business might be at stake.

1.3.15 Management of Distributed Projects Might Turn out More Challenging than Expected

Given the long distances between buyer and vendor and between development team and domain experts, management of distributed projects may turn out to be more difficult than anticipated. (See Chapter 7.)

1.4 CHECKLIST FOR STRATEGIC SUCCESSFUL OFFSHORE OUTSOURCING

The following checklist provides a number of questions that can help a customer evaluate the maturity of its offshore outsourcing plans and assess the chances of success.

Objectives (Chapter 2)

- Are the customer's objectives explicitly stated?
- What are the success criteria? Are these goals realistic?
- Most IT projects have a strong impact on business processes. Is the interaction between the IT project and the business processes

■ Are these expectations realistic? Do these prospective savings match published numbers for similar scenarios? How will costs evolve in the future? What costs should customers expect in a few years' time?

Support for offshore plans (Chapter 6)

■ Are the offshore plans fully supported by top management and marketing and sales departments?
■ What are customers and end-users thinking about these plans?
■ Does the offshore scenario need support from in-house IT staff? How will such support be achieved?

Contract (see Chapter 9)

■ Does the customer have access to truly qualified consultancy regarding software projects, outsourcing contracts, and legal problems in an international context?
■ Has the customer clearly set out the negotiable and nonnegotiable parts of the agreement (e.g., terms of contract, pricing model, control rights)?

Protection of commercial secrecy (Chapter 10)

■ How important is commercial secrecy?
■ Does the cost advantage justify the loss of control over staff?
■ How will business know-how be protected in the long run?

Offshore relationships (Chapter 5)

■ How is the power in the offshore relationship distributed? Who makes the decisions *de facto*?
■ How will power be distributed in a few years' time?
■ What is the conflict resolution strategy?
■ What importance does litigation have in the conflict resolution strategy? Note that litigation has rarely been very beneficial for the customer in offshore scenarios to date. How much experience does the customer have with international litigation and how efficient are courts in the context of international business, including business with developing countries?

Remote project management

■ What processes will be used to control, manage, and oversee

- Is the information about other application of these processes reliable? Have the processes been successfully applied without university staff, without research and development funding, and outside of the scope of influence of the inventors of these processes? (See Section 5.4 to Section 5.6.)
- How are requirements defined? (See Section 9.1.)
- Who will engineer the requirements documents? Do these people have enough experience? Do they have experience in writing requirements documents in the context of international projects? (See Section 9.1.)

Exit plan (Chapter 11)

- Is there an exit plan that shows a way in which the offshore scenario can be discontinued? Does this plan include a strategy for how the business will be continued after the collaboration ends? Does this exit plan include contractual provisions as well as commercial strategies and tactical day-by-day business decisions?
- Is the exit plan realistic? What is the evidence that this exit plan will work? Has this strategy ever been tried (e.g., in another scenario)?

1.5 OPINIONS AND HARD NUMBERS ABOUT GLOBAL SOURCING

At the time when this book was written, widely accepted hard numbers were difficult to find. Many organizations that submitted such numbers had vested interests to influence the public opinion about global sourcing in one or the other direction. This might explain why even numbers submitted by governmental statistical institutions exhibited huge differences, depending on which government controlled the respective institution.

Another reason for not including extensive surveys and studies in this book is that the numbers from these studies become outdated rather quickly. In particular, "expert prognoses" that refer to the future are prone to require "corrections" soon after they are published. Thus, only a few selected numbers and expert opinions that are currently under discussion are presented here.

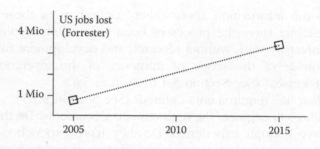

Figure 1.1   Expected loss of jobs due to outsourcing. (*Source*: Forrester Research, August 2005.)

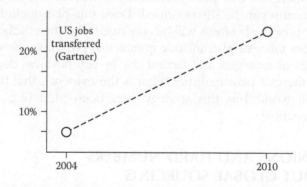

Figure 1.2   Expected number of jobs transferred abroad. (*Source*: Gartner, 2004.)

The number 3.4 million sounds dramatic. Forrester, however, emphasized that it represents less than seven percent of jobs in the categories covered by the study, which include "management," "computer," and "legal." Ironically, Forrester concluded that the heated discussion of offshore outsourcing in the media has accelerated the process by making executives aware of the trend. In another study in April 2005, Forrester reported that 58 percent of the surveyed 139 North American firms are not using or planning to use IT offshore service providers.

According to Gartner's report, in 2004 about five percent of jobs have been moved to foreign soil. However, researchers expect 25 percent by 2010. (See Figure 1.2.)

Gartner vice president Ian Marriott told the attendees of an IT confer-

AU7017_book.fm Page 13 Thursday, March 16, 2006 5:07 PM

loss of competitive advantage and inability to focus on growth through innovation."

Deloitte Research announced a prediction that 275,000 jobs in the telecom industry will have been shifted abroad by 2008. These are about five percent of the total 5.5 million employees in that industry. Telecom companies that are already using global sourcing models — or planning to do so — expect 20 to 30 percent reduced costs within four years.

Interestingly enough, the numbers published by U.S. government institutions are much less spectacular and alarming. According to a report from the Bureau of Labor Statistics (BLS), 4633 jobs were lost to overseas relocations during the first quarter of 2004. Given that nearly 240,000 jobs were lost in that time, offshore outsourcing accounted only for the moderate contribution of less than two percent.

Notice, however, that this report is only taken from companies that laid off 50 or more employees. Thus, this statistic covers only a small fraction of the real job turnover at that time.

These differences make it obvious that reading such data requires a good deal of experience, as well as knowledge of where the numbers came from and how they came into existence.

The World Trade Organization (WTO) analyzed, in their World Trade Report, the gap between the numbers in surveys from research institutes such as McKinsey, EITO, and Gartner compared to other numbers derived from national Balance of Payment (BOP) data. The report analyzed the 2003 data on bilateral trade between the United States and India. Based on the country's IT services association, the National Association of Software and Service Companies (NASSCOM), India exported $6.8 billion of IT services to the United States. The U.S. BOP data, however, is different; according to this source, only $0.9 billion of computer and information services (CIS) have been imported from India. (See Figure 1.3.)

A radically different opinion comes from the Information Technology Association of America; their analysis showed that offshore outsourcing not only boosts the U.S. gross domestic product but also helps *generate* jobs in the United States.

According a Deloitte study (conducted in late autumn 2004), the organizations participating in the study spend about $50 billion on outsourcing. The U.S.-focused study reveals "that 70 percent of participants have had negative experiences with outsourcing projects and are now exercising greater caution in approaching outsourcing. One in four par-

14 ■ The Insider's Guide to Outsourcing Risks and Rewards

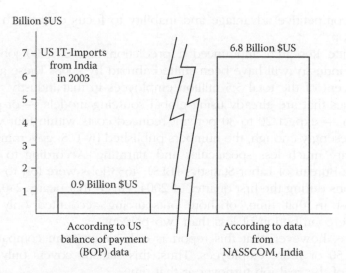

Billion $US

US IT-Imports from India in 2003

0.9 Billion $US

According to US balance of payment (BOP) data

6.8 Billion $US

According to data from NASSCOM, India

Figure 1.3 Differing estimates of U.S. IT imports from India-based providers.

it is not delivering the value as promised, and its appeal as a cost-savings strategy will also diminish as the economy recovers from recession and companies look for differentiated solutions to support their growth."

A report from India's NASSCOM estimated the total value of outsourcing to India at $17.2 billion, or 44 percent of the worldwide total. In 2004 about 80 percent of the Fortune 500™ companies outsourced at least one operation to India (an increase from 60 percent in 2003). These numbers include companies that have their own centers in India as well as companies that are working with Indian technology providers.

The situation in Western Europe requires a separate analysis because salaries are lower than in the United States and the employment laws and business culture are different.

In summer 2004 the institute IDC surveyed 500 medium-sized and large organizations in Western Europe. Eighty percent of them do not have plans regarding offshoring IT services. Only 10 percent are currently using offshore outsourcing. This study included areas, such as application development, where offshore providers are traditionally strong.

The data suggests that offshore outsourcing has not yet led to deep-rooted changes in Western Europe as dramatic as those described by analysts in the United States. One observation, however, might be impor-

This rather relaxed picture of only 10 percent of companies outsourcing seems to contradict the numbers of Forrester Research; according to their study about 1.2 million jobs will be lost in Western Europe due to offshoring by 2015.

1.6 DEFINITIONS OF TERMS

Offshore outsourcing has developed its own vocabulary. This section provides a concise overview of the terms used and includes references to the chapters where these concepts are explained in more detail.

The term *outsourcing* is used if services and business functions are provided by an external organization. The organization that receives the services is called *client, buyer, customer,* or *project owner,* and the external organization is called *outsourcer, vendor,* or *(service) provider.* Frequently, the buyer is located in a leading industrial nation (such as the United States or one of the countries of Western Europe), and the vendor is based in an emerging country (e.g., India or China) — so-called *offshore outsourcing* or *offshoring.* One of the most important motivations for offshore outsourcing is that the salaries in the emerging country are much lower.

The term *offshore* usually implies that buyer and vendor are on separate continents, i.e., for a customer in the United States a provider in Eastern Europe is "offshore." However, if the buyer is located in France, an Eastern European vendor would be considered *near-shore.* The present book does not usually make this strict distinction. If there is no danger of confusion, a vendor in an emerging country is called "offshore" irrespective of where the customer is located. In some industrialized countries, the term offshore outsourcing carries the connotation of "losing jobs." To avoid resentment, some authors use the term *global sourcing* instead.

Before the offshore cooperation can start, the partners have to collect the necessary information about each other — so called *due diligence* (Section 5.2). Some prospective buyers submit a questionnaire to various vendors before they decide on their provider. This *Request for Proposal (RFP)* outlines the project that is to be outsourced (Section 5.1). The invited vendors answer such requests with offers and proposals.

The top-level architecture of the cooperation, the day-by-day practices and the contracts involved, is called the *offshore scenario* or *business*

small), in the industrialized country, that is owned by the offshore vendor and facilitates communication with the customer (Section 7.4). *Liaisons* (also known as *straddlers*) are employees of the vendor who visit the customer for a certain time or periodically, e.g., to install intermediate work-results and discuss new requirements (Section 7.4). An *envoy* is an employee of the customer who visits the vendor (Section 7.4). A *customer's representative* is similar to an envoy; he or she is a person trusted by the customer who oversees the work of the offshore team and makes decisions on the customer's behalf (Section 7.4). The difference is that the customer's representative lives permanently in the emerging country, but the envoy visits the vendor only temporarily. When the envoy comes to the developing country, the envoy is usually embedded into the vendor's team during the visit. The customer's representative might be part of the vendor's team as well; however, there are also customer's representatives who run an independent office geographically close to the vendor, visiting the vendor's site only occasionally.

The buyer may decide to work with a single, exclusive provider — so-called *single sourcing* or *sole sourcing*. The *multi-sourcing* model, in contrast, includes two or more providers (Section 7.5).

In *on-site offshoring* the vendor sends workers to the buyer's site — so called *loan workers* (Section 7.2). They work under surveillance of the customer's management. For the time of their stay the vendor is only responsible for some basic discipline — e.g., that the workers come at a certain time to the office. The onshore management guides the efforts, oversees the work of the loan workers, and is accountable for the final success of the project. A related model is the *body leasing agency* (Section 7.2). These agencies are usually based in the industrialized country. They take on staff in offshore or onshore countries and send these loan workers to the customer's site where they work under surveillance of the customer's management.

The vendor may *subcontract* part or all of the work to third parties — i.e., the *subcontractor* does the work on behalf of the vendor. If the subcontractor is running another network of sub-subcontractors, the business architecture is called a *daisy chain* (Section 7.2). Frequently these sub-subcontractors and freelancers are smaller, cheaper, and less reliable than the initial vendor; sometimes, the owner of the project is not aware of this chain of subcontracting relations and would not have agreed to it if informed.

certain project (Section 7.2). A strategic alliance can include one or more joint ventures.

Even after the offshore scenario is established many buyers keep some IT experts in house, although the number is much smaller than before. This *steering committee* oversees the work of the offshore team and facilitates communication (Section 5.4). Another important task of the steering committee is governance of the relationship. In the course of the cooperation some disputes might arise. Litigation is almost always the worst solution to such disputes. Thus, the outsourcing contract might include a clause which applies *Alternative Dispute Resolution (ADR)* — e.g., *mediation* and *arbitration* (Section 5.5). *Arbitration* is similar to a court trial that leads to a final decision in favor of a plaintiff or defendant. The procedure is usually shorter, easier, and less expensive than a trial at an official court. In addition, the parties can choose a specific arbitrator — e.g., an expert in that field. During *mediation,* a trained mediator helps the parties to find a mutually acceptable solution; one can think of mediation as kind of marriage counseling for companies. Mediation does not lead to a decision by the mediator; the parties have to find their own, mutually accepted solution.

If the price for the outsourced project is agreed on in advance, the contract is called a *fixed-price contract* (Section 9.2). An alternative is the *unit price contract,* which is based on a payment per working hour (or working day), as discussed in Section 9.3. Some buyers decide to outsource a part or all of their IT services for a certain time (e.g., five years); this leads to a *service agreement* (Section 9.6). A service agreement usually specifies the monthly fees, the *term* of cooperation (e.g., five years), the *services* that will be provided by the outsourcer, and some so-called *service levels* (e.g., network availability or the average response time when problems have been reported). These items are discussed in Section 9.6.

Many service agreements include a *benchmark* clause (Section 5.6). The *benchmark audit* is conducted by an independent third party — the *benchmark provider.* During this audit the performance of the vendor is measured and the fees are compared to other outsourcing contracts in the benchmark provider's database. The conclusion of the benchmark audit might be that the vendor has to resolve identified problems within a certain time or that the fees will be adapted.

A software project includes a number of important files. The engineers are developing a set of text-files — the so-called *source code* (e.g., in

on a computer; the source code cannot be. Nevertheless, the source code is of crucial importance for the project because it is needed whenever any changes are to be made.

When a certain team is responsible for source code, it is said that they "*own*" the code. This "*ownership*" does not mean that they own the code in a legal sense of copyright law; it is just an expression indicating that they have the last word about which changes and extensions they consider necessary.

When the first version of the program is finished, it usually still contains some errors. The incorrect behavior that can be observed by the user is called a *defect*. Defects are found during testing. The reason for a defect — e.g., the wrong line in the source code — is called a *fault*. In jargon the process of finding and fixing faults ("bugs") is called *debugging*.

The term "debugging" stems from an old anecdote.

> The circuits of a certain telephone center had a nasty error that turned out to be difficult to find. The engineers had strong suspicion that a certain switch was responsible for the wrong connections. Tests, however, showed that the device seemed to be all right. The engineers even changed the entire unit. Surprisingly enough, the problem persisted.
>
> Finally, they found the reason: a small bug was occasionally sitting between the contacts of the (mechanical at that time) switch, preventing electrical contact. Tracing the problem to that switch was difficult because the bug would leave its place and come back another time.

2

DRIVERS

ABSTRACT

Motivations in the Offshore Decision-Making Process

The potential cost reduction is a compelling argument in favor of offshore scenarios for many companies. Due to its dominant role in a considerable a number of offshore projects, an entire chapter of this book, Chapter 3, is dedicated to cost aspects.

In addition to the obvious financial motivation of cost reduction, commercial (strategic) or technological issues might be taken into consideration, such as:

- *Efforts to acquire and maintain IT know-how*
- *Access to scarce talent*
- *Additional flexibility*
- *Focus on core activities*

2.1 TECHNOLOGICAL DRIVERS

Gaining access to leading-edge technology may be an important reason for considering an outsourcing scenario. In many cases the customer wants to outsource the IT-specific know-how, although the domain expertise and business know-how should remain in house. A technologically strong vendor specialized in IT offers attractive advantages including economies of scale and access to top talent. The outsourcing step, however, may lead to strategic risks for the buyer in the long run, such as loss of direct

2.1.1 Efforts to Acquire and Maintain IT Know-How

For most organizations software development is not the core of their business. For example, the core business of a company providing transport services is transportation of goods or people. If such companies develop software at all, they do it because they need the software for their principal business. Nevertheless, the software might provide a competitive advantage or a crucial success factor for the business.

In these companies the know-how consists of four major components:

1. Domain expertise
2. General IT skills
3. Technical details about already-existing projects
4. Knowledge regarding the interaction between IT processes and the business

2.1.1.1 Domain Expertise

In the example of the transportation business, the component of domain expertise includes knowledge about trucks and streets. This know-how is not usually considered for any outsourcing activity and is not affected by IT outsourcing. It constitutes the core of the organization's business.

2.1.1.2 General IT Skills

Programming skills and mastering the latest technologies are examples of this component. These skills are at the center of interest if an organization considers an IT outsourcing scenario. The IT business in general and software development in particular are fields of extremely high complexity. Attaining and retaining technological currency requires large investments. IT is a fast-changing landscape; for many organizations it is challenging to keep pace with these breathtaking changes, especially if IT is not their main business. The latest technology, however, is the basis for excellent service delivery and high user satisfaction. Enlisting the help of a specialized service provider can be an important step toward solving this challenging issue.

Due to these challenges even companies that are specialized in IT or software development have to occasionally employ some outsourcing strategies to access knowledge that is rarely used but of crucial importance

2.1.1.3 Technical Details about Legacy Projects

The software team might have developed other projects in the past that will probably require future maintenance; defects that are discovered must be fixed, extensions have to be included, and adaptations to new versions of operating systems and hardware might become necessary. This type of maintenance requires in-depth understanding of the technical details of these projects — understanding the source code and understanding why some technical decisions have been made in a certain way. In general, it is difficult for a completely new team to maintain "legacy" software without extensive support and substantial help on the part of the initial authors of the software.

2.1.1.4 Knowledge about the Interaction between IT Operations and the Business

This component includes the following topics:

- The business reasons for the features of the software — i.e., the motivations for why certain functions operate in a particular way.
- The motivation for quality requirements (e.g., response time, per-formance, security, portability).
- The mapping of business goals to software features. Which business goal is achieved with that software? How is this business goal achieved and which features are crucial? What alternative ways exist to achieve these business goals? What other technologies are available? Which of these alternatives have been considered or tried already and why have they been rejected?
- What can be done in certain unfavorable circumstances — e.g., if an error occurs, if some components fail, or if an overload is reported.

The third and fourth know-how components listed above have to be transferred if a company decides to outsource its previously internal IT department. Even if the vendor already has adequate IT skills (item 2 above), it will need the specific business element to provide a background for these skills — i.e., items 3 and 4. Without this know-how, it is usually impossible to carry through a software project successfully.

2.1.2 Advantages of Vendors Specialized in IT

The larger vendor can afford to employ specialists who maintain in-depth knowledge in various fields.

Access to Scarce Talent

Outstanding young developers are very attractive for quite a number of potential employers. Unfortunately, small companies are not very attractive for these young stars, particularly if the organization's main business is not IT. Such engineers are more interested in the future prospects offered by large organizations specialized in IT. There they find challenging projects and senior colleagues ready to take on the role of mentors.

2.1.3 Consequences of Know-How Transfer

Control over Technical Staff

Unless the customer continues to employ a significant number of IT staff, direct control over this kind of know-how may be lost. In the future this know-how will be at the disposal of the vendor — a fact that makes the customer vulnerable and might become a problem if the customer wants to move the IT business back in house or switch to another vendor.

This problem is not limited to an outsourcing scenario: Even if the know-how is in house it can be lost one way or another — e.g., by attrition. Nevertheless the situation of an in-house IT department is more-or-less under the control of the management. The control of the customer's management over an in-house department is much stricter than control over a software team that belongs to the organization of the vendor. For these reasons some analysts consider the loss of crucial knowledge as one of the greatest risks related to offshore outsourcing.

Hidden Contributions of IT Departments

Studies have revealed that full-time employed software developers occupy only about half of their time with what they are in fact expected to do: developing software. During the other half of their working hours they contribute to meetings, discuss technical issues with colleagues, and evaluate new ideas and potential improvements of business processes. Last but not least they answer questions of upper management, write reports, and explain consequences of technical decisions to their superiors.

Explaining the strategic effects of a technological decision to top management for just one hour might have a greater positive impact on the organization than working for an entire week at the keyboard would.

Outsourcing this other half of added value is even more challenging than just outsourcing software production. It is difficult to find stipulations for the outsourcing contract that provide for these services. If services of this kind are included in the outsourcing contract, there is a high risk that these provisions will entail nothing but costs on the part of the customer and very limited benefits — at least unless there is a relationship of deep trust between customer and provider. In addition, these services require a high degree of loyalty. Permanently employed staff members usually have more reasons to be loyal to their organization than an independent vendor does. If a company outsources software production to an external provider, it also has to find a solution for the future provision of these "hidden contributions" of IT staff.

Secrecy of Business Know-How

The know-how might include intellectual property or competitive advantages. Transferring this crucial know-how to another, legally independent organization (perhaps offshore) can have far-reaching impacts on the business. For this reason, careful assessment is required. (See Chapter 10.)

2.1.4 Retaining and Developing Strategic Knowledge

A number of decision makers consider the loss of key information an important source of risks in the context of outsourcing. Forestalling or solving such hazards requires identifying essential business knowledge and providing the necessary infrastructure to keep it in house in the long run.

For many customers knowledge worth protecting includes the following items:

- Strategic business goals of the organization
- Information about competitive advantages over other companies
- How the customer's various products and services are related and which business goals are achieved by using each service
- Insight into the customer's business culture
- Knowledge of the *real* distribution of power
- Understanding of the industry's business processes at the service

AU7017_book.fm Page 24 Thursday, March 16, 2006 5:07 PM

2.2 COMMERCIAL AND STRATEGIC DRIVERS

An advantage of outsourcing is that the buyer gains a certain degree of flexibility: staff must be paid only as long as needed. To some extent fixed costs are turned into variable costs. The validity of this outsourcing advantage must be questioned, however, and assessed in the particular scenario at hand; the customer is frequently keen on staff stability on the vendor's side. Continuity of staff in the context of cost efficiency requires a certain degree of continuity of orders.

The outsourcing relationship allows the customer to focus on its core activities. The other side of the coin is a higher dependency on the external vendor providing crucial IT services.

Many of the published success stories of offshore outsourcing refer to rather large organizations — say, those with at least 50 in-house IT staff. Small organizations have access to offshore outsourcing as well, but they need more creative solutions.

2.2.1 Flexibility vs. Continuity of Staff

In some outsourcing scenarios the customer's flexibility is improved: the IT staff not needed for projects pertaining to that customer is available for other projects and does not have to be paid by that customer. If more staff is needed, the outsourcer will provide it. At first glance it seems that a large vendor has many projects and a lot of IT staff. This should give it the necessary flexibility if some projects require more or less staff.

This is only one side of the coin, however. The reverse is that many customers require the vendor to always assign the same staff members to their projects. The reason behind this request is that most software projects need quite a lot of specific customer know-how and domain expertise. In addition, customers prefer working on a permanent basis with the same partners (employees of the vendor) because they gradually come to know each other, and cooperation is smoother if they have known each other for some time. For these reasons, it is desirable that the same staff members work for the same customer. Hence, some continuity of staff is necessary.

Continuity of staff is possible only if the orders from the customer have some continuity as well. If longer breaks between orders occur, the staff has to be assigned to other projects from other customers unless the

well. This request limits flexibility, especially for offshore vendors in emerging software industries. Because many offshore companies have only limited funding and low margins, they can employ staff only if they have projects for them: low prices and low margins require that capacity be used to almost 100 percent. Gaps between projects cause problems in continuity.

Full flexibility is therefore hard to achieve when continuity of staff as well as the lowest prices possible are requested. Given all these reasons, the promise of flexibility and its real validity must be carefully evaluated in any planned offshore outsourcing scenario.

2.2.2 Concentration on Core Activities vs. Dependency on the Vendor

The policy of the customer's organization of concentrating on its core business might be an important motivation for an outsourcing decision. However, outsourcing the IT department causes dependency on the vendor; this may have disadvantages in the long run, so it has to be considered carefully. (See Chapter 11, in particular Section 11.2.)

2.2.3 Size of the Customer's Organization

Most of the published success stories of offshore outsourcing refer to rather large organizations and IT departments with several dozen in-house employees. Some analysts say the minimum number is about 50 in-house IT employees; other analysts estimate a minimum of 100 staff. Many of these successful customers are "global players" — large organizations that have been active in an international market for many years.

One reason why small companies may have difficulties in launching an offshore scenario is that offshore outsourcing requires a lot of upfront work to establish the partnership and negotiate the contract. In addition, overseeing the work of the remote development team is significantly more demanding than managing an in-house software project. Small and mid-size organizations are not excluded from offshore outsourcing, but these scenarios require more creativity. One obstacle is that small organizations frequently have smaller margins, less funding, and smaller prospective cost savings. On the other hand, small organizations do not necessarily need an up-scaling scenario. (See Section 7.2.)

2.3 ALLOTTING DRIVER PRIORITY

Technological, commercial, or financial drivers may play a role when designing offshore plans. Depending on the degree of priority assigned to each of these factors, the outsourcing scenario will look completely different. For this reason it is of foremost importance that the customer fully understand its motivations and establish its priorities.

Outsourcing the production of software is different than, for example, outsourcing the production of screws. In most cases producing software does not boil down to the work done at the keyboard for developing several modules. More often than not the first step is for the software team to find out what the customer really *needs* — which is almost always something other than what the customer says it *wants*. The author of this book has encountered quite a number of software projects that would have ended in utter dissatisfaction on the part of the customer if the software team had simply delivered what it was asked for. Nevertheless, in many cases the projects ended more-or-less successfully because the software team questioned the orders it had received and made suggestions for improving the requirements.

Traditionally, production of software is associated with high-quality consulting. The vendor does not usually write an invoice for consultancy; instead, these costs are included in the price of the project. For this reason many customers are not fully aware of the importance of this consultancy process in the context of the project, especially in the early preparation phase. In addition, few customers are aware of the cost for this consultancy and want to think about it. This extensive consultancy practice is in line with the recommendations made by most software engineering books, and for many customers it is the only way to reach acceptable requirements. Nevertheless, this practice causes additional costs on the part of the vendor.

A customer that wants to outsource its IT department might not be aware of the importance of consultancy and the related costs. If the managers had technical questions, they would call their IT experts for a meeting and expect that the engineers would show up with a well-prepared analysis. If this customer is now about to decide in favor of using a "cost-efficient" vendor, the managers have to consider whether

vendor selection process and has to make these motivations known to the vendor. If the customer, for example, wants excellent consulting it cannot work with the cheapest provider; the customer's drivers are technical, the vendor's offer is placed on the financial axis. In most cases premium consultancy quality is not available at the lowest prices.

The customer must be aware of its own motivations — i.e., must understand exactly why it wants to enter an outsourcing relationship. If the main motivation is technical (e.g., access to leading-edge know-how), the optimum outsourcing scenario will look completely different than if the main motivation is cost reduction. Hence, understanding and assigning priority to offshore motivations is of crucial importance for a successful offshore scenario.

For hard numbers pertaining to the motivations for offshore outsourcing, see Figure 2.1.

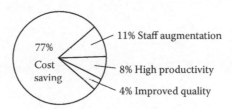

Figure 2.1   In May 2004, www.cio.com conducted a poll among its readership regarding the primary motivations for offshoring.

3

COSTS

ABSTRACT

American and Western European companies receive offers for software development from emerging countries such as China, India, and Eastern European nations almost every day. Sometimes the prices put forward are as low as 25 percent of the price offered by onshore providers for the same services — in extreme cases, even below this rate. These numbers suggest that cost reductions of at least three quarters should be expected if software projects are outsourced to offshore vendors. Nevertheless, most case studies report savings of only 15 to 30 percent. Even these considerably smaller savings are achieved only after the offshore relationship has been established and the cooperation has found its rhythm; the first few projects frequently involve no savings at all and sometimes entail even higher costs than in the case of onshore workers. This raises the issue of the reasons why this could happen.

Offshore projects include a number of hidden costs of which first-time customers are frequently not aware — e.g., costs for governance and communication. In failed offshore scenarios, adequate governance often was lacking. In other cases high communication costs led to reduced communication and consequently to compromised management quality.

3.1 REALISTIC ESTIMATION OF COSTS

An offshore cooperation implies a number of hidden costs that blunt the cost advantages. Managers who are new to the business

expected. Failing projects may, in turn, lead to consequential damages. Last but not least, the customer has to work out a realistic plan of business continuity if the relationship with the vendor is to be ended.

3.1.1 Finding Partners

Before the offshore relationship can actually be inaugurated, a vendor must be selected, offers must be analyzed, Requests for Proposals (RFP) have to be written, and the contract must be negotiated. It might be a good idea for the customer to visit the offshore country and meet one or more potential partners. All these steps involve additional costs. (See Section 5.1.)

3.1.2 Transition Period

More often than not know-how must be transferred from the in-house IT staff to the vendor's team. This entails meetings, travel, and accommodation. There might also be an emotionally tense situation, and existing staff might refuse to cooperate because they fear losing their jobs. To solve these problems additional efforts could be necessary. For example, in the case of layoffs of onshore staff, employment contracts might require substantial financial compensation. (See Section 6.5.)

3.1.3 Communication

The offshore project is carried through in a context where the customer and the vendor are separated by long distances. Meetings become very expensive due to the high travel costs. This adds to the high cost of telecommunication, which can be surprisingly expensive in emerging countries. The higher costs might lead to less communication between vendor and customer, which increases the probability of misunderstandings leading to expensive additional rework. (See Section 3.3.)

3.1.4 Governance

Even after the outsourcing relationship is established, the customer has to keep employing technical staff to oversee the work of the offshore team and manage the relationship with the vendor. This steering committee

The steering committee's main responsibilities are supervising the vendor and overseeing the work of the offshore staff. In addition the governance team has to help other in-house departments tackle the changes in business processes that may become necessary when IT services are switched to an external vendor.

3.1.5 Upgrading the Customer's Organization

Managing an offshore project demands skills that differ from those needed to develop software in house. Cooperation within a software project where the vendor is far away requires a high level of maturity of the software management process, even on the customer's side. The requirements-engineering process has to be established, and the software specifications have to reach a high level of quality, for example. Many customers do not meet the necessary standards of process maturity when they enter an offshore cooperation. Catching up requires additional training and new infrastructure, which come at a cost.

3.1.6 Structured Software Engineering Process vs. Improvisational Programming

The software engineering institute at Carnegie Mellon University has published a classification schema with five levels of software process maturity (CMM). The highest level, level 5, implies a highly structured and optimized software engineering process. An increasing number of leading offshore providers are in possession of CMM level 5 certificates. Large Indian vendors especially have made tremendous efforts to reach this level. A high CMM level on the part of the vendor has many advantages for the buyer — higher quality, for example. Most customers' internal IT departments are only on level 1 or 2 of the CMM classification — i.e., they use rather improvisational methods. The mismatch between the process's maturity on both sides can cause problems because the vendors need structured input of high quality — e.g., mature requirements documents. Adapting the infrastructure and upgrading the internal processes to reach the necessary level might require significant restructuring, which usually constitutes a substantial investment.

3.1.7 Cultural Differences

use in emerging countries, and therefore the Indian developers were not exactly sure whether real problems with the specification existed. Their limited experience and lack of self-confidence prevented them from reporting their pertinent observations to the onshore team. Even though the specification was in fact wrong, they did not dare challenge the instructions from their supposedly superior American customer. As a result of their lack of assertiveness and self-confidence, they implemented the software just as it was specified in the requirements document. In this case they considered themselves to be on the safe side by not challenging the decisions of the American team: they did exactly what they had been asked to do.

Software developers in industrialized countries are expected to carefully check the requirements documents they receive to safeguard the project from implausible statements and contradictions. If problems exist, they send the requirements back to the customer asking for clarification. In emerging software industries, software developers might consider some statements in the requirements document utterly nonsensical. Nevertheless, they implement them because it appears to them that any kind of objection may challenge the higher authority of the customer, whom they feel they have to obey. They think: "If this is the way the customer wants it, we can give the customer exactly what it wants!" They do what they are asked for, without interpreting any of the orders they receive, just like in the army. In many cases this attitude leads to costly rework.

Things will improve as offshore outsourcing becomes more mature; both shores are constantly learning — the buyers learn how to provide higher-quality requirements, and the vendors comprehend that identifying mistakes in the specification can be a precious contribution. Nevertheless, maturity of the outsourcing relationship can only be achieved in time, and throughout the first stages of a project, cultural differences can cause additional costs.

3.1.8   Integration and Customization

Software projects are rarely "lonely islands" in the customer's organization. Most projects need to be integrated into the existing framework of applications and systems. If the project is developed by an in-house team, the

3.1.9 Maintenance

Certain maintenance tasks can hardly be performed by offshore teams —
e.g., solving problems that entail visits at the user's site. If this is an issue
in the conceived scenario, the customer has to think about how these
problems will be solved.

A related problem is a country's specific holidays; an onshore task
force may be needed to allow prompt response to emergency problems
on those days. In both cases the onshore team has to contribute to the
maintenance of software that has been developed offshore. Maintaining
software that has been developed by another team is more difficult.

3.1.10 Failed Projects

Offshore projects have a higher risk of failure than an onshore cooperation
does. This is particularly true for the first few projects of an offshore
scenario or if the buyer is adamant to bargain for the lowest prices. Even
if the customer does not have to pay anything for the failed project, the
fiasco has costs. For example, there might be lost opportunities, the fact
that other departments rely on the availability of the software, or a decline
in the customer's reputation on the market.

3.1.11 Termination of the Cooperation

For a number of reasons it may become necessary to end the relationship
with the service provider; the customer may be dissatisfied with the service
standards, new business situations requiring radically different IT services
may arise, or the vendor changes its pricing structure — to mention just
a few possibilities. In these cases the client might wish to switch to another
vendor or move the IT services back in house. The transition will cause
additional cost.

These hidden costs of offshore outsourcing contribute to the fact that
the "theoretically possible" savings of three quarters of the costs are rarely
achieved.

3.2 COST DYNAMICS

*Initial costs are only one component of the calculation. The
prognosis of cost evolution is no less important. The rather high
costs of establishing the offshore scenario are present only during*

largest and most mature vendors in India have already started asking why the price has to be lower if the quality is higher.

3.2.1 Components of the Cost Structure

The following observations are important when analyzing costs:

- Some of the hidden costs enumerated in the last section occur at the beginning of an offshore relationship. They are investments made to establish the offshore outsourcing framework. Once the framework is established, these costs will gradually diminish. The first project in a newly established offshore relationship rarely reports any profits because both sides have to invest in the cooperation and frequently the vendor has to offer the first test-project at a promotional price. Usually, the reduction of costs only becomes visible during subsequent years.
- Part of the cost savings is due to the relative youth of the entire offshore business. Although offshore outsourcing is already much easier than it was a few years ago, further improvements can be expected. In the future things will probably go more smoothly; vendors and customers will learn from experience, successful patterns of cooperation will be configured, and outlines of reliable contracts will be published. For this reason the timing may have an influence on the costs; the questions of how long to wait and when to launch an offshore cooperation might be of crucial importance.
- Cooperating with a more mature vendor usually reduces the costs of establishing the relationship. The vendor is already familiar with many pitfalls of the offshore business and can avoid them. However, more mature vendors usually charge higher prices. In addition, the experienced provider might be tempted to use its superior knowledge to its own advantage — not necessarily to the advantage of the customer.

The large discrepancy between the salary differential (up to three quarters lower and more) and the only moderate savings reported in published case studies (15 to 30 percent decrease of costs) is surprising for most managers who are new to offshore business. For the time being, this discrepancy is a matter of fact in many offshore scenarios. However, it comes as a challenge for management to analyze where this discrepancy

Some projects are more suitable than others for offshore outsourcing. Often it is better to outsource an entire project instead of individual modules. The general rule is that outsourcing "entire things" is easier than outsourcing "parts." (See Chapter 8.)

3.2.2 Costs for Offshore Salaries

The costs at a certain time or for a certain project constitute only one aspect to be considered. Because most offshore cooperation is designed to be carried through over longer periods of time, the prognosis of costs' evolution in time is also a particularly important matter.

In most offshore countries, the salaries for software developers have been continually growing over the past few years. Future further growth is to be expected. The differences in salaries between countries may become smaller as time goes by. This possibility should be considered when estimating whether the investment for setting up the offshore cooperation will pay off.

In addition to this constant and to some extent foreseeable growth, sharp salary peaks in times of high demand can occur. In a matter of a few months' time, salaries might rise dramatically. In industrialized countries, IT payments can grow in periods of high demand as well. However, the relative growth of the IT salaries in emerging software industries is much more dramatic than in industrialized nations: sometimes prices can more than double, and such peaks are hard to predict.

> This happened during the so-called dot-com hype at the end of the millennium. At that time, a number of Web sites pertaining to Internet companies (www.something "dot-com") reported high profits, which generated great worldwide demand for software services that outstripped the supply. In an extremely short time (only a few months), software developers in emerging countries asked for much higher payment. In some countries the salaries more than doubled in this period of time. The boom was further accelerated by the software companies being caught in binding contracts that they had to complete — even though the terms of trade were not profitable anymore. Quite a number of small vendors left the market as a consequence of this experience. This added to the general decrease in demand for

To some extent it is possible to keep existing staff at the negotiated conditions during the critical period. However, even this can turn out to be difficult because in developing countries written contracts are not as reliable as in industrialized nations; the staff might leave and take on a better-paid offer without fulfilling their period of notice. In any case, keeping the staff at the negotiated conditions requires a lot of background political work and future promises. All in all, it will clearly be successful only for a very limited period of time.

Anyway, staff that is to be hired during a "boom" period must be paid at the high prices of the market at that particular time. This becomes relevant if staff must be replaced because of natural attrition or if the organization wants to expand at this time. One reason for expansion can be that a project has been started with only a few developers during the requirements phase and is to be extended to its full-blown size during implementation. If the expansion must take place in the difficult circumstances of the peak period, and the vendor is bound by a legally valid contract with fixed prices, the vendor's executives might have a problem: they signed a contract at a low price, hoping that they would be able to employ low-paid staff when they need them. Now they are faced with an empty labor market and extraordinarily high prices. However, they have a legally binding contract and the customer might not be willing to renegotiate the prices.

The obvious action of cutting costs on the vendor's side is usually not possible. Most offshore companies already work cost efficiently. Further reductions of costs are hard to achieve. Because many offshore companies have rather limited funding, the provider has only two options: it can decrease its quality and service level — or it can go bankrupt.

Somebody has to pay for the additional costs — either the customer or the vendor, depending on the contract. If the customer wants to order a new project during the heated period, the offer will be calculated according to the high salaries imposed by the boom. If the contract has been signed before the time of the boom, the vendor might have to cover the costs. It might be wise for the partners to consider the possibility of dramatically changing salaries in emerging software industries and try to find an answer to how this situation will be handled.

3.2.3 Necessary Changes of Contracts and Specifications

Most projects pass several rounds of changes and extensions even before

other times the contract is no longer adequate due to technological evolution that makes the terms of the contract outdated. From a purely technical point of view, the vendor will usually understand the need to change the contract. Perhaps the vendor itself would suggest some technical changes. Nevertheless, the vendor has by no means as urgent a need to adapt the contract as the customer does. A vendor will negotiate the desirable changes of the contract, but it should be noted that the vendor has a rather strong position in this negotiation because it has a valid contract. If necessary, the vendor could go on with the existing contract as well. It is the customer who needs the changes and not the vendor. Even though most outsourcing contracts include provisions concerning the vendor's obligation to agree to necessary technical adaptations of the contract, these provisions leave a lot of space for interpretations on prices, schedules, and other conditions. In some cases the necessary extensions constitute an important basis for improved margins on the part of the vendor. (See Section 9.2.)

> Some providers of printers follow a similar strategy: the price for the printer sounds reasonable. However the ink cartridges are very expensive. At first glance the customer believes he or she is buying an inexpensive printer. In the end it turns out that the total costs per printed page are anything but cheap.

3.2.4 Pricing Strategy of Offshore Vendors

Another reason why the finally achieved cost reduction is surprisingly low might be that vendors do not necessarily offer the lowest price possible. Some vendors put forward a price that is low enough for the customer to accept the offer but no lower. Vendors can put forward different prices depending on whether the customer comes from the United States or from Western Europe. The salaries for software developers in the United States are usually much higher than in Western Europe. If a project is offered to a customer in the United States at a rather high price, the customer will still achieve a reduction of costs compared to the alternative of carrying through this project at home. In Western Europe the vendor's offer must be considerably lower, or no reduction of costs is possible.

Offshore vendors are on the lookout for high-level (and well-paid) projects in industrialized nations. In particular, the largest Indian providers

In the long run the cost difference between industrialized nations and the leading vendors in emerging countries, such as India, may disappear — not only due to increasing salaries in emerging countries but also because the vendors change their pricing policies.

3.2.5 "Back-Loading" Contracts

A number of vendors apply the so-called back-loading of contracts. This term refers to allotting the high costs of setting up the relationship throughout the entire term of the contract. In this way the early years come at a rather low cost for the buyer. The vendor compensates for its unsustainably low margins in the beginning of the contract term in the following years.

This argument sounds perfectly reasonable, and in many cases it has been used by the vendor's marketing team to attract the customer into the relationship. For the client's managers, it is particularly appealing because they can immediately report high cost savings to their shareholders. So it is not surprising that a number of outsourcing scenarios have applied this practice.

This explains how back-loaded contracts frequently come into existence: top management decides that they need X percent savings. The provider engineers a financial plan that leads to these savings — in the first few years. Most of the costs, however, are back-loaded toward the end of the contract when cost savings are considerably lower.

Many clients signed this type of contract in the times of plenty of the late nineties, especially in scenarios where the entire in-house IT department was outsourced. A few years later, when the economic context dictated strict cost efficiency, the contract became rather expensive because it came into the phase where the vendor recouped the investments made in the early years. In this period, some customers are simply not able to pay the high fees that appear towards the end of the term. In the face of the pressure of the economic situation, some outsourcing scenarios found "creative" solutions: The customer brought back in house some low-margin services; in exchange, the contract fees were reduced. Due to compelling economic problems and the provisions of the contract, the customer lost its negotiation leverage and had to allow the service provider to take the pick of the bunch. From the accountant's point of view regarding cost calculation, this option may be feasible. From the strategic and com-

not appear as such in the accounting papers. Sooner or later this credit has to be paid back.

Another serious disadvantage of back-loaded contracts is that they contradict the provision of "termination on convenience." (See Section 11.1.) The option of terminating on convenience is included in some outsourcing contracts and grants the customer the right to cancel the contract without any reason, even if the vendor is doing a great job. In this case the customer has to pay a reasonable termination fee that balances the vendor's investment but not lost profits. Termination on convenience is an important steering instrument for the customer; in quite a number of outsourcing scenarios, it is the single most important management tool.

3.3 COMMUNICATION COST

Long distances between service provider and buyer make communication more expensive. If the two firms are separated by many time zones and have only few common office hours, apparently commonplace things such as phone calls can become a real issue. Unless the partners on both shores speak the same native language, at least one of them has to communicate in a foreign language. Depending on language proficiency, the quality of communication may suffer. Expensive and difficult communication can result in simply less communication, which may in turn lead to a breakdown of management quality. (See also Section 7.4.)

Due to the hazards of communication cost, the customer is well advised to consider communication cost carefully in the very first outline of the offshore scenario. This applies especially if the projects are prone to having extensive communication needs — e.g., innovative products. (See Chapter 8.)

Communication problems are major obstacles for a successful offshore scenario with full leverage of the global differences in salaries and probably one of the strongest factors limiting the potential cost reduction.

The communication costs consist of several components:

- Distance between customer and service provider, which leads to higher telecommunication and transportation costs
- Time zones, making synchronous communication such as phone

AU7017_book.fm Page 40 Thursday, March 16, 2006 5:07 PM

Distance between Customer and Service Provider

Long distances make communication more expensive. Telecommunication costs are higher, and traveling to meetings is more expensive and more time consuming.

Time Zones

Synchronous communication (such as phone calls and video conferences) requires that both parties master a common language and share common office hours. This is utterly different from the possibilities of asynchronous communication (such as e-mail). If the service provider and the customer are separated by many time zones and have only few common office hours, synchronous communication can become a serious issue.

E-mails are not a bad thing — not at all. In fact, there are issues that can be better solved by asynchronous communication. For example, problems that require well-prepared suggestions for their solution might be more easily tackled by e-mail than by phone calls. In other cases, however, a phone call or a meeting might be much more efficient — e.g., if misunderstandings may exist or if the discussion has become stuck.

> A user in the United States reported a serious defect in an existing software project. In response, the developers in Eastern Europe requested data necessary to reproduce the problem on their computers. The users uploaded the requested data. Further analysis carried out by the software team, however, revealed that additional data was necessary. The team requested the missing data and the customer provided it. When the vendor's staff downloaded the archive they noticed that the data was still not complete. They suspected there was a misunderstanding and asked for a complete data set. The user's team was confused and said their archive was complete. To verify this statement they downloaded their own archive again and checked it; it turned out to be complete. When the users reported this result, the vendor's team downloaded the archive again. It was still the same archive with the same size and the same date of creation — surprisingly enough this time the data was complete. Obviously a transmission error had occurred during the first download. For mysterious reasons the archiving software did

likely that analyzing a reported failure requires several "itera-tions" until the problem is resolved.

Notice that if the software team had been in the same time zone as the user, the problem could have been solved rather easily. In the worst case, it should have been a matter of a few hours. In this project, however, the customer and the vendor were separated by a difference of 10 hours between time zones: when the software team noticed that something was going wrong with the data the users had already left the office — and vice versa. For this reason, each cycle of communication took up a full day. Hence, a rather simple problem needed almost a week to be resolved.

The delay was nobody's "fault." The main problem stemmed from the fact that the two parties were separated by many time zones. In this anecdote, the lack of synchronous communication turned out to be a significant problem.

Time zones constitute an important difference between "offshore" and "near-shore" outsourcing — where the partners are separated only by few time zones. Customers in the United States consider countries like Canada and Mexico "near-shore." Leading economies in Western Europe look for partners from the eastern part of their continent.

The "challenges of phone calls" are greatly reduced when near-shore partners cooperate. If real-time interactions are an issue in the relationship, near-shore outsourcing may become a very attractive alternative even though the wages are higher than in offshore countries.

Foreign Language Interface

Unless both parties share the same mother tongue, at least one side must communicate in a foreign language. Depending on proficiency in the language, this restriction might influence the quality of communication. In addition, access to the entire labor market of that country can be impeded. Notice that workers can contribute to the offshore relationship only if they have a satisfactory degree of fluency in the common "business language."

If the customer is located in a non-English-speaking country, the onshore staff may have to communicate in English (or Japanese). Most computer scientists in the leading industrialized countries have sufficient

Communication Volume and Quality

If communication is expensive and difficult, one possible consequence can be that its volume is reduced. Consequently, misunderstandings can accumulate, and the project management may lose quality.

In quite a number of the envisioned offshore scenarios, communication costs are not adequately considered. In many of these cases, offshore plans fail due to problems related to communication cost or quality — and implicitly, management quality.

Projects with Intensive Communication between Customer and Vendor

Some projects have inherently "weak" requirements. For innovative products, for example, it is usually difficult to write reliable specifications in advance because users and other project participants are learning a lot about the new product as the project is unfolding. The results of these new experiences should be incorporated into the final product, of course. Hence, the requirements frequently turn out to be rather premature as initially stated and undergo substantial changes throughout the project.

Innovative products are just one example. Other scenarios may also require intensive communication. In eXtreme Programming environments, for example, a representative of the users is expected to stay permanently with the development team and make the vast majority of the day-by-day decisions on behalf of the customer. Teams using eXtreme Programming have reported a great success for Web applications where time-to-market is one of the top priorities. If such projects are handled in the context of a conceived offshore scenario, the customer is well advised to address the communication issues in the very first blueprint of the business architecture.

3.4 BUSINESS CONTINUITY IN CASE OF WAR OR DISASTER

Once the offshore scenario is established, it has growing importance for the buyer. Thus war or disaster in the emerging country can have a serious impact on the customer's business continuity. Some countries are more prone to political instabilities or disasters and others are less vulnerable. If emergency situations are likely to occur, the customer might want to establish a disaster

- The continuity of projects currently under work, which might be of strategic importance for the customer's organization.
- The ability to develop future projects. The customer's capacity to perform in IT-related issues is based on the know-how that has been transferred to the vendor when establishing the offshore scenario.
- Developing countries have only a limited infrastructure that can be used in the case of disasters. In addition, some important countries in the offshore outsourcing network have little political and military stability. India, for example, is a nuclear power in a tense relationship with its neighbor Pakistan, which also has nuclear weapons.

War could affect either country, of course. But in some countries, e.g., in Eastern Europe, this risk is much more remote than in others.

3.4.1 Disaster Recovery Plan

To forestall the loss of business continuity in case of war or disaster, the customer might want to work out an emergency plan that includes:

- Transfer of key personnel in case of crisis. This includes practical facilities, such as availability of flights or other transportation means in emergencies.
- Employees who are citizens of the developing country might have defense obligations in their country (in the case of an imminent war). This issue should be taken up with the offshore government when designing the emergency plan.
- Transfer also includes legal issues (e.g., visas) that might need clarification with the customer's government well before an emergency situation occurs.
- Backup procedure for crucial data and project files.
- Strategy for destroying confidential material or protecting it during the crisis.
- Compelling justification of the plan. Support at all management levels and agreement on the procedures for triggering the execution of the plan.
- Financing the emergency plan. The funding should include

much more anxious than governments are. It is quite likely that the customer would like to trigger the plan long before the government sees any reason for declaring a "state of emergency." Thus, it is important for the customer to retain the right to trigger the emergency plan.

Experienced practitioners do not trust untried plans very much and consider them unlikely to work smoothly at first trial. It might be worthwhile to test and practice the crucial parts of the procedures in advance — i.e., in peaceful times. In any case, seeking the advice of a local expert about emergency situations when designing the recovery plan is recommended.

Some analysts advise customers to ensure priority over other clients. This step might be considered, and the advantages should be compared with the costs. In many cases, however, the provision of "most favored customer" has led to litigation. Thus, customers must have some guarantee that they will really obtain the priority treatment they have paid for in case of war or disaster.

4

COUNTRIES: DECIDING ON AN OFFSHORE LOCATION

ABSTRACT

Partners from at least two countries contribute to the offshore scenario. The responsible managers should have some basic knowledge
about these countries. This information has to come from reliable
sources; otherwise, it is useless or even harmful. The governments of
the developing country or institutions closely related to the government are not necessarily the best sources in this instance because they
are likely to make biased statements; most governments throughout
the world are vying for foreign investors because such investors are
highly attractive for their countries' economy. For obvious reasons, a
government might be tempted to paint its country's image in exaggeratedly bright colors. Thus it might be better to enlist the help and
common-sense expertise of independent sources. Foreigners who have
worked in the country's software industry could be reliable advisers.
Organizations that provide ratings of the investment climate in various
countries are another source of information.

This chapter provides a checklist of what should be known about
the countries and companies involved. Some items might not be
answered, and others might have limited relevance for the offshore
scenario at hand. Some of the questions could have an obvious answer
for some managers but not for other members of the offshore relationship. The questions offer some guidance for further investigation
and may help prospective participants in an offshore relationship
avoid potentially costly information deficiencies. The checklist identifies items that may qualify as truisms in industrialized countries but

4.1 IMPORTANCE OF BACKGROUND INFORMATION ABOUT THE CONTRIBUTING COUNTRIES

When preparing for setting up an offshore relationship, the management of all contributing companies should be in possession of at least some basic knowledge about the situation in the respective countries. In addition, they should know as much as possible about their future partners. This background information is necessary to cross-check the calculation made on an offer. It helps executives anticipate risks that might arise in future projects and find possible mitigations. It may even provide some essential information that might lead to the cancellation of future cooperation before it has actually started. One reason for canceling the cooperation might be that there is no acceptable solution for the anticipated risks: sometimes it is better not to start cooperation at all rather than to have it end in a fiasco.

Even if the Western customer only has the intention of giving orders to offshore vendors and does not have any plans for developing a more profound activity in the emerging country, some basic knowledge about the offshore country is important. This information provides the support necessary for the management's evaluation of the plausibility and reliability of the partner's statements as they are formulated during negotiations. An offshore engagement lacking in this background information has little chance of success. Conversely, background information shared among all contributors is an important component of successful and smooth offshore cooperation.

The onshore management can try to get this information on its own or can employ a consultant. The consultant should have broad experience in the offshore country as well as in-depth understanding of the situation in the onshore software industries.

The following anecdote provides a motivating example of a situation in which background info is necessary.

A software engineer in Bucharest, Romania applies for a job. He shows up 45 minutes late for the interview, which was taking place somewhere in the city center. He blames the town's disastrous system of public transport for the delay.

In a Western country the delay would be considered an

The truth is that the public transport in Bucharest does not achieve the clockwork-like precision expected in industrialized countries. Nevertheless, it should be possible to arrive in the city center within a time window of, say, 10 minutes. In addition, taxis are rather cheap in Romania — even students can afford to occasionally use a taxi. Moreover, the fact that a meeting with a foreign partner is a rare event for most candidates justifies leaving the house well in time. Therefore, I would conclude that the statement sounds fabricated and the applicant shows signs of unreliability. In addition, he might have a rather low degree of honesty and integrity. In this case I would carefully look for other traces of subtle implausibility during the interview.

The example supports the general observation that people in developing countries tend to overemphasize their poverty and the problems of infrastructure in their countries, particularly when they are talking to foreigners who have only recently come to the country and who have only superficial knowledge of the situation there. However true it might be that many people in developing countries are poor and the infrastructure has its shortcomings, some persons pretend to be even poorer than they are and maximize the problems in the country by making them sound even more dramatic. Their motivation is that they might get some privileges in the negotiations that they would not get if the partner had in-depth knowledge of the situation in the country.

4.2 INVESTMENT CLIMATE

The political situation in the offshore country can greatly influence the long-term success of the offshore scenario. Political instability or territorial conflicts might lead to war, which makes business virtually impossible. Potential natural disasters are other reasons for an emergency plan. There are huge differences in the way foreign managers perceive the level of security in everyday life in emerging countries. If personal freedom or human rights are overly restricted, a smooth work flow may become impossible.

- Are there any laws regarding intellectual property and to what extent are they enforced?
- Are the citizens of that country or foreigners faced with restrictions on exercising their personal freedom?
- How are foreign investment protection mechanisms enforced? Is there any risk of arbitrary confiscation of the assets of foreign investors?
- Have there been cases of governmental corruption or criminal acts — or rumors of such cases?

Undue governmental regulations are an important risk to the long-term feasibility and viability of an offshore scenario:

- How easy is it to get visas? How long does it take to get a visa? What overhead is necessary to manage the visa issues of the offshore scenario?
- How easy is it for citizens of the emerging country to get visas for the buyer's country?
- How easy is it to leave the country?

4.2.2 Governmental Support

How much importance does the government attribute to software outsourcing? How important is the software industry to the national economy? Many emerging countries still have problems with their legislative systems. If the relative importance of software business is high, however, there is a better chance that problems with legislation and the infrastructure will be solved in the near future. In addition, the software faculties at universities will receive wider support, and the qualifications of graduates are expected to be higher.

In some countries software production has a low contribution to the national economy in comparison to other fields. In these countries copyright laws against software piracy are not yet very well-established. Many companies cannot afford the high prices for modern Western software. Enforcing the existing copyright laws would slow down economic growth in other fields. The likelihood is that these problems will be solved in time. In countries that rely heavily on software production and international outsourcing, however, the process of enforcing the copyright laws might be faster than in countries where this business has only a marginal

AU7017_book.fm Page 49 Thursday, March 16, 2006 5:07 PM

war breaks out in the country where the offshore unit is located, proceeding with the software development is unlikely.

Important questions in this context are:

- How stable is the country from a political point of view?
- Are there political tensions between neighbors?
- Is the territorial integrity of the country questioned? Are there disputes regarding the borderlines?
- Is civil strife or ethnic tension an issue in the area?
- How friendly is the relationship between the vendor's country and the buyer's country? Are there treaties between the two countries?
- Is exporting the technology that has to be used in the operations of the offshore unit permitted?
- What import licenses are necessary? How easily and rapidly can they be obtained?

4.2.4 Natural Disasters

Other situations that might create the need for an emergency plan are natural disasters. (See Section 3.4.)

- What kinds of disasters can occur in the region — e.g., earthquakes?
- Is the offshore government prepared for disasters? What standards of infrastructure are to be expected in the days and months following a potential disaster?
- Are there risks of pollution or destruction of the environment after a natural disaster (e.g., nuclear accidents)?

4.2.5 Everyday Security

In most offshore countries the indices of security do not reach the standard level in industrialized countries — e.g., in Western Europe. However, even among borderline neighbors there might be considerable differences in the perceived level of "insecurity." Romania, for example, is thought of as rather peaceful, but some foreign managers consider Ukraine, a neighbor on the map, more dangerous.

What importance do violent crimes have in the lives of the people in that country (foreigners or natives)? What preventive measures are usually considered necessary by foreign managers to provide protection to persons

of Eastern Europe. Problems may arise only if very specific hardware and software subject to export regulations are involved. Telecommunication and Internet access might be surprisingly expensive. International phone calls in a developing country can be orders of magnitude more costly than telephone calls between industrialized countries.

How efficient and how reliable is data and voice communication? What is the highest bandwidth available in the region? What are the prices for various bandwidths? Is it easy to establish communication channels?

How long does it take to travel within the country? The traffic system in some developing countries is in an incipient form, and therefore internal routes can be quite costly in terms of time. This is particularly important for sites that are not close to an international airport.

Is the environment polluted? How reliable is the supply of everyday goods and services: electricity, telecommunication, medicines, and even drinking water?

> A few days after I rented an apartment in a good area in Bucharest, Romania, my wife told me that we did not have any hot water.
>
> "What happened?" I asked.
>
> "Well, it seems that they turned off the hot water," my wife responded.
>
> "For how long?" I asked.
>
> "Oh, I don't know yet — perhaps a few hours, perhaps several weeks."
>
> In this case the problem was resolved after "only" a few hours. But once we really did not have hot water for three weeks — in winter time, in the bathroom, with a baby!
>
> If something like this happened in Germany, I would have called the block's administrator. If he could not resolve the problem within a reasonable time, I would think of consulting a lawyer. In Romania having or not having hot water is not a reason for "much ado."

4.2.7 Software Engineering Classes at Universities

in that country and in comparison to software classes in other countries? Some universities in offshore countries cooperate with universities in industrialized countries. Several of these cooperation projects are already rather mature, and the degrees are considered equivalent. Do such systems of cooperation exist in the country under consideration?

How much time do students invest in their studies? Even if time is not the only component, the invested time is generally strongly correlated with the results. Do students have to work their way through university? How do they provide for their living expenses?

Talent is very important for software engineers. Do top talents receive adequate support? Are they successful at international competitions? Many young people in developing countries leave their country even before university to study in industrialized countries. Others emigrate immediately after graduation. Usually the most talented leave the country. This raises questions about the qualifications and talent of those who are available on the labor market in that country.

4.2.8 Going by Car

Driving a car in an offshore country requires some precautions.

You should have a cell phone number of a lawyer of that country at hand whom you could call even outside of usual office hours, at night, or during the weekend. This number is very helpful if you are stopped by the police or if you are involved in an accident. Try this contact before you really need it: does your cell phone work in that country? Is the number valid? Do you find a lawyer at the other end of the line or a secretary? Is there enough proficiency in a common language to discuss issues of traffic, police, and accidents?

Discuss with that lawyer or another trusted person what precautions are necessary for foreign drivers. In some countries it is not advisable to drive at night or in certain areas. In other countries foreigners are well advised to always drive in convoys with other drivers — groups that are formed in advance (not on the way) because criminals might attack single cars. Another reason for forming a convoy is the possibility of an accident: when you travel in a convoy the other drivers see how the accident happened, and they are witnesses at court. In some countries, people who are sitting in the same car cannot be fully valid witnesses for each other. You should also have some basic photographic equipment at hand

4.2.9 The Health System

Staff from industrialized countries might have to spend fairly long periods of time in the developing country. In this case the level of the health system might play a role in decision making. What is the maximum quality of the health services that can be provided in a particular country? What are the costs for various levels of quality? Health assistance at a high level might be even more expansive than in industrialized countries.

> While I was writing this book, my son had to stay for a day in a hospital for a small routine treatment. My wife called me from the hospital asking me to bring food and mineral water because these resources were in short supply there. In an industrialized country, a hospital where drinking water might be a problem would be beyond imagination.
>
> By the time when I arrived at the hospital, my wife had already resolved the issue: she had arranged with the doctor that the child would sleep at home and come back to the hospital the next morning. The main reason for this decision was that all beds were already occupied — by two children each.
>
> Another time our child was scheduled for a vaccination. In an innocent voice the doctor said that we would have to bring a certain serum (notice: we have to bring it!). My wife opened her handbag and gave the doctor a small box. Now the doctor was really surprised: "Where did you get it? It is not available in Romania right now."
>
> My wife said she bought it the previous winter when the child received the first vaccination in this series and kept it in the refrigerator; she had already considered the possibility that there might be a shortage of this serum at the time when the child was scheduled for the second immunization.
>
> Then my wife insisted that she be present in the room when the doctor prepared the injection and treated the child. Later I asked her why this was so important. "Well, there is still the possibility that the doctor might give our child another injection (e.g., salted water) and keep our serum for 'better friends' — who love their children too," she said.
>
> The child of an offshore manager did not have an appetite

The desperate parents discussed the issue with a friend of the family, a medical researcher. He suspected that there might be certain parasites in the child's intestines. They caused pain when food was digested, and this might have been the reason why the child refused food. The friend suggested the child should take a test for these parasites. The test, however, came back negative.

The treatment against these parasites may cause side effects. For this reason it is indicated only after a positive test — not as a preventive measure. The medical researcher was convinced that his suspicion was valid and urged the parents to repeat the test. Finally, the third test brought a positive result. The child was treated and the problems disappeared immediately. It seems that the first two tests had not been done at all — the nurses just checked "negative" on the form.

The test in question is rather time consuming and requires reagents that are not quite cheap. If the test is not done at all, the medical laboratory saves time and does not have to buy the reagents, but they still can bill the result. Just checking the "negative" check-mark has advantages — from the point of view of the lab.

In industrialized countries few persons share this type of experience — and few know how they should deal with it.

4.2.10   Lawyers and Accountants

Foreign managers might encounter difficulties finding reliable lawyers, accountants, and other authorized staff. This problem even more important if the foreign management has only a limited knowledge of the emerging country's language, as the following anecdote illustrates.

A small offshore company worked with an accountant in that emerging country to keep their books. It turned out that the accountant worked very sloppily — he put incorrect numbers into the documents and did not submit mandatory documents to the authorities. Of course, the foreign management did not know of this. The managers wanted to earn good, honest money

the accounting documents. Only then did they start to understand that their papers were a desperate mess.

In this case the authorities were understanding, and the company was allowed to fix the problems without severe punishment. They asked what they could do to avoid this kind of trouble in the future. The authorities suggested employing two accounting companies — one checking the other.

This advice sounds obvious and is expected to work: if the vast majority of accounting companies are honest it is unlikely to meet two unethical accountants in a row, simply from statistical considerations. This is the common sense point of view. My own experience is summarized in the following anecdote.

I bought a construction site. The situation was a bit more complicated than usual because I bought parts of multiple small, adjacent properties from different owners and "merged" them. For this reason, I had to order a topographical study regarding the exact limits of my property. This document had to be double-checked by an independent topographical expert and validated by the authorities because it might have far-reaching legal consequences.

I have to admit that I am far from a topographical expert, so I could do hardly more than accept the work of the expert "as is" — leafing through the file and admiring the many signatures and seals of various forms and colors. However, the proportions of the drawing looked different from the real site as I had it in memory. And applying Pythagoras' Formula led to a result which appeared to be wrong by more than 20 m.

Further investigations revealed that the topographical expert had never seen the site. When I scheduled a meeting at the site he had even the nerve to call my cell phone asking for guidance to the site because he had trouble finding it. He simply took coordinates from older documents and merged them on paper. In this process he made a "small mistake in calculation."

But what about the second expert who was paid to double-check the results? Well, the two "experts" have known each for a long time; they trust each other and "cooperate smoothly."

and do not have the time to worry about each piece of land that might have been sold. They simply have better things to do.

So either you have someone whom you can trust or you do not. Paying a second "expert" for double-checking will definitely increase the costs. Whether it also improves the reliability is something you might find out later.

4.3 ECONOMIC FACTS IN THE OFFSHORE COUNTRY

Cost efficiency is a prime issue in most offshore scenarios. This is why potential investors should know some basic economic facts about the emerging country, including average income, cost of living, and prices for office space and other real estate. Taxes are important, and the prognosis for labor cost influences the long-term feasibility of the offshore relationship.

4.3.1 Average Income and Cost of Living

Living in offshore countries can be rather cheap. However, this is applicable only as long as one lives according to the offshore country's long-established practices. In the course of the offshore relationship, it might be necessary to relocate staff from industrialized countries temporarily or permanently to offshore sites. If the living standard, the level of accommodation, and Western eating habits are to be maintained, the cost of living can reach even higher levels than in Western society. The main reason is that accommodation at high standards has a low level of availability and is consequently expensive. In some emerging countries there are only a limited number of supermarkets that follow the Western model, leading to high prices. Certain kinds of food that are very common in Western countries, can be hard to find — and quite expensive.

The average income in the country might be a particular point of interest for the potential investor. The official numbers are not always reliable because in emerging countries a significant part of the money available to private persons comes from sources that are not covered by the statistics. Knowledge of the average income helps the manager to evaluate the plausibility of applicants' and partners' statements. Thus, the options of partners become clearer and negotiations are more efficient.

4.3.2   Prices for Real Estate

How expensive is it to buy or rent acceptable office space and personnel accommodation? How expensive is it to protect offices and apartments against unauthorized access? How expensive are hotels? In some offshore capitals, hotels are even more expensive than the equivalent accommodation in Western cities.

Do not think that land in emerging countries is necessarily cheap: in 2006 a construction site in a good position in Bucharest, Romania cost more than $2000 per square meter. The price for a five-star hotel ranged beyond $200 per night.

4.3.3   Taxes

How high are the taxes for companies and for private persons?

How sharp is the difference between the net income of a typical software engineer and the company's total cost for that employee? In some emerging countries, this difference can be surprisingly high: the final costs for the company may well be three times the employee's net income due to high taxes and social security contributions.

How large is the discrepancy between the company's profit and the net amount of money that ends up in the pocket of the entrepreneur?

Are there special tax regulations for foreign capital companies or for international business relations? How high are the customs duties?

Taxes are just one part of the equation. The other important variable is the rigidity or generosity of the finances authorities when establishing borderlines and their rigor in checking accounting papers.

4.3.4   Long-Term Labor Cost

Salaries in emerging countries are quickly evolving. In many important countries, offshore outsourcing payments have been constantly growing over the years, especially in the case of qualified young software engineers who are fluent in English. The long-term cost prognosis depends on several factors, such as:

▪ The expected demand for software services in that country.
▪ The supply of qualified workers. Some countries, such as China, have relatively large and untapped pools of workers. In other countries the market is rather narrow, and the prices are sensitive

level of qualification — i.e., assistants. So far, this resource has been available in developing countries at affordable prices. The increasing speed of offshore outsourcing raises the question whether the emerging software industries can scale up fast enough while maintaining both quality and cost efficiency.

■ The capacity of the education system in that region: how fast is it possible to produce new talent?

■ The pricing policies of the vendors. Indian vendors, for example, have decided to climb up one step of the supply chain and try to erase the price differences.

■ How attractive is the software industry in this country in comparison to other businesses? What options does the country offer for intelligent and motivated young people? Emerging countries enjoy high economic growth and provide quite a number of attractive positions even in low-tech industries. In some cases the low-tech alternatives are even better paid than high-tech software jobs.

In some Eastern European countries car mechanics were among the best paid workers at the end of the millennium. This stemmed from the fact that many of the circulating cars in these post-Communist countries were in desperate condition. Some experienced mechanics (many of them were autodidacts) bought cheap, old, secondhand cars in Western Europe, rehabilitated them, and sold them at high profits in their countries. "Why should I worry about high-tech software when I can earn three times as much by selling old cars?"

4.4   LEGAL SYSTEMS

The executives of all contributing companies need a basic understanding of the legal systems in the other countries involved. There are huge differences in the practical aspects of legal systems in emerging countries and in industrialized countries. In practice, the differences are even larger than the study of the published laws may suggest.

4.4.1   Establishing and Running an Offshore Unit

58 ■ The Insider's Guide to Outsourcing Risks and Rewards

- Can foreigners own 100 percent of the subsidiaries?
- Are there special laws for companies owned by foreigners?
- How much overhead is caused by bureaucracy and management of the contact with the authorities?
- Can foreigners own land and other real estate?

4.4.2 Employment Contracts

Pertinent questions regarding employment contracts include:

- What are the labor laws?
- Which legal provisions are mandatory? To what extent is it possible for the contract partners (employer and worker) to negotiate a contractual agreement?

Drafting a valid employment contract can turn out to be a difficult task in a developing country. This is especially true if a small company wants to take on new staff, in which case even finding a capable lawyer can be tricky. The legal systems are rather unstable in many emerging countries. If it comes to litigation, crucial provisions of the contract might turn out to be invalid. This can also be quite an issue in industrialized countries as well. However, the probability of this happening is higher in a developing country.

In general, employees do not have much legal experience either. For this reason it seems that power is "balanced on a low level." This can change, however, if the cooperation comes to its end and the contract is to be closed.

A small offshore company hired several software developers. Neither the company's manager nor the employees were very experienced in legal matters. So they enlisted the help of an arbitrarily chosen lawyer for legal consultancy regarding the employment contract. The contract included a period of notice that seemed reasonable to all participants; at least, all participants signed it.

After some time one of the software engineers wanted to leave the small company. He had an attractive offer from a very large international organization. He had changed his mind and was no longer fond of the idea of a "period of notice." Instead

as fast as possible. Large companies have access to qualified legal consultancy — even in developing countries. The large organization's experts were much more qualified than the lawyer "from the street corner" who had drafted the contract. Important parts of the contract turned out to be invalid, and the employee could leave without a period of notice.

This anecdote shows that the employment contract must be drafted in such a way that it can be protected even against the intervention of a large international organization. This challenging task is beyond the possibilities of most small offshore companies and beyond the skills of many offshore lawyers.

4.4.3 Costs for Lawsuits

How expensive is it to be involved in a lawsuit? Some offshore managers are shocked when confronted with the prices for a single consultation with an onshore lawyer.

4.4.4 Damages, Indemnities, and Compensation

The amount of money for compensation for nonmaterial damages (such as disclosing a business secret, disturbing a customer relationship) might be ludicrously low in emerging countries. On the other hand, the sentenced compensation in industrialized counties might be beyond the wildest nightmares of an offshore manager. How high is the typical amount of compensation in the particular country?

A Romanian TV station made headlines by breaking a certain law and stirring up a huge scandal. Consequently, they were fined approximately 5000 Euros. In Western countries, it would be considered hilarious if a TV station were sentenced to compensation that low.

4.4.5 How Reliable Is the Legal System in Practice?

In some Eastern European countries software piracy is not at all persecuted, even if it is officially condemned. The latest

An offshore lawyer faked his client's signature. The documents were perfectly all right. The lawyer, however, was just too slothful to make an arrangement to have the papers signed by the client himself. Other lawyers took bribes from his adversary.

An offshore manager litigated against a disloyal partner. From the legal point of view, the situation was crystal clear. For this reason the manager did not worry very much but asked a lawyer to take care of the issue. The manager was more than surprised when he finally received a letter from the court that the case had been decided — against him. Further investigation revealed that the lawyer was simply absent from the trial; probably he was occupied with something else. The judge had an easy job: he decided in favor of the only party who was present at the process. The manager and a second lawyer needed quite some time to correct the first lawyer's dubious practices.

In fact it may be difficult to find a lawyer who has both integrity and high professional qualifications.

4.4.6   How Long Does It Take to Finish a Process if the Legal Situation Is Obviously Clear?

An offshore manager bought a site to construct a house for his family. A neighbor brought some old cars to the site and started an (unregistered) business for secondhand parts for cars. For this reason, the manager could not start work on the house. The cars were there without any agreement from the site's owner. So the offshore manager employed a lawyer to solve the problem. However, he had to fire the lawyer because there were clear indications that the lawyer was cooperating with the adversery. Probably he had been bribed, although this could not be demonstrated. A second lawyer also had to be fired because of doubtful integrity. Obviously, the owner of the old cars was very skilled in using unfair tricks such as bribes. A third lawyer turned out to be trustworthy. However, he could hardly repair the wrong done by the first two lawyers. It took years until the authorities took the old cars away from the site.

AU7017_book.fm Page 61 Thursday, March 16, 2006 5:07 PM

of contracts are respected. This raises the question of how the validity of agreements is usually ensured in practice — for example, concerning the measures necessary to make sure that employees do not disclose business secrets and observe their periods of notice.

There are rumors of cases where managers put tremendous (sometimes illegal) pressure on the families of employees to make sure that the employee "behaves correctly" — "correctly" according to the definition of the offshore management.

Such cases are particularly likely to occur if the employee has been sent abroad to an industrialized country where the employee is protected by the police of that country. The family of the employee, however, is protected only in a limited way by the less-efficient security system of the developing country.

> An offshore engineer had to visit a customer in an industrialized country. Visa regulations required that this employee be paid according to the level of payment in the Western country, at least for entire period of his stay. The offshore company would have liked to get this rather important sum of money into their own pockets instead of rightfully giving it to the employee.
>
> Before the employee left for the industrialized country his family had to sign a so-called "credit contract." They would never receive the money that was stipulated in the "credit contract." The contract stated that those were costs for "training" — which was meant to smooth the employee's adjustment to a new working environment. Once the employee was in the industrialized country, his family had to pay back their so-called debt — i.e., the money that was stipulated in the credit contract and which they had never actually received. The only way they could pay back their "debt" was to resort to the employee's paycheck, and thus the employee was forced to send a large part of his rather high salary home. Thus, much of his salary ended up in the pocket of the company in the developing country.

Extreme cases of this kind may be the exception, even in developing countries. However, when entering an offshore engagement it is important to know how these kinds of problems are usually solved in the respective

5

PARTNERS: CUSTOMER–VENDOR RELATIONSHIP

ABSTRACT

It's all about relationships in outsourcing business. The first decisions for the emerging relationship are already made before its actual onset at the time when the customer selects a vendor and the two parties negotiate the outsourcing contract. This preparation task constitutes a significant part of the investment in establishing the offshore scenario, but a carefully structured process of vendor selection can greatly diminish the costs of establishing the relationship. The customer's first step is defining the vendor selection criteria and clarifying the motivations for the outsourcing decision: financial, technical, or commercial. After both sides have elicited reliable information, the exact stipulations of the contract can be negotiated. Once the outsourcing scenario is established, the customer must manage the vendor and oversee the work of the offshore team. When the cooperation gains speed, it is quite likely that sooner or later disputes about technical or contractual issues will appear. Litigation is almost always the worst solution. Therefore, many outsourcing contracts include a dispute resolution procedure, which usually starts with forwarding the conflict in a predefined way to higher management. If the issue remains unsolved, the partner can apply mediation or arbitration in an attempt to find a mutually acceptable settlement before taking the ultimate step of going to court.

One widely applied method of government and vendor management is benchmark audits; an independent third party provider of benchmarking services helps to analyze the relationship and evaluates the vendor's performance by comparing it to that of peer companies. The benchmark study should determine whether the service level still matches the state of the art and whether the prices are appropriate and the contractual provisions are fair. The benchmark report may conclude that the vendor has to solve any identified problems within a reasonable time period or that the fees need adaptation. Benchmark clauses are adopted in many outsourcing contracts. For the customer, they are a way to keep the vendor honest. A successful benchmark audit can increase customer satisfaction and thus improve the customer–vendor relationship.

In scenarios where the customer works with a single provider, this vendor can gain undue influence because of its monopoly position. Some customers try to avoid these problems by working with more than one vendor in parallel. Such so-called "multisourcing" scenarios can have a number of advantages because they introduce a competitive element. However, coordinating multiple vendors who are competitors on the market creates other challenges and requires advanced skills in project management and information technology (IT) politics: the work atmosphere might become tense, and the project can reach a crisis because the various service providers do not cooperate smoothly but try to undermine each other's reputation in front of the customer.

5.1 VENDOR SELECTION AND CONTRACT NEGOTIATION

Vendor selection and negotiation of the outsourcing contract are major items on the list of costs in the process of establishing the outsourcing relationship. However, it is possible to save costs by applying a well-defined, carefully considered, and structured process evolving from the first informal discussion to the signed contract in a systematic way.

The Steering Committee

The customer establishes an internal task management team that has the responsibility for and is empowered to develop the outsourcing plans. In many cases enlisting the help of external outsourcing advisers who are knowledgeable on the topic of the offshore outsourcing of IT projects and have been through this process before is recommended. (See also

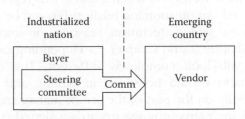

Figure 5.1   The steering committee consists of employees of the buyer. They oversee the work of the offshore team and facilitate communication.

An outsourcing deal is a complex mix of administrative, legal, and technical components, and therefore a balanced mixture of skills is required; managers, outsourcing experts, and people with solid IT backgrounds should take part in the preliminary discussions. Because the various business and legal aspects of an outsourcing deal are closely intertwined, a business-oriented attorney with experience in offshore outsourcing should be available to the steering committee. Even in the early stages of the discussion, some legal issues have to be considered. Otherwise, the customer's negotiating position is quite likely to undergo substantial changes afterwards, resulting in costly rework due to the necessary reopenings of apparently closed issues. It is of foremost importance that the steering committee's members have the necessary skills and inclination for the tasks at hand and are convinced of the advantages of the outsourcing plan.

It often happens that individuals within the organization have serious concerns about the advantages and risks of outsourcing and doubt that this step is for the best of the organization overall. Such concerns should be dealt with as soon as possible and should be analyzed and confirmed or refuted before the process is given the green light for the later step of contacting potential providers.

Gathering information

Offshore outsourcing is a challenging field of international IT management. For this reason, the responsible persons have to compile a multitude of information in various fields — offshore countries, potential partners, business models, contract architectures, and selection of suitable projects — to mention just a few.

have to coalesce their views and reach a consensus regarding the business goals to be achieved. An outsourcing relationship can be driven by various motivations — cost saving, technical reasons, or strategic commercial decisions. (See Chapter 2 and Chapter 3.) Depending on these priorities, the entire deal will look completely different. The objectives of the outsourcing scenario should be stated in writing and require a broad consensus, especially on the part of the senior management. The priorities can be refined as the plans progress towards a signed contract. However, the customer has to be aware that substantial changes in the objectives will cause substantial rework and costs for both customer and vendor.

Vendor Selection Criteria

The customer's steering committee has to define the attributes of the ideal vendor and the limitations of the vendor selection process: which properties are strictly mandatory, which are optional, and which features of the service provider are to be prohibited (e.g., working for competitors).

Defining an Evaluation Process

A number of analysts recommend that the customer should define in advance the steps to be followed in the discussion with various vendors. Which phases should the evolving negotiation pass through? What milestones should be reached? What are the entry and exit criteria for moving from one phase to the next? The explicit definition of the process keeps the main directions of negotiation with potential business partners structured and efficient. In addition, it helps the customer maintain leadership in the ongoing discussion, instead of just reacting to the provider's marketing strategy.

To achieve an efficient process the customer has to set deadlines and ensure that they are met. Reliable deadlines also require that the customer itself maintain a certain discipline; otherwise, it will lose credibility in the eyes of the vendor.

Some vendors might try to shorten the outsourcing evaluation process and directly contact senior management for a quick decision. One reason is that the disciplined process takes a lot of time and resources, and the vendor may want to avoid it. In addition, the vendor might risk being ruled out in one of the earlier phases of the process. If the respective

Not only vendors but some customers as well are not fully convinced of the necessity of a structured and carefully carried out vendor selection and negotiation process. In particular, first-time customers try to apply shortcuts: signing incomplete contracts, insufficient coverage of the market, not using outsourcing expertise. In many cases this strategy backfires: incomplete contracts, for example, frequently turn out to be to the disadvantage of the customer.

A clearly defined process has the additional advantage that the steering committee can easily explain to higher management how the partner was finally selected and why it was preferred over others.

The Request for Proposals (RFP)

An RFP is a document that is sent to potential service providers. It includes a set of requirements and invites service providers to send a list of prices, terms, conditions, and suggested solutions. A related document is a "request for information" (RFI), which asks a potential partner to send general information regarding its strong points and details about the services it can offer. Frequently, RFPs are rather lengthy documents, and the elicited responses are rarely shorter. Thus, writing RFPs or the corresponding suggestions from scratch is not inexpensive. This explains why in practice both RFPs and the suggestions on the part of the vendors are frequently derived from generic patterns. Only some specific details are adapted to the needs of the project at hand. In addition, RFPs can be sent to quite a number of potential service providers. Thus, the vendor only has a limited statistical chance to win the project selection competition when it responds to an RFP. This is why the provider has to limit the resources to be invested in the proposal. Most vendors avoid investing too much into the RFP and send stock answers instead, which are just sufficient to allow the vendor to remain in the selection process.

On the buyer's side, the situation is not much better: detailed analysis of the lengthy responses would require significant resources. It is doubtful that the stock answers justify this investment. Instead, the answers are frequently just glanced through. Hence in many cases, the RFP process does not ensure the desired efficiency. The following hints can help the buyer make its RFP process more efficient:

■ *Short RFPs* with precise questions call for concise answers. Longer

◼ *Background information* about the buyer may help the vendor assess the importance of the emerging relationship. Note that vendors have to concentrate their scarce resources on the most promising prospective buyers. Thus, some data and the current outsourcing policy may help the vendor get a clearer image of the RFP-submitting organization.

RFPs can be an important tool for preselecting potential partners, and the customer will want to make sure that the responses are true and valid. For this reason, it could be advantageous to work with a business attorney when drafting the RFP because the answers should be directly incorporated into the contract.

Confidentiality of Requirements

In many projects, requirements include important business information about the customer's strategic plans. For this reason they should be kept confidential, at least to such an extent that they should not leak out to competitors. In addition, offshore outsourcing plans are usually very sensitive information, and many organizations avoid disclosing them too early to their in-house IT team to avoid tension, backlash, and reduced productivity. Although the receivers of the RFP may have some obligations regarding confidentiality of the RFP, the process is not usually considered very secret, particularly if the RFP is sent before a contract of cooperation with the addressees is signed.

Selection of Potential Business Partners

For some customers, it is advantageous to discuss key issues of the envisioned outsourcing scenario with a number of vendors and then to narrow the list to the few most promising candidates. Notice that discussions between potential future outsourcing partners are not cheap for either side. For this reason the customer is well advised to keep the number of considered vendors as small as possible — without compromising the coverage of the market, of course. Strictly limiting the number of potential partners helps the client focus its own resources on the most promising candidates. Providers that are unlikely to win the contract competition should be eliminated from the evaluation process as early as possible. This clearing-up process makes resources available for negotia-

AU7017_book.fm Page 69 Thursday, March 16, 2006 5:07 PM

Communication of Serious Intent

Like clients, vendors have to manage their resources. Many prospective buyers contact quite a number of vendors — at least in the early stages of the selection process. For this reason, the vendor only has limited chances of winning the game — from a purely statistical point of view.

If the customer wants to be given proper consideration, it has to communicate serious intentions. Otherwise, it will not have access to the vendor's most qualified analysts.

The Vendor's Point of View

Some customers have already decided on a favorite vendor but keep one or more other bidders in the selection process to encourage competitiveness and to negotiate the lowest prices possible. Such so-called stalking horses never had a real chance of winning because the customer's decision for the preferred bidder was already made but not made public. This makes the stalking horses different from a "losing bidder" who had in fact a realistic chance of success. Although the losing bidder is informed as soon as it is out of competition, stalking horses do not know anything about their status. On the contrary, the customer is particularly careful not to disclose this fact, especially because stalking horses do not receive compensation for their efforts. That is why the role of the stalking horse is rather dangerous for the vendor. If a service provider is frequently caught in this role, it is likely to leave the market very soon. The roles of stalking horses and losing bidders are only one reason why the vendor can lose its precontractual investment. Another cause can be that the project is cancelled at an early stage. For this reason the vendor tries to assess whether the customer's intention of making an order is really serious. The vendor will want to know:

■ Is the customer discussing the project with other vendors as well? How many bidders are involved? Who are these competitors?
■ Is there a preferred vendor? How much attention do the other bidders receive?
■ How much has the customer already invested in the deal? How many people are currently working at the client's site preparing the outsourcing scenario? How much of their time are they spending on this project?

An engineer in a lower position might want to make an impression on his superiors with an allegedly "prodigious" idea for a new software project and to this purpose may even solicit offers and business proposals from various potential vendors, without management even being informed about these contacts. In such cases it is rather unlikely that these feeble attempts of promotion on the part of an overly ambitious employee will ever lead to a signed contract.

■ Are the outsourcing plans stifled by heavy politics? Do some individuals disagree with the goals of the deal? Who are these individuals and how much influence do they have? What are their motivations? Projects that are opposed by key players are likely to be cancelled at an early phase. (See Section 6.5.)

Informal Discussion with Selected Vendors

The first rounds of discussion should be carried out using informal business language — i.e., in plain English instead of contractual provisions. Negotiating the wording of the contract at too early a stage implies the risk of process blockage due to adversarial debates about contractual details that are of minor importance to the strategic outline of the outsourcing relationship.

Although the details of the contract's wording and legal discussions are avoided in the phase of informal negotiations, the representatives of both sides should have the necessary background know-how to assess the legal consequences of the outlined business architecture. They also must be authorized to speak in the name of their organizations. Otherwise it is quite likely that apparently closed topics will have to be reopened in the later stages when law specialists enter the process. Such cycles of reopening are at best a nuisance and at worst may cause considerable costs due to prolonged negotiations or even lead to a cancellation of the relationship.

Delaying the wording of the contract does not mean avoiding the crucial topics. Some outsourcing partners waste a lot of time with rather academic discussions about philosophy and partnership. In many cases, these discussions have a very limited impact on the contract and the future cooperation. It is often better to use this time to discuss "hard topics" such as prices, service levels, and governance. Discussions between service providers and buyers are rather expensive. Especially if the partners are separated by long distances, negotiation time is quite precious. During the informal discussions phase, the customer's team has to make sure that

the final contract are very important as well. Nevertheless, the blueprint of the cooperation already exists before the contract is drafted. The author has personally seen more outsourcing relations fail because the entire architecture of the cooperation was not suitable than because of details of the contractual provisions. If the outsourcing relationship results in unfavorable dynamics, it is quite likely that the wrong decisions were made in the very beginning during informal discussions, not during the negotiation of the final contract's wording.

Rethinking the Basic Decisions

After all information is compiled and all cards are on the table, the steering committee may want to rethink the decision for outsourcing the project — i.e., whether the outsourcing deal is to the advantage of the organization as a whole. In this phase it might be reasonable to ask the most senior management for final confirmation based on complete and updated information.

> One of my friends, a gunnery officer in the army, told me that whenever he has finished all the calculations for inclination angles and directions of the artillery's guns, he takes a bite of his sandwich while glancing through his calculations — before he gives the command to fire.

Discussing with Only One Potential Vendor?

Negotiations with multiple vendors have advantages and disadvantages. The customer obtains much additional information if it discusses with multiple vendors in parallel. It learns about alternative commercial business processes and innovative technological solutions. Parallel negotiations, however, require significantly more effort. In addition, the providers may hesitate to invest in the emerging relationship because there is only a limited chance of winning the contract. In a scenario based on parallel negotiations, it will probably take longer to set up the outsourcing relationship. Taking into account all these pros and cons, the customer has to decide whether parallel negotiations are desirable in the scenario at hand. In any case, the number of vendors that make it to the later stages of the selection process should be strictly limited.

AU7017_book.fm Page 72 Thursday, March 16, 2006 5:07 PM

accept a contract to work below a "decent" margin — except perhaps in the case of a first very small pilot project that is meant to establish the relationship. In the long run the vendor has to cover its costs, forestall risks, and report reasonable results to its shareholders. When fighting for lowest prices, the customer might seem to obtain a bargain — at least for the time being. In time, however, this strategy may backfire and work to the disadvantage of the client.

One reason for exaggeratedly low prices can be that the vendor is rather inexperienced. In this case the provider will probably leave the market very soon, most likely before the project is finished, leaving the customer with an unfinished, failed project. Another possible reason for surprisingly low prices can be that the provider is rather experienced and already has a well-prepared strategy of counterbalancing its initial losses — e.g., via change requests. The low prices are only a tactic to attract the buyer into the contract. (See Section 9.2.)

Notice that there are many ways in which customers can lose money in the IT outsourcing business; some of them are outlined in this book, others are just being invented.

Balance of Power

Paying customers are very much sought-after in the IT business, as in most other businesses. The polished manners and the amiability displayed by numerous vendors might give the customer's representatives the impression of being by far the stronger party at the negotiation table. To some extent this is true: the client can, for example, cancel negotiations with a vendor for almost absurdly insignificant reasons — and soon more than enough competitors will be eager to take the place of the candidate who has fallen into disgrace. In fact, the buyer has rather strong negotiation leverage — at least before the contract is signed. Thus the customer's team usually negotiates a contract that "looks quite respectable" to present to their superiors. It often happens that the negotiated price and some other contractual details seem to be to the advantage of the buyer.

In other cases, however, this subjective impression of power can be misleading. Some large vendors have taken part in hundreds of outsourcing projects and gained tens of thousands of hours worth of experience in the ensuing negotiations. Most of their customers, on the other hand,

predicting the most likely evolution of this relationship than does the partner who is in love for the first time.

Another source of inequity is the outsourcing contract — a long and complex document covering technical, financial, and administrative aspects. Large outsourcing deals are detailed in a text up to 1000 pages in length — sometimes even more. The providers are far more experienced in managing this complexity than are their rather green partners. Sometimes the buyer does not really penetrate the architecture of the contract, and it might not grasp the future evolution of the relationship.

These observations lend credibility to suspicions regarding the parity of the outsourcing partnership. Sometimes it reminds me of the story of the sly old wolf and Little Red Riding Hood. In this analogy, however, Little Red Riding Hood is rather well-off, making decisions worth tens and hundreds of millions of dollars — and the poor old wolf is feeling a bit hungry.

5.2 DUE DILIGENCE: ELICITING INFORMATION ABOUT VENDORS

Any outsourcing relationship (not only offshore) is based on trust. Before the customer can enter this relationship, it has to do some due diligence and collect some basic data about the future partner:

- *Cost reductions are a strong motivation in many offshore scenarios. If the vendor is overly cheap, this may be an indication of economic instability, which is against the best interests of the customer.*
- *Because the vendor's team is part of the customer's extended enterprise, the buyer has to validate the qualifications of the offshore workers. A particular problem of teams in emerging software industries is the worryingly high attrition numbers.*
- *Many customers ask for references from the vendor to evaluate its reputation in the market. However, reading and interpreting recommendations requires experience and a good deal of skepticism.*
- *Most offshore scenarios are designed for long periods of time. For this reason, many analysts suggest that synergy*

In many scenarios it can prove difficult to elicit reliable and complete information regarding the listed items. The vendors might have good reasons to disclose only part of the required information or give misleading or even false information.

Financial Analysis

An efficient way of eliciting pricing information from various vendors is a pricing table — i.e., an empty matrix that the bidders fill with their actual data. Thus, the buyer gains access to this crucial information in a standardized way by drawing comparisons between competitors more easily and efficiently.

Cost efficiency is a key issue in many offshore scenarios. For this reason, the customer has to thoroughly understand the conditions under which the vendor will be providing the contracted services and how the price calculation is derived because the pricing strategy involves some hidden risks. Is the price too high? This problem can easily be identified and resolved, for example, by comparison with competing offers. Is the price too low? This issue is more complex and raises doubts concerning quality. Another reason for low prices could be that the vendor has undisclosed plans regarding its future pricing policy. The provider could raise its prices when it is more difficult for the customer to switch to another vendor. In this way, vendors compensate for losses made at the beginning of an offshore relationship. In any event, surprisingly low prices require further analysis.

Economic Stability of the Vendor and Continuity of Its Organization

Basic economic numbers might be interesting: How large is the company and how many employees are on their payroll? How many of them work as software developers? How many of them are permanently employed? Does the company work with freelancers? If yes, for what reason? How long has the company been in business?

Even though the profits might have been published or can be made accessible in another way, the customer should try to get some information about the vendor's economic state of health. The client has to make sure that the vendor will still be present on the market when the project is finished.

In case of liabilities and indemnities, the vendor has to have enough assets to pay compensation. These assets have to be within the access of the court that decides on the indemnities.

because the stars are busy performing other tasks — e.g., meeting new customers. Thus the customer should know:

- Which people will work on its projects? What exactly are their qualifications — their formal education and university degrees as well as their practical experience? How much experience do they have with the technologies that will be used for the customer's projects?
- Team members who are working for several projects at the same time can cause serious management issues. It is more difficult to schedule meetings. They might have a conflict of loyalty if more than one project at the same time needs extraordinary efforts. Thus it is important to determine whether the workers assigned to the customer's project have additional duties concerning other projects. To what extent are they available for the customer's project?
- What roles will specific team members be assigned within the project? Are they available full time, for periodic supervision, or only for "emergency" consulting?
- Outstanding software engineers can have a strong positive impact on a software project even if they only contribute occasionally. This raises the question: what access does the vendor have to top talents? Only a few customers are in the position to assess outstanding talent. However, there are international competitions that enjoy a high reputation, such as the ACM Contest. The winners of such competitions are usually software whiz kids.
- High consulting quality rarely comes at low prices. This is why the customer has to set its priorities.

Retention of Staff

Many offshore software companies have a problem with attrition of staff, causing a serious drain of know-how and experience. Was the attrition rate worryingly large in the last few years? What measures have been taken to forestall this?

Low pay can be an important reason for weak retention numbers. Thus, a customer might be interested in the average monthly pay received by the vendor's software developers. How are these salaries ranked in comparison to the average national or local pay?

What are the qualifications and experience of the workers who decide

Reputation in the Market

The customer should have a look at some references from former clients of this vendor. Unfortunately, not all providers are completely honest, and in some cases testimonials might be forged or bought. In other cases the vendor might have participated in a few "prestigious" projects for the main purpose of obtaining impressive credentials. Anyway, the vendor will provide only references from content clients and successful projects; the professional fiascos remain carefully hidden skeletons in the closet. In all these cases, the testimonials paint a biased picture of the vendor's professional standards. Hence, reading and interpreting testimonials requires some experience and a good deal of skepticism.

Some customers might ask the vendor for references from clients who were less than fully satisfied. Discussions with dissatisfied partners can reveal more interesting information than talking to the buyers of showpiece projects would — e.g., they may reveal how the vendor deals with difficult situations and projects in crisis. The vendor may refuse to provide the customer with the names of unhappy buyers under the pretext that it has not encountered failure so far. In this case skepticism is indicated because vendors who have never been through a crisis are considered to be "red herrings" among insiders. However, the vendor might have legitimate motivations for refusing to provide references from unhappy customers. Someone could use these references to systematically collect doubtful competitive information against the vendor and perhaps even publish it. In this case, the vendor's entire business could be in danger. For this reason, it is difficult in many cases to get such references, desirable as they may be.

Vendors Working for Competitors

Large vendors have many customers. Of particular interest is whether the vendor has been carrying through projects in the customer's business field. In this case the vendor already has a lot of business background and domain expertise, which greatly accelerates the upfront work of establishing the relationship and of training the provider's team. On the other hand, if a vendor works for the customer's competitors, it raises serious issues regarding the confidentiality of intellectual property and business know-how: how are the teams separated in this case — are they separated at all? Will they still be completely separated in a few years? In time some team members will be assigned to other tasks within the vendor's orga-

the know-how of multiple customers. The client only has access to its own know-how. Given this strong position, the vendor might sooner or later consider entering the market as a competitor of its clients: the vendor has more comprehensive know-how than its customers and competitive costs, and it controls the technical staff — what could prevent it from succeeding?

Strategic Goals of the Vendor

The offshore outsourcing market is changing at a breathtaking pace. The economic conditions in some offshore countries are even more fast paced. The offshore scenario, on the other hand, is designed for durability and continuity due to the high cost of setting up the relationship and the difficulties of switching to another vendor. For this reason, many analysts consider synergy of goals to be very important for the long-term success of the offshore scenario.

In practice, however, it is sometimes difficult for the customer to simply find out the vendor's true strategic plan — let alone to match it with its own plans. The buyer has hardly any means to verify the validity of the provider's statements regarding its strategic plans. Thus a document with the title "strategic plans" is probably authorized not by top executives but by the marketing department and contains statements that are meant to please the customer's ears. Anyway, these "strategic plans" are by no means legally binding.

Security

Security is not cheap, and offshore business is very price sensitive. Consequently, the vendor might be tempted to save costs at the wrong end. Because security vulnerabilities can cause high consequential damages, the customer may want to verify the security measures that the vendor has in place. (See Chapter 10.) The following topics are important:

- *Networks*. Assessing network security outwits most customers. Thus, it may need a closer look from an expert.
- *Confidentiality*. What protections against breach of confidentiality and espionage are implemented? How is movement of digital resources controlled? If the vendor develops software for several (perhaps competing) customers, how are networks and teams separated?

AU7017_book.fm Page 78 Thursday, March 16, 2006 5:07 PM

An offshore manager reported three break-ins in his apartment and one attempted forced entry in his organization's office during only five years' time.

It might be reasonable to send someone to inspect the security measures; verbal promises are not always valid. Note that some vendors have multiple sites — one that is shown to visitors and another where the actual work is done. Thus the customer's representative should make sure to visit the latter office.

Collecting Reliable Information about the Future Partner

It might seem rather easy to e-mail an RFI to numerous vendors, which will respond with a more-or-less stock reply. However, in many practical cases it can be quite difficult to find out correct, complete, and reliable answers to the questions listed above. Two examples explain possible obstacles:

1. The vendor might have a pricing strategy that is based on low prices in the beginning. The low prices provide the basis for entering the market and achieving an attractive market share. Later on, when customers can switch to another vendor only with considerable effort, the margins are dramatically changed.

   This pricing policy will be carefully protected as a business secret of the vendor. It will be made public only after the vendor has reached a reliable position on the market where it is unlikely that the success of its pricing policy can be undermined.

   Even if only few of the most mature Indian vendors have so far published this pricing policy, it is quite likely that other providers will follow because it is a quite obvious strategy. The customer has to decide whether it still wants to enter an offshore scenario even under the risk that the vendor might raise its prices almost to the level of onshore providers in a few years' time. Or, as an alternative, the customer has to find a way to reduce this risk — e.g., by owning parts of the vendor's organization or by founding its own foreign subsidiary.

2. The details of how the vendor is providing the services are another example of information that the vendor might hold back from the customer. These details may lead to cost advantages on the vendor's

who are cheaper than full-time employees but less reliable, for example, regarding the risk of breach of confidentiality.

These examples explain why the customer has to find out as much as possible about its future partner. In addition they shed light on the reasons why it might be difficult to get a correct and complete picture about the vendor's organization and its strategic plans.

In many cases vendors know more about the business of IT outsourcing than their customers do. And almost always the vendors know much more than their foreign clients do about their (offshore) country's software industry. This is why the vendors are in a better position when the customer wants to obtain information about the provider's organization — information that the vendor resists giving. If the customer insists on getting the required information it will in many cases receive false, incomplete, or misleading information. It might even be difficult for the customer to evaluate the reliability of the provided information. Many customers — especially smaller companies — do not have enough background knowledge to spot subtle implausibility and contradictions in the vendor's statements. Thus they think they know enough about the vendor — but this is not always true.

5.3 VENDOR'S NEED TO GARNER INFORMATION REGARDING THE CUSTOMER

Like customers, vendors need information about their prospective partners. The offshore team should have a profound understanding of the client's business culture and the values promoted by the buyer's organization — i.e., how things are done at the customer's site. The differences in labor costs are a key motivation for many offshore scenarios. For this reason, the offshore team has to be aware that protection of the onshore working time is of high priority. Most buyers are fair and serious, but there are a few exceptions involving somewhat nasty customers. To avoid future problems, the vendor will want to assess the "rating" of the customer as early as possible.

Organizational Culture

Which values are considered important within the organization — for

the offshore company can work according the onshore company's values, it has to know and understand them.

The cooperation will be much smoother if a convergence in organizational cultures is present. Usually this means that the company in the developing country adapts to the organizational culture of the company in the industrialized country (although there are a few exceptions to this rule). In many offshore relationships, a "liaison" — one or more persons who work for a certain time in the onshore office and then return to the emerging country — is a good way to transfer knowledge about the organizational culture. Such liaisons are excellent agents for cultural transfer. (See Section 7.4.)

Costs for Working Hours Onshore

Some engineers working in emerging software industries do not have the faintest idea how much costs may rise, particularly when the onshore staff has to invest a considerable amount of working time. In fact there is a huge difference between the few U.S. dollars-per-hour net income that an offshore developer gets and the gross costs for an onshore manager. The offshore team must be aware that saving the working time of the onshore staff should be a matter of high priority. For example, if a problem can be solved by buying a book, then this is almost always cheaper than asking onshore staff — no matter how expensive the book is.

Rating of the Customer's Fairness and Seriousness

Some basic facts about the organization in the industrialized country are important for the offshore management:

- How much time is supposed to pass between sending an invoice and receiving the money?
- How good is the credit rating of the customer? This might be important especially if the project is partially or totally paid only after it is finished.
- How "tough" is the customer when it comes to legal problems involving employees, business partners, or third parties. If the organization is known as very litigious, it might be necessary to take additional precautions before entering the cooperation.
- Has the customer worked with other vendors? Is the customer still working with these vendors? Why have these past business rela-

5.4 GOVERNANCE: MANAGING THE RELATIONSHIP WITH THE VENDOR

The buyer is well advised to implement strong and cautious management, carried out by people who fully understand the content and strategic goal of the outsourcing deal, oversee the work of the offshore team, and manage the relationship. This steering committee constitutes an interface to the offshore team, facilitates dispute resolution, and serves as an internal advocate of the offshore scenario.

In many practical cases, it turns out that overseeing the work of an offshore team is no easier than developing the software in house. The customer's team usually needs additional training to deal with the challenges of remote project management.

Importance of Governance

A rule of the thumb says that about four to ten percent of the entire project team in offshore scenarios is needed for governance of the relationship. That is, if the customer wants to outsource an internal team of 100 programmers, it has to retain between four and ten IT professionals in house to manage the relationship with the vendor.

First-time buyers frequently underestimate the importance of governance and either assign too few people to this task or choose staff lacking in adequate skills. Inexperienced managers on the customer's side frequently consider vendor selection and contract negotiation much more important than governance. In fact it should be the exact opposite; governance deserves more resources than precontractual investments do. This is why some analysts consider inadequate governance among the highest risks for an offshore scenario.

Establishing the Steering Committee

The members of the steering committee are frequently selected from the existing internal IT department. They may be considered good choices because they have the necessary know-how regarding the interaction of IT projects with the business.

Some analysts, however, advise against this practice because software

language — skills that are in short supply in many IT departments and that are hard to acquire after a certain age. A person who has been working for decades as a sailor is not necessarily the best candidate for, say, port manager.

Coordination of the Information Flow

A typical software project includes input from numerous sources on the customer's side: management, marketing, and various user groups among them. These viewpoints usually contribute opinions that are in the best of cases similar; in the worst case they are conflicting. Usually, the software team is overwhelmed by this multitude of overlapping and contradicting opinions if they enter unfiltered into the software engineering process. Even if the team is in house, it needs a kind of mediator to filter and coordinate the continuous in-stream of opinions and tell the software developers what the final, valid decisions are and what they have to do. In the case of an in-house team, this role can be taken by the project lead or by the owner of the project. These individuals have adequate contacts with the related departments and enough overview of the political camps. In an offshore scenario, this solution is not possible: the customer must actively assign a steering committee (or a single person) to act as a clearing office for all traffic between customer and vendor. All opinions and instructions from the various departments of the customer have to pass the filter of the steering committee.

Requirements Engineering

If software is developed in house, the users and the software team are in close contact. Even if they are working in different departments, issues such as the cost of travel to meetings are not important. In addition, the software team has much background know-how about the users' work. This working relationship contributes greatly to the users finally getting the software they need. In fact, this close contact is one of the main reasons why the rather informal software process used in many in-house IT departments is successful — at least to some extent.

If the software is to be contracted to an offshore vendor, a requirements document that will be the basis of the new software project must be engineered. Perhaps even the internal IT department had used "a kind of

Engineering a high-quality requirements document requires new skills such as precise and eloquent usage of language — skills that are not easy to learn or to teach after a certain age and that are completely different from developing source code. The task is more similar to the work of a technical writer than a traditional C++ programmer. (See Section 9.1.)

Client Feedback

Many software projects require much user feedback and approval of intermediate deliverables — such as prototypes and beta versions. Evaluating these work products is not easy. It requires:

- Skills in the field of software technology, at least at a basic level, to assess what is possible according to the state of the art.
- Knowledge of the state of the art in usability.
- Domain expertise.
- Social skills and negotiation experience; the feedback might be critical and the relationship should not be unduly perturbed by social tensions.
- Some basic understanding of international business law because in the course of the discussion the customer's representative should give legally valid statements. The requirements may require modifications, or other contractual provisions may need renegotiation. Even if the steering committee is not officially authorized to sign for the customer, the committee members will still prepare the decision.

Change Control

The requirements of almost all software projects undergo numerous changes until the project is finished and installed. These changes constitute a serious risk for a software project — so-called "requirements creep" — i.e., the requirements are slowly but constantly changing. The danger stems from the fact that the development team is kept busy working on numerous small change requests from various factions, and they do not have time to implement new features. Consequently, the project hardly makes any progress at all.

To avoid this problem, software engineering books recommend using

the software developers. These change councils are beneficial for both sides: the users have a forum where they can discuss changes they wish to make, and the software developers have longer periods of undisturbed work between the meetings of the change council.

Assessment of Quality and Service Level

The quality of the vendor's services may worsen over time. For this reason the customer has to install a rigorous control system to ensure on a permanent basis that the vendor delivers the necessary quality and conforms to the provisions of the contract.

To avoid possible disputes, the contract should stipulate what service level and quality will be provided. This provision, however, requires insight into how subjective quality requirements such as "usability" and "maturity" of a software project are measured and how they can be validated.

Note that the validation of such quality requirements is very different depending on whether the software is developed by an in-house team or by an external provider. If there are disputes about the delivered quality in the case of an in-house team, the two departments can ask their bosses for a decision, i.e., they have a kind of "built-in" arbitration. The service provider and buyer, however, are independent organizations, and a higher service level implies additional costs on the side of the vendor. Thus it is not surprising that service level is among the most frequent reasons for dispute.

Validating the Final Product

When the development of the new software project is in its final stages, the customer has to give a formal acceptance of the final product. The acceptance means that the customer gives an official, legally binding statement that:

- The software is in conformity with the requirements.
- The product has the necessary quality and maturity — i.e., it does not have too many defects.
- The agreed-upon quality requirements such as "usability" are met.

When the acceptance is signed, the project leaves the development phase and enters into maintenance. Even though most contracts include

These facts constitute an important difference from in-house projects. For this reason the acceptance demands additional skills on the part of the customer's team:

- Experience is needed regarding the risks and technical problems that often occur in projects of this kind, and particular attention should be paid to such hazards.
- Soft skills are needed in the offshore relationship. Notice that the customer's decisions might be negative. Litigation is almost always a much poorer solution than mutual agreement on a solution.
- Software test methods need to be well understood.
- Some legal background is a prerequisite. After all, the acceptance is a legally valid act.

Contract Monitoring

Outsourcing contracts are frequently long and complex documents. The steering committee has to gain insight into the wording and spirit of the agreement and verify that the vendor delivers according to the contract.

Benchmark Audits

Many outsourcing scenarios are designed for long-term cooperation. Over time, the services available on the market and the level of costs are prone to change. To facilitate the necessary adaptations of the outsourcing agreement, some contracts include a so-called benchmark clause. During the benchmark audit the prices and service levels of the contracted services are compared to those of the vendor's peer companies. The audit can conclude that prices have to be adapted. Another possible result is that the vendor is obliged to solve the identified problems within a reasonable time limit. In the benchmark audit, the steering committee assumes the role of the customer's representative. (See Section 5.6.)

Internal Advocate

Outsourcing the work of a former internal IT team to an external provider can have a strong impact on other departments in the customer's organization. The steering committee supports the affected departments and helps modify their business processes to adapt to the changed situation.

team and reduce cultural distance. Usually, the liaisons are members of the steering committee or work in close cooperation with this team. (See Section 7.4.)

5.5   DISPUTE RESOLUTION

During the long term of an offshore cooperation, it is quite likely that disputes about technical and contractual issues will appear. Frequently, litigation is the last and least desirable option. For this reason, many offshore contracts provide for a set of procedures for conflict resolution that defines a way in which the partners can express their concerns and search for a mutually accepted solution without resorting to costly litigation. This so-called escalation procedure includes alternative dispute resolution (ADR) and a reasonable number of preliminary levels before the ultimate step of legal action.

Steering Committee

Many customers implement a "steering committee" that facilitates communication between the customer's various departments and the offshore software team; all communication and particularly all disputes should pass the steering committee. Similarly, most vendors assign spokespersons or liaisons who maintain contact with the customer. (See Section 5.4 and Section 7.4.)

Informal Dispute Resolution

Many procedures of ADR use face-to-face discussion as an initial step. Settlement based on mutual agreement is always the best solution sought by reasonable parties. In a first phase, the representatives of the departments between whom a dispute exists try to solve the conflict. If this attempt fails, the problem is put forward in a so-called escalation sequence to senior executives — one from each side. These executives are identified in advance — before the conflict happens. They are chosen so that neither is involved in the daily business activities performed within the project. This informal dispute solution separates individual egos and emotions from the problem.

If even the executives fail to settle the differences, the issue is passed

The procedure is attractive for many offshore scenarios and is frequently used as a first step of conflict settlement. Some analysts, however, recommend skipping this step and starting directly with mediation or arbitration.

Mediation

During mediation — another method of ADR — a trained conflict manager assists the parties in finding an acceptable solution. The mediator helps the parties explore alternatives that they might not have previously considered and brings new ideas into the discussion. You can think of mediation as a kind of "marriage counseling for companies."

The mediator is not a "judge"; mediators have no authority to make binding decisions; they only help the disputing parties find their own solution. This makes mediation different from arbitration.

Arbitration

The arbitration procedure is carried out by a trained arbitrator. The arbitrator can be a lawyer, a judge, or an expert witness in the field, for example. The arbitration procedure can be compared with a hearing in court to some extent. It will end with a final decision in favor of one side or the other. The difference, however, is that it assures a faster solution, in most cases it is cheaper, and the procedure is easier. In addition, the contract partners can decide on an arbitrator who has expertise in the field. Some official judges are rather green in the inner secrets of information technology. Did you ever try to explain the details of an IT project to a judge who is unable to set the clock on a camcorder?

In a "binding" arbitration, the result of the arbitration is valid and legally enforceable. In addition, the arbitrator's decision is usually considered final; no appeal is possible. Notice that the judgment is not subject to review; there is no appeals court, even if the arbitrator commits errors of law. For this reason, drafting a binding arbitration clause is a legally challenging task with far-reaching consequences and needs the professional hand of a specialized and experienced business attorney.

In some special cases the arbitration is binding only for one side — e.g., when the parties have very different economic power. Some banks, for example, suggest that their private customers search for the solution to a dispute via arbitration by an ombudsman. The result of the arbitration is binding for the bank. However, the private customer is still free to ask

Selecting Mediators and Arbitrators

The selection of the mediator or arbitrator is of crucial importance to the success of ADR. In some cases, a mutually acceptable mediator is specified in the contract. An alternative is that each side names a spokesperson. The two named individuals decide on a third and final mediator/arbitrator.

Some analysts consider mediation more time and cost efficient than arbitration. In addition it is more likely to reach a mutually accepted result. This is not a general rule, however. Other contracts prefer arbitration over mediation.

Litigation

Litigation is the last and least desirable option in many cases because:

- Litigation can seriously damage a relationship and frequently indicates the end of the association between the partners. This has disadvantages on both sides. The vendor loses a customer. The customer has to find a new vendor — a step which might entail further investment (for transfer of know-how to the new vendor's team, for example).
- Sometimes it is hard to predict the outcome of a lawsuit in the context of international business, especially if the lawsuit involves developing countries.
- Litigation is time consuming and expensive and can cause undesirable publicity.
- A lawsuit entails high costs — for the attorneys on both sides and the court fees. This money is essentially taken away from the potential settlement.

Nevertheless, there are situations where the relationship is damaged, and a mutually acceptable settlement is no longer possible.

5.6 BENCHMARK AUDITS

During a benchmark study the service levels and prices of the deal are compared to the conditions of the vendor's peer companies. Usually an independent third party, the benchmark pro-

AU7017_book.fm Page 89 Thursday, March 16, 2006 5:07 PM

results are used as a basis for discussion without immediate legally binding consequences.

Not all analysts agree on the methodological reliability of a benchmark audit. Some object that most IT projects are unique and not really amenable to a like-to-like comparison. Another objection is that the quality of the relationship can hardly be measured by means of normalized comparison.

What Are Benchmark Audits?

In a benchmark study the contracted services, prices, and conditions are compared with similar outsourcing scenarios of other vendors. Usually, benchmark audits are used if the customer outsources a set of IT services for a certain time. If the scope of the cooperation is limited to a specific project, benchmarks are rare. The benchmark study can be conducted periodically — e.g., to adapt the price regularly, or it can be triggered when the cooperation reaches a crisis and the customer is dissatisfied with the service provider. In the latter case, the benchmark audit can help clarify the relationship by collecting facts to validate or refute the subjective impression of poor performance or inappropriate pricing. If the benchmark is successful, the customer's satisfaction improves and the customer understands more clearly what it is paying for.

The benchmark study should answer questions like:

- Is the service level still adequate according to the state of the art?
- Are the conditions of the contract fair?
- What problems can be identified in the outsourcing cooperation?
- What are the reasons and the actual facts behind "perceived subjective dissatisfaction?"
- What are the anomalies in the cooperation and what are the reasons for them — e.g., technology, business processes, or management reasons?

The Benchmark Provider

Usually, the benchmark study enlists the help of an independent, third-party vendor of benchmarking services. This "benchmark provider" guides the benchmark audit and draws the final conclusion. The comparison with

consequences (e.g., price adaptations). Some outsourcing contracts include a list of mutually acceptable benchmark providers. When the benchmark is prepared, the customer can select one provider out of the list to conduct the audit. Other contracts specify from the beginning only one benchmark provider.

Scope of the Benchmark Audit

In the scope definition, the partners specify what exactly should be studied in the benchmark audit. The scope definition is of utmost importance when preparing for a benchmark audit because the scope determines whether the benchmark will deliver what the outsourcing partners need — especially what the buyer needs. Because the scope definition is legally binding, it is usually stipulated in the outsourcing contract. In addition, it should be discussed with the benchmark provider so that the benchmark provider's expertise can be incorporated into it and to make sure that the benchmark provider is prepared to conduct a study with the specified scope.

The scope of the benchmark usually includes price and service level. Gartner identified three potential scope definitions:

- *Vision and alignment.* Whether both parties can meet their strategic and operational goals and respond to business and technology changes
- *Contract and relationship.* Whether the management of the contract and relationship meets the needs of both parties
- *Customer satisfaction.* Whether the business unit end users are satisfied

Monitoring Period

Before the audit can take place, the partners have to collect performance data. Therefore, they have to install monitoring facilities that help answer questions such as: Which services have been provided by the vendor over a certain period of time? Did these services reach the specified service level? What was the response time? How did the vendor perform? The elicited data and the benchmark clause in the outsourcing contract should be compliant with the benchmark provider's database. For example, the granularity of the elicited data must match the granularity of the database.

maintenance prices "per site." Consequently, the data for preparing the benchmark audit must be elicited on a "per site" basis. This mismatch between the granularity of the elicited data and the database of the benchmark provider will probably lead to results of limited usefulness.

To avoid such problems, the benchmark provider should be included rather early in the discussion, usually even before the contract is signed, because the benchmark provider must help draft the benchmark clause. This observation contributes to a number of outsourcing contracts specifying a single benchmark provider. In any event, if the contract leaves the option between multiple benchmark providers, the details of the benchmark clause have to be discussed with all of them.

Consequences of the Benchmark Test

The details of the benchmark audit are frequently specified in the outsourcing contract. The contract can stipulate that the audit is purely informative. More often, however, the result has certain enforceable consequences: the price may be adapted automatically or the vendor is forced to solve the identified problems within a certain term.

Methodological Acceptance of Benchmark Audits

Benchmark studies are adopted in many outsourcing contracts and are widely applied. The benchmark audit is frequently used to adapt fees periodically. Nevertheless, some analysts express methodological concerns regarding this method. The objections of these commentators are:

- Most IT projects are unique, which makes it difficult to compare two given IT scenarios on a like-to-like basis.
- The data used by some benchmark providers does not have the necessary methodological quality: the data is too old or it refers to scenarios with large geographical differences.
- The monitoring period is rather short. Thus, the data might be inaccurate because of special efforts made by the vendor during the short monitoring period.
- The quality of the relationship in outsourcing scenarios is very

provisions are. Some analysts warn against connecting the results of a benchmark study to legally binding consequences — e.g., price adaptation. Those researchers suggest using a benchmark study as a starting point for discussion and analysis. If this informal discussion or facilitated mediation should fail, the customer can consider its "termination on convenience" clause, which has legally binding consequences and which is usually one of the strongest leverage mechanisms for the customer's postcontractual negotiations. (See Section 11.1.)

List of Top Ten Concerns

A variant of a benchmark audit can be used when the relationship is seriously damaged: the customer provides a list of top ten concerns that must be solved. The list can be complemented by raw data elicited in a period of monitoring the vendor's performance.

When the list of top ten concerns is established, the contract partner can use various methods of ADR (Section 5.5) — informal discussion, mediation, or arbitration — to review the list of top ten concerns item by item. Once the outsourcing partners agree on the validity of the concerns, they can start developing a solution for the identified problems. The vendor is given a certain period of time to implement the agreed-on course of action. The mutual agreement is followed by another period of monitoring that ensures the actual implementation of the proposed solutions. The list of top ten concerns can be a very helpful tool when the relationship reaches a crisis. Notice, however, that both the elicitation of the list of concerns and the implementation of the monitoring facilities require considerable efforts and can cause significant costs.

6

STAKEHOLDERS: INTEREST GROUPS IN THE OFFSHORE RELATIONSHIP

ABSTRACT

The offshore relationship has quite a number of different groups with an interest in the relationship ("stakeholders"). Obviously, both companies (onshore and offshore) and their executives are important. However, other viewpoints should be considered as well, including those of:

- *The developers in the emerging country — who are working for relatively low pay*
- *Onshore technical staff — many of whom will probably lose their jobs*
- *Offshore managers and entrepreneurs — who might face conflicting interests*
- *Envoys of Western companies — who have to work temporarily or permanently in emerging countries*
- *Offshore liaisons — who are visiting the customer's office in the industrialized country*

All these groups have a say in and an important contribution to the success of the offshore cooperation. These stakeholders can have secret plans for the future, which may not necessarily be in line with the contract. Only rarely do the other parties involved consider these

6.1 CONFLICTING VIEWPOINTS: AN INTRODUCTORY CASE STUDY

Offshore relationships usually involve numerous interest groups with divergent interests, some of which are disclosed, although others are kept secret. The following case study offers an illustration of how the secret interests of various stakeholders may turn a potentially successful offshore scenario into a failure.

A Western European software company intended to establish a near-shore cooperation relationship with a small Eastern European vendor. The Western top manager discussed the matter with his software lead and asked him to select a suitable project to test the soon-to-be cooperation. The test project should have been technologically challenging but not too large — just to keep the investment within reasonable limits. Of particular importance was the request that the project not be of strategic importance for the customer — to limit the risks in case the test project failed. The software manager considered the procedure reasonable and promised to have some materials ready.

Meanwhile the top manager talked with the vendor. The manager asked that the project lead should come at least once a month for several days to the customer's site to deliver intermediate results and to discuss further steps. The vendor promised to do its best to make the new customer content.

So far, everything indicates a very usual near-shore project. This, however, was only what the participants were *saying*. Let us have a closer look at what they were *thinking* — the hidden agendas and secret plans:

The customer's top manager. In the long run I need a near-shore company that is under my full control: in fact, I need a foreign subsidiary. It is risky to build up something new from scratch because I do not have enough background information about that country; I lack experience and reliable contacts there. If I am content with the vendor I will try to buy this company. If the company is not for sale or the price is exaggerated, I will headhunt some of the vendor's best staff. They will provide me with a starting point

The customer's software lead. This damned outsourcing deal is serious danger for my team and for my own career. In the long run the company's entire software business will go abroad because of the lower costs. Management will fire most of my team. If they do not have a software team anymore, they will not need a software manager either; they won't want me anymore. I am in my forties; how shall I continue my career in a time when the entire country's software industry is downsizing? For the moment, I have to steer a cautious course and do not dare place myself in an open conflict with top management's policy. However nothing is lost yet; I have more than enough ways to detrimentally influence the test project and bring it into a no-exit situation. I am going to do this in a secret and hidden way so that no shadow of suspicion will fall on me. The best that can happen is that the project fails and top management thinks it failed for technical reasons. This would be a big step toward canceling this entire outsourcing idea.

The vendor's top management. I will buy this offered project: I will put forward such a cheap price that this new customer will simply be unable to turn it down. The project is rather small. Therefore, it can only influence my company's balance sheet in a very limited way. If I ask too large or too small a sum of money for it, it will not make a very big difference because both losses and profits will be accordingly small due to the small size of the project. However, cooperating with the new customer is of strategic importance. If the customer is content with us, it will eventually move its entire software business near-shore. A general law of outsourcing says that it is very difficult to get rid of an outsourcer once it is involved in projects that are of strategic importance to the customer. Then the time will come when I will tell the customer what the real prices are.

The vendor's projects manager. In the long run I would like to start my own software company because this would provide me a higher income. However, it is too early to take this step now, when I'm lacking good contacts in industrialized nations. These trips to Western Europe are exactly what I need now. I will establish contacts with the top management there and maintain friendly relationships with my colleagues. These new friends must have contacts in other companies. Last but not least, I will have some leisure time there; I can arrange meetings with other companies in the evening. That

viewpoints are also rare. For this reason, it is best to develop a basic understanding of the background and possible motivations of all stakeholders involved in offshore relationships before entering that game with real money.

6.2 CUSTOMERS AND VENDORS

It has been said that an offshore scenario has to be a win–win situation. To some extent this is true; if the deal is overly unbalanced the relationship becomes unstable, and it is quite likely to end in a lose–lose situation — i.e., in a way that is unsatisfactory for both sides. Skepticism regarding a long-term successful offshore relationship is especially justified if the prices are unrealistically low and not sustainable for the vendor in the long run. Unfortunately, the harsh reality is that outsourcing is not an inherent win–win scenario. In many respects, customers' and vendors' interests are poles apart. The balance of prices is one obstacle against a win–win strategy. Another obstacle is that the business models are prone to change with time: vendors become better qualified and accumulate additional capital for more ambitious plans. Customers, on the other side, shift their focus to their core competencies while losing power and control in the IT field. It is difficult to predict where this dynamic will lead to in, say, ten years. Both shores will make long-term strategic and commercial plans — which are to their own advantage, of course, and not necessarily to the advantage of their current business partners.

This section will outline some areas where customers' and vendors' interests are diametrically opposed.

6.2.1 Costs and Fees

Reducing costs is a major strategic purpose for many offshore scenarios. The customer wants competitive pricing during the entire contractual period or at least that prices do not soar up. In the worst case, the prices should remain those agreed upon in the initial contractual provisions; otherwise, the customer's calculation of the offshore scenario's profitability is no longer valid.

As IT offshoring is gaining speed, the cost structure in the entire

The vendor, on the other hand, wants to make money. The better the prices, the higher the profits. The prices of the currently negotiated contract are important. However, they are only one variable of the equation. The other side is the price development prognosis. The most attractive prospect is for the vendor to gain access to well-paid projects — i.e., the vendor is looking for projects that are paid according to onshore prices. Going offshore and ending up paying onshore prices is not exactly what the customer wants.

6.2.2 Initial Cash Layout

Many offshore vendors have only very limited financing. In some cases, the lack of capital becomes an important obstacle in the way of the company's expansion. For this reason, vendors try to limit the initial cash layout necessary for starting a project.

6.2.3 The Vendor's Strategic Plans

The offshore outsourcing market is undergoing breathtaking changes and a rapid process of concentration. Thus, the most likely prospect for most small and midsize offshore vendors is that they will have left the market a few years from now. Some providers, on the other hand, will be much larger than they are now. In this context, it is rather difficult for offshore vendors to make valid strategic long-term plans.

6.2.4 Dependency on the Vendor

It is usually difficult for the customer to discontinue working with the service provider once the vendor is involved in important projects. In many cases it is quite challenging to switch to another provider or to bring the IT business back in house. For the vendor this dependency is a big advantage because competitors are ruled out. This situation can help the vendor increase prices or improve margins by lowering service quality. The customer tries to keep the option of collaboration with other service providers open to keep the scenario competitive and to ensure vendor loyalty.

6.2.5 Risk

6.2.6 Scope of Contract

The vendor's interest is a scope of services with a clearly defined limit because additional services are to be paid extra. The customer would like to have a contract that includes as many "general services" as possible (without additional fees).

6.2.7 Extending the Contract

In many outsourcing relationships the customer's dependency on the provider grows with time. Thus, outsourcing contracts have a natural tendency to expand, especially if the customer outsources all its IT services for a certain time (not just a single project contract). The vendor will try to accelerate this tendency and expand contracts and relationships as much as possible.

6.2.8 Existing Infrastructure

Usually, the vendor already has some infrastructure before the cooperation with the new customer starts. This existing infrastructure enables the vendor to provide certain services more cost efficiently than others. Because this infrastructure has been established for earlier projects with other customers, it will most likely not exactly match the needs of the new customer. Nevertheless, the vendor will try to leverage its existing infrastructure by influencing the customer — i.e., the vendor will try to sell what is most profitable for its own organization, not necessarily what the customer really needs.

6.3 STAFF IN DEVELOPING COUNTRIES

Employing and organizing employees in emerging countries is quite different from managing an onshore software team. These differences are particularly important for customers who want to establish their own foreign subsidiary and not merely work with an independent vendor.

6.3.1 Choosing Candidates

Evaluating a graduate's transcript requires detailed knowledge of the

A serious challenge for job interviews in emerging countries is the lack of reliable references. References might be forged or bought. Due to rapid changes on the market it is difficult to verify the validity of references; a few months later, at the time when the reference is presented, the organization that issued it might have already disappeared or the manager who signed it might have left the company. Thus, in developing countries references do not have the importance they have in industrialized countries.

Reading resumes is similarly difficult: high attrition of staff is a frequent problem in emerging software industries. Thus, frequent changes of jobs are not necessarily an indication of unreliability of the employee. Unreliability can be a reason, but there might be other reasons as well: the candidate can claim that the employers were not fair. In emerging countries it is quite possible that this is true. Another possibility might be that the candidate has received a sequence of increasingly better offers and frequently changed jobs for this reason.

For these reasons potential employers rely largely on elaborate techniques for interviewing and testing candidates. Presented documents have only limited importance in emerging software industries. The papers might provide some guidelines for preselection, however, to improve the selection process's efficiency.

6.3.2 Plausibility of Candidate's Statements

Not all candidates are completely honest during the interview. For this reason, ascertaining whether the candidate is telling the truth is important. One indication that the candidate is lying is that the statements contain subtle contradictions. The person who conducts the interview must have extensive background knowledge to identify the subtle implausibility of statements. Managers from industrialized countries frequently lack the necessary background information. For this reason, it might be wise to include people who have the necessary knowledge and training as well as loyalty and integrity on the interviewing board.

A talented young offshore software developer applied for a job. Tests showed that he had achieved a high professional level. The candidate said that he did not currently have a job and therefore could start working immediately. He even offered to work without any legal contract because this arrangement saved the company taxes and social insurance contributions.

Most applicants in this situation ask for a permanent contract. The contract provides them with continuous income, social insurance, and health care. This candidate even suggested of his own free will to give up signing a contract. What was going on here? The situation obviously required further investigation.

Finally it turned out that the candidate had serious plans for emigration to an industrialized country and that in few months' time he would leave the country. His visa papers were already pending; he just wanted to use the time before he left to earn some additional money. A working contract would just impose obstacles in his emigration plans because such contracts usually include a period of notice.

This anecdote shows the importance of background knowledge about the life of the typical candidate. The interviewer must know what a candidate's future plans usually look like. How do these plans come across in the case of candidates who intend to go abroad (temporarily or permanently) and what do they look like in the case of candidates who want to stay in the country for good? In the example, it was crucial to notice the surprising fact that the candidate did not ask for a contract.

6.3.3 Work Ethics, Professional Attitude

Most offshore developers are rather well informed about the salaries of their American and European colleagues, particularly the maximum pay in regions where the living standards are especially high. The high cost of living in these countries is not as well known by these employees. If the maximum gross pay in countries like the United States is compared to the average net pay in developing countries (ignoring the different cost of living), offshore developers get the impression that they work almost "for free." However true it might be that there are really significant differences between the standard of living of American software developers and their colleagues in developing countries, the gap is not as dramatic as the numbers might suggest.

For some offshore developers, this comparison may have a significantly deflating impact on their working morale. Some developers consider that showing a blatant lack of discipline and professional attitude is more than a fair and well-deserved response to this discrepancy. Some employees consider they have a green light in terms of professional ethics to break

Discrepancies are unavoidable as long as offshore companies get significantly lower prices than onshore providers; high costs for customer
acquisition, traveling, communication, and management are imposed; and,
last but not least, the cost of living is lower in developing countries.
Employees who cannot accept these arguments are free to try their luck
abroad; quite a few of these emigrants have returned after a while.

6.3.4 Authorized Employee Claims

The offshore organization has to take care of all promises of senior
management to avoid discontentment afterwards. The workers try to assess
how reliable their boss is. Even among offshore entrepreneurs there are
some black sheep — and most offshore employees have heard of them.
Thus, the validity of verbal commitments and promises is of particular
importance. Although these promises and verbal statements have limited
validity — at least in a purely legal sense — the company should take
care to stick to them. Otherwise, the workers will probably classify the
company as "unfair." In many cases the workers will be disgruntled. As
a consequence, productivity may suffer or the reliability of the workers
may decrease dramatically. The author has analyzed the history of some
cases where employees were outrageously unfair and unreliable. In many
of these cases, broken promises or invalid verbal commitments on the
part of the company had occurred earlier. As a consequence, the workers
labeled their superiors as unfair — and "with unfair bosses you cannot
behave in any other way than dishonestly."

6.3.5 Integrity and Loyalty

> A well-paid offshore manager had to make decisions concerning
> employing new staff. Ignoring other, more qualified candidates,
> he gave the jobs to some of his acquaintances. This demon-
> strates that even though he was well paid, he was not loyal to
> his organization. It never entered his mind that his high pay
> should come with a corresponding degree of loyalty.

Experience has shown that it is difficult to buy loyalty, integrity, thor-
oughness, honesty, and similar virtues. In an industrialized country, well-
paid employees will probably try to keep their jobs and their perks by

AU7017_book.fm Page 102 Thursday, March 16, 2006 5:07 PM

To avoid potential misunderstandings, it is important to state that in emerging countries some people maintain high standards of integrity. However, trying to impose moral values on someone who is utterly lacking in such an attitude can turn out to be a complete waste of time and money. High salaries are not always efficient deterrents against bribery and do not guarantee a sense of loyalty.

We have all heard the proverb "you get what you pay for." In offshore business this statement should be slightly changed: "you definitely do not get more than you pay for."

In some offshore countries, corruption and lack of integrity are part of a long-established tradition. For foreign investors this has several detrimental effects:

- Once corrupt practices have become part of someone's work behavior, one can not easily change that person's habits again. In countries where corruption has a long tradition, it might be difficult to find partners who have integrity as well as intelligence and skill.
- Many people have learned to live with corruption. There is a rather low awareness level concerning this issue, and many share the feeling that this is a minor peccadillo.
- The rich experience some have in resorting to such illicit practices makes it easy for them to use elaborate techniques to conceal their activities. For this reason, it might be difficult to discover these tricks, particularly in the case of a foreign manager who is inexperienced as far as corruption is concerned.

In some Eastern European countries in the nineties corruption was widespread; it was necessary to bribe practically all public employees just for doing their jobs. They would not even say in which building you could get the form that has to be filled out unless they received a small amount of money, some cigarettes, or the like. They would just pretend that they did not know about such things; it was not their responsibility to know about the forms of other departments.

In the years since then, governments have taken measures to fight corruption, and things have changed. Public employees are doing their jobs even without bribes. However, it takes much longer and the officers create more difficulties for you if you do

AU7017_book.fm Page 103 Thursday, March 16, 2006 5:07 PM

months, the first step is to find a trusted agent. Such agents take not only the cash for bribes but also a fair fee for their own work, of course. Then the agent meets the officer without witnesses and gives the officer the bribes — at least this is what is supposed to occur. It is all about trust in offshore business.

Romanian television reported the example of a high-ranked customs officer who bought a residential building for his family. The value of the house was equivalent to his legal pay for about 380 years.

These anecdotes show that in cultures where corruption has a centuries-long tradition these mechanics can be rather tricky and hard for an outsider to penetrate. If a foreigner just urgently needs a document to prolong a visa, for example, corruption might be considered just a minor nuisance providing a basis for funny anecdotes. However, some managers have hard feelings if, for example, their software lead is bribed by a customer or by a competitor — and they find it out only when it is too late.

6.3.6 Professional Training

Highly qualified employees are of core importance to each software company. For this reason, many organizations invest in professional training. Regarding professional skills two components must be considered:

1. Specific skills that are important to a certain project or valuable only to the respective company
2. General skills that can be applied in many working environments (e.g., programming languages and certifications)

Both kinds of skills are important to the success of the company. General skills, however, also make the employee attractive to headhunters and other companies. Even if the company paid for the training necessary to acquire those general skills, the employee will probably ask for higher compensation. For this reason, some companies hesitate to pay for training in general skills.

An offshore company sent some of its employees to a training

have a certificate that they could show to other, competing companies. The employees could pay for the certification exam out of their own pockets, of course. However, the prices for these exams are rather high compared to monthly net income. Few employees could afford this option.

6.3.7 Culture at Work: Closure of the Employment Contract

An offshore manager reported the case of a software engineer who simply stopped coming to work in the morning, without any prior notice — let alone respecting the period of notice. Another software engineer announced that he does not intend to keep his period of notice because he considered the (agreed and signed) period of notice unrealistically long. He stayed for a few days more and then he left the company.

The company sought legal consultancy. The lawyer confirmed that the company stands a good chance of winning the litigation, but that this might take several years. At the end of the trial the company would receive a compensation of only a few hundred U.S. dollars at best. If the dishonest employee is still in the country at that time, the company has a good chance that the court's decision can be executed.

The management decided not to start litigation.

A German company wanted to carry through an Enterprise Resource Planning project (ERP). They worked with an Indian vendor to apply so-called Onsite-Offshoring — i.e., the vendor's staff was working permanently at the customer's site. The project made good progress, and the client was content with the vendor's team. Suddenly all the Indian specialists quit their jobs at the same time. The employment contract between the Indian vendor and the respective engineer provided only for a few days' period of notice. For this reason, the step taken by the Indian staff was completely legal. Because all the Indian workers quit at the same time, it was obvious that this step was a carefully conceived action and not mere coincidence. The project was in full progress, and the customer did not have any chance of finishing the work in due time if it had to train

The developers were fully aware that the project was a matter of high priority to the customer and there was not the slightest chance to finish the project in time without their contribution. They carefully planned the perfect moment to quit, a time when an optimum base for negotiation could be obtained. Given their strong position, they simply did not accept any lower offer. They did not have anything to lose but there was much to win: if this strategy failed they would go back to India and apply for new jobs — everything would go on as if nothing had happened. If their plans turned out as they expected, however — as it finally happened — they would finish their project in Germany. When they came back to India, they would be rich — at least according to the standards of their country.

In emerging software industries, employees are subject to little risk if they quit their jobs in an unfriendly way or even by breaking a contract. Perhaps parts of the last month's salary will not be paid. However, there is little risk of more serious legal consequences beyond this calculable amount. In industrialized countries, references and a mature legal system perform the necessary control functions: employees who leave jobs in an unfriendly way may risk a process for serious damages. In any case, such employees will not get good references, which may prove rather troublesome afterwards when searching for a new job.

The level of compensation and indemnities is established according to the average income in the particular country — which is rather low in developing countries. In some cases the compensation might be ridiculously small and does not have the necessary deterrence effect. Due to the lack of validity of references and the immature legal system, the long-established controlling mechanisms in industrialized countries have only limited effectiveness in developing countries.

Some companies try to solve this problem by including reasonably high contractual penalties in the employment contract. Drafting such contracts, however, requires excellent business attorneys with profound understanding of the countries' employment legislation. Such experts are hard to find in developing countries. Without an excellent lawyer, the contractual penalties might turn out to be invalid if it comes to litigation.

However, important differences exist. High attrition of staff is a serious problem in emerging software industries. Because most software projects require a certain degree of continuity, the offshore management has to pay particular attention to controlling the retention rate. A specific part of the attrition problem is represented by emigrating software engineers, who constitute a significant fraction of the young graduates. If someone decides to leave the country, the offshore company usually cannot make a competitive offer to keep this person on the job.

In some offshore countries, there are excellent top talents at a high professional level. For IT companies, it is very attractive to hire these young stars. However, even in emerging countries these talents are a scarce resource. Thus finding, hiring, and retaining outstanding talents requires specific management skills and a lot of background information.

6.4.1 Forestalling Attrition of Staff

In emerging software industries, attrition is a bigger problem than in industrialized countries; it is not very surprising if a software developer changes jobs for the third time just one year after graduation. Because most software projects require some continuity of staff, companies strive to achieve maximum retention. This goal requires a carefully designed plan including monetary and nonmonetary elements.

Many software developers in offshore countries have rather exact, detailed, and up-to-date information regarding the state of affairs on the labor market at the local or national level. A stable employment relationship requires that employees be paid according to their value on the market. Nonmonetary aspects are important as well. However, pay under the market level usually makes the relationship immediately unstable. Even a fascinating project, interesting learning opportunities, or social contacts have very limited influence if pay falls below standards. Offshore business is very price sensitive.

Many offshore companies use incentives to consolidate the employee's connection with the organization. These incentives are given with a certain delay: e.g., the incentive for the previous year is paid in the late spring of the following year. An employee who quits the job loses the fidelity bonus. Other companies offer their employees cheap credit — e.g., for buying an apartment. This benefit is available to employees who have

AU7017_book.fm Page 107 Thursday, March 16, 2006 5:07 PM

Social relationships at work are especially important in developing countries because many young software developers, relocated to other towns, have limited possibilities of finding new friends. To some extent this network of social relationships discourages quitting the job.

Long-running projects are exposed to the risk of the project lead or other key personnel leaving the organization in the middle of the project. Some projects might be less prone to this risk; for others it might be a disaster. In such cases it might be wise to have some reserves in the project's budget to prevent key staff from leaving — at least for a limited time until replacement workers can fill in for them.

6.4.2 Emigration

In times of IT boom many computer scientists in emerging countries emigrated to leading economies where good jobs and high incomes were promised. In some countries, more than half of the graduates went abroad during the first year after graduation. Others followed later.

Quite a few emigrants come back after a while. Many of them earned money abroad, acquired important technical and business skills, brushed up on their foreign language abilities, and established important contacts in the industrialized country. This put them in a position where they could start businesses of their own or take on greater responsibilities in other organizations.

Temporary emigration can bring many advantages to the emigrant and — in the long run — to the emerging country's software industry. However, at the moment when young engineers leave the country, emigration constitutes a big problem for their former employers. Whenever developers leave a company, they take a part of the company's precious know-how with them, causing a corresponding loss of experience, background know-how, and domain expertise in their current teams.

Another problem stems from the fact that most projects require a high degree of continuity: at the time when the software engineer announces a plan to leave the country, that individual might have substantial responsibility in the company. Perhaps this person is a project manager or possesses rare and important technological skills. The engineer might have exclusive knowledge about some technical details of the current project. Almost always the emigrant colleague is involved in a current project that is in progress at that very moment — and that has to be finished one way or another. Note that it is usually difficult to replace software devel-

a similar economic situation. There are minor differences, of course, but the general economic context is usually comparable to some extent. This means that the headhunting offshore company usually cannot make a significantly better offer. In many cases the resigning engineer's current employer can outbid the headhunter, unless personal or nonmonetary reasons are responsible for the employee's desire to resign. If absolutely necessary, the engineer can usually be kept by offering enough money — at least for a certain period of time until a suitable replacement is hired.

If a software developer decides to leave the country, the situation is utterly different. Usually the proposal from abroad is so attractive that the former employer cannot make a similar offer. For this reason software companies have to find out the longer-term plans of candidates. If possible, the company should try to foresee emigration plans even during the interview. Candidates who have mature emigration plans will probably not be considered for long-term projects. In this case it is quite unlikely that the candidate will be employed.

The candidates, on the other hand, are aware that companies are very sensitive regarding emigration due to the serious problems created by emigrating employees. For this reason, some candidates try to keep possible emigration plans secret.

The person conducting the interview can take into consideration some indications: Certain groups have an increased tendency to emigrate, especially highly qualified young singles with good knowledge of at least one foreign language. Many of them already have some experience in foreign countries before they make the final decision to leave their country for good. They are often acquainted with the realities of their destination country. Some of them have already established private or professional contacts there.

In this author's opinion, if candidates fit into the outlined profile, it might be worthwhile to verify carefully the reasons why they might not want to emigrate. If they really have decided to remain in the offshore country for good, they will give strong reasons. A candidate might have ill relatives who need support, for example. Sometimes, personal reasons are important: "I stayed there for three months but I felt homesick."

In addition to strong reasons, an honest candidate will have a clear, mature, and plausible outline for an alternative plan of life — a plan that does not include emigration. That plan might need to be tested for plausibility: do facts fit together, is the plan realistic, and does it match

6.4.3 Rolling Stones Gather No Moss

When experienced programmers want to quit their jobs and announce that they want to go abroad, the company might consider offering more money and thus keeping them. Because the cost of living is lower in developing countries, the promised net income will not reach the average income in industrialized countries. In many cases a reasonable standard of living is enough to keep developers from emigrating. This is especially true if the engineers grew up in that country and are used to the regional peculiarities. They are likely to have family and friends in that country. These nonmonetary facts might hinder plans of emigration. After all, people do not leave their native countries permanently only because of a gradual change in the standard of living.

In many cases, however, these facts do not apply. It requires a rather high income to ensure a standard of living comparable to that in a well-developed country — even if the difference in the cost of living is taken into account. Most offshore companies cannot afford such high salaries, at least not for ordinary software developers. Otherwise the company would not be able to make competitive offers to clients.

There might be exceptions when the company chooses this alternative irrespective of high costs: for example, in the case of a trusted person with a high record of integrity in an executive position — i.e., a manager who is difficult to replace. For part of the technical staff, this step might be justified if the engineer in question has very specific and important skills. Some software developers have a high productivity rate that goes far beyond the average — sometimes up to five times higher. The company might consider investing some money to keep its "star."

Offering money does not always work, however. The employee might reject the offer due to doubts whether the offer can be counted on in the longer run. Making serious emigration plans usually requires a considerable investment of time, energy, and money. If there are suspicions that higher payment would only be temporary, employees will probably not give up their carefully conceived long-term plans of emigration for the short-term income increase. For these reasons, offers must be backed up by solid indications that the income increase will be stable in the long run.

Most people are fond of their native country, the region where they grew up, where they use their mother tongue effortlessly. The emotional links to the country form an obstacle in the face of emigration — even if income is lower. Some people, however, want to emigrate even if the

An excellent Romanian mathematician announced to his boss that he was planning to go abroad. The boss tried to keep him and offered a salary that allowed a reasonable standard of living in Romania. The mathematician turned down the offer. He said that money was not an issue and that he would leave anyway. A few weeks later burglars broke into the boss's apartment. When the mathematician found out he asked his boss: Do you understand my reasons now?

6.4.4 Top Talents

In the most important offshore countries, computer scientists maintain a high professional standard, comparable to the level of their Western colleagues. In addition to the high average, in some countries a small elite group exists at a level difficult to find even in industrialized nations.

In Eastern European countries, this group has developed in the context of the old communist elite training. The communist regimes have disappeared, but the infrastructure responsible for producing top talents is still intact. Trainers are still active, and there is a broad consciousness of outstanding performance and talent-oriented upbringing among parents and teachers. These groups of top talents are small, however. Even in Eastern Europe there is only a very limited number of elite professionals.

Studies have shown that outstanding software engineers have a productivity rate that can be as high as five times the capacity of an "average" programmer. These so-called hyperproductive software developers, however, constitute only about two percent of the programmer population. Some headhunters have a clear understanding of the relationship between talent and productivity and search for employees particularly within this segment of hyperproductive programmers.

Attracting such top talents is not easy; it requires headhunters who know where to find such people in the first place. Experts are needed to assess them and evaluate their talent: it is not at all easy to tell whether someone belongs to the most talented two percent of programmers or "only" to the best 20 percent. Once a prodigy is identified, a carefully prepared offer must be put forward; money is important, of course. However, as experience shows, money is not everything; it is only one part of this game. For these individuals, other aspects, including professional opportunities and personal preferences, are important as well. The offer must fit the long-term plans of the future employee.

way, the young talent may not achieve full potential, or other competitors will come and offer more "enticing alternatives."

6.5 THE CUSTOMER'S IN-HOUSE TEAM

The customer's in-house team is vital when offshore plans are evaluated. On the one hand, the offshore scenario will need the active support of as many members of the onshore team as possible to train the replacement workers. On the other hand, most of the members of the in-house team will lose their jobs once the offshore cooperation is established. Those who will contribute to the offshore cooperation will be needing new skills and significant training.

6.5.1 Internal Communication of the Offshore Plans

Reducing costs is one of the core motivations of offshore outsourcing. The consequence is that a significant part of the rather costly onshore IT staff must be fired unless the offshore activity is compensated for by simultaneous expansion (which is rare). For the onshore employees, this step has serious consequences. Unlike the IT boom period, this is not the best of times to try to find a job in the IT business. Not just one company is involved in offshore activities; the entire software industry is working with offshore vendors. This means that there might be a lack of well-paid jobs in the industrialized countries' software industries.

The situation is particularly difficult for older software developers who will have difficulty finding other jobs. If they lose their jobs in a downsizing industry during a period of crisis, it will be almost impossible for them to find new positions with similar pay and prestige.

6.5.2 Adequate Retained Functions

The onshore company will still take on IT staff after the offshore relationship has been established, but to a much lesser extent than before. In addition, this steering committee will need a range of very different qualifications compared to the initial team because an organization needs different skills for governing outsourcing agreements than for providing IT services internally. Purely technical acumen loses ground in favor of

importance within the onshore team that they will have after the offshore step is completed. Thus, additional training will be necessary.

6.5.3 Employees' Resistance against Offshore Plans

Software specialists do not enjoy a particular reputation for excellence in social and verbal skills. In addition, these skills are known to be difficult to learn and to teach as well — at least after a certain age. For these reason only the smaller part of the team employed so far will be able to complete the transition successfully and will contribute to the offshore cooperation. Because most of the work is done offshore, only a fraction of the onshore staff is needed anyway.

The other staff members who are not able to make the transition or whose services will no longer be necessary are in a rather desperate position. Many of them are too old to switch smoothly to a successful career in a completely different field. For most, the only alternative is to accept a lower-level position — which often implies a significantly lower salary.

The offshore cooperation might require that onshore staff relocate temporarily or permanently offshore. This could have a dramatic impact on the family life of the onshore employees.

6.5.4 Balance of Power

Obviously, there are more than enough reasons why the onshore staff would be skeptical of any kind of offshore activity. This is only one side of the coin, however. The other side is that the most important part of an organization's IT know-how is its technical staff. Of course, there is printed documentation as well, but this type of material is rarely complete and almost always out of date. For gaining access to substantial information, there is no way around the in-house experts.

This places management in a paradoxical situation; to go offshore they need the active support of as many of their existing onshore staff as possible — the onshore team has to make their knowledge available to the replacement workers. The in-house employees even have to train the offshore staff, who will soon be replacing their "teachers."

It is obvious that management faces a difficult communication challenge. The following anecdote shows a scenario where the management cancelled profitable offshore plans because they did not want to take the

deliver higher quality at a much cheaper price. Not surprisingly, the onshore software team adamantly opposed the offshore plans.

Due to legally binding contracts, the customer's organization was required to deliver software updates quarterly. Therefore, continuous and stable software production was of vital importance to the organization.

The company ordered a small test project, which the offshore vendor completed with flying colors. A second, larger project ran into trouble: the customer's in-house team provided very low-quality requirements documents and refused any form of cooperation with the offshore vendor. When the onshore management tried to force them, they replied that they were too busy carrying out other tasks and did not have the necessary time for the offshore project. If active cooperation with the offshore provider was to be included in their agenda, the quarterly updates would be at risk, they said.

Eventually, the plans were cancelled because the management did not want to take the risks that it would face during the transition period.

6.5.5 Public Announcement

Offshore plans can cause serious tension, backlash, and breakdown of productivity in the customer's organization once they are made public. For this reason the timing of the public announcement is crucial and needs careful consideration. Some companies rely on open communication from the onset; others keep plans secret for as long as possible.

In many cases the customer needs the support of the existing onshore team to facilitate a smooth transfer of know-how. This steering committee that will manage the offshore relation and oversee the vendor's work has to be established. If the steering committee is made up of existing IT staff members, they will need additional training to be prepared for their new tasks. Training, of course, takes time. This means that a rather large group of persons is informed about the offshore plans. Big groups of confidants increase the likelihood of rumors being spread. In this case, rumors are almost always worse than controlled information management.

asked to do, but the transition period is frequently accompanied by high tension, and disputes often arise due to the employees' feelings of humiliation and betrayal.

> A large American organization announced that the in-house software department would be outsourced. Because the organization had already established connections to a well-known onshore vendor, the employees expected that the department would be outsourced to this provider. For this reason the situation remained rather relaxed; many of the employees expected that they would continue working for their former superior even if they were now to take the role of consultants. The stress-free atmosphere radically changed when the management announced that an Indian company, not the onshore provider, would in fact be the outsourcer. Under the circumstances, the company offered the equivalent of three months' pay to those who were willing to train their Indian colleagues. The employees did what they were asked to do. The money was too tempting for them to do otherwise, especially because the alternative was immediate unemployment. Eventually, some onshore employees expressed serious concerns about the visa status of the offshore employees, noting that it might not be in line with U.S. visa laws. This scandal caused serious trouble for the emerging offshore cooperation. A trade union even filed suit because of the visa situation. Finally, even though the union managed to stir things, it could not prevent the organization from going offshore and replacing most of the onshore workers.

As the anecdote shows, in most cases employees cannot hinder management's plans to take their business offshore, especially if management is really determined to do so. This is particularly applicable to large organizations because there is always a fraction willing to take the money and break solidarity. In small organizations, success is not completely certain; details about the group dynamics within the software team might become important. One of the anecdotes earlier in the chapter showed how a stable front of solidarity can impose serious pressure on management and cause careful reconsideration of offshore outsourcing plans.

6.5.7 Legal Obstacles to Firing Onshore Workers

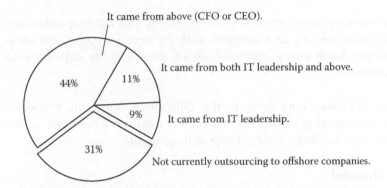

Figure 6.1 In November 2003, www.cio.com conducted a poll among its readership regarding who had the initiative of offshoring.

apply the strategy outlined above; whoever is willing to train the offshore workers will receive compensation because the company has to pay the money anyway, whether the existing IT team supports the offshore plans or not.

Especially in the United States but also in other countries, the pros and cons of offshoring are intensively discussed in the media. Because governments are concerned with its impact on the jobs on the internal labor market, they have discussed or established legislative barriers that permit dismissals due to outsourcing only under certain conditions. A poll conducted by www.cio.com shows that IT people are not particularly fond of outsourcing. More frequently the initiative comes from management (see Figure 6.1).

6.5.8 Going Offshore in Two Steps

Some large organizations with internal IT departments go offshore in two steps: In the first step they separate the IT department from the company and make it a legally independent business. Even if little else is changed, the newly established IT business is a company of its own with its own name and separate balance sheet. In the second phase (after a reasonable period of time), parts or all of the IT company go offshore. Because the IT company has meanwhile become independent, the management of the large (mother) organization is no longer responsible for its actions. This step may help to avoid unwanted negative publicity for the mother organization.

*vendors encounter problems with finding and holding onto expe-
rienced leaders, as managers with the necessary business experience have many options both in the emerging country and
abroad.*

Several factors contribute to the difficulties that some software companies in emerging countries, especially small and mid-size companies,
encounter in finding qualified top management.

High Demand

Some emerging countries are enjoying high economic growth not only in
the software industry but also in other fields. Many startup companies are
appearing, and existing organizations are expanding, thus generating a
huge demand for qualified managers in those countries.

Few Candidates

These countries do not generally benefit from long-established industrial
tradition. Only a few people have the necessary experience as top managers. Training classes for executive positions are just beginning to be
established, and hence there are few qualified graduates who can be
assigned such positions.

Virtues

The manager must first of all be loyal to the company and should have
high standards of integrity — virtues that might be difficult to find in
some developing countries. If loyalty is to be found at all, it is often due
to interpersonal relationships rather than a sense of duty. Loyalty according
to a written contract or manifested towards an international organization
is not very much ingrained in the mentality of developing countries.

High Qualifications Necessary

Successful top managers in offshore software companies should have a
high level of professional qualifications, including leadership ability and
proficient technical, business, and social skills. They must have international and multicultural experience as well as fluency in foreign languages.

company offers software at prices ranging between $12 and $25 per hour in industrialized countries and has to cover costs between $5 and $10 per hour, the margin is not at all substantial. This becomes obvious when considering additional factors that might further decrease the profits; usually, the outsourcer cannot use its full capacity because of gaps between projects. What is more, unexpected technical problems can occur or employees might break the terms of their contracts. Customers might run into financial problems, in which case invoices remain unpaid. Thus, for many reasons offshore companies cannot pay their managers lavishly.

Once the high level of skills necessary for offshore software management and the corresponding average pay enter the equation, it does not come as a surprise that quite a number of software managers in offshore countries are willing to consider other offers. They are especially looking for opportunities in industrialized countries, where people with similar qualifications are better paid, or they might take executive positions in other (low-tech) industries. Even if the top manager is the owner of the company, low margins might prompt a search for other opportunities, especially in the case of owners of small companies.

One obstacle that prevents qualified people from getting more attractive positions in industrialized countries is that they are denied access to Western labor markets — mainly because they do not have the appropriate passports or visas. Another obstacle is the lack of good business contacts with Western customers. Interestingly enough, both problems can be solved by taking a position as software manager, even if the financial remuneration is not exactly satisfying. The organization will provide its manager with the necessary visas and will pay for trips or relocation abroad; thus, the manager will easily develop interesting business contacts. After working for a certain time for an offshore software vendor, the manager might be in a good position to start a software business. Another option is that of finding employment in an industrialized country, perhaps even with a customer of a former employer.

Nevertheless, most offshore companies consider this unfair and try to forestall such situations. Because the legal systems in developing countries are not yet standing on solid ground, companies have very limited possibilities of stopping managers from first ensuring their own future financial security, instead of listing what is best for the company as a priority. To reach stable cooperation, some offshore companies allow their managers to somehow be part of the profits' allotment, e.g., they give them shares

country — e.g., as customer's representatives. These so-called envoys take an important role in the communication mechanisms of the offshore relationship.

In developing countries, costs of living are usually lower. However, if the envoy wants to keep up Western living standards, the cost of living might be even higher than in industrialized countries. As compared to the low per capita income in the developing country, the envoy is considered rather well-off; such individuals are attractive targets for crimes with economic motivations.

6.7.1 Security

During the offshore cooperation, it might become necessary for managers or technical staff to relocate temporarily or permanently to the offshore country. In an industrialized country, the family of an ordinary software manager with moderate monthly expenses would not be of particular interest to criminals. If the same family spends the same amount of money per month in a developing country, they are considered "extremely rich" and consequently are confronted with security problems; they are attractive targets for economically motivated crimes, and thus even older children may need adult surveillance when playing in public places — otherwise, they might be in danger of kidnaping. Permanent surveillance requires extra effort. In addition, the children might be hindered in their development if they do not have the opportunity to interact with other children without "Mommy's help." In most cities in Western countries, only celebrities face this kind of problem.

In general, all foreigners are labeled as "rich" in developing countries. They are easily recognizable due to their physical appearance, accent, behavior, and manner of dealing with money. Because of this, Western business people might consider additional security measurements necessary.

6.7.2 Cost of Living

Usually, the cost of living in most developing countries is lower than in industrialized countries. This, however, is true only as long as the envoy gives up a Western lifestyle and adjusts to the new state of affairs — e.g., adapts to the eating habits. If the manager wants to continue a Western lifestyle, cost of living can be even higher than in industrialized countries.

6.8   OFFSHORE STAFF WORKING IN INDUSTRIALIZED COUNTRIES

Liaisons are employees of the offshore vendor who work for a certain time at the customer's site (see also Section 7.4). In many offshore scenarios, liaisons facilitate international communication and narrow cultural gaps. The liaison usually bears a lot of responsibility within the project. For this reason, these people are very qualified and carefully selected — which makes them particularly attractive to headhunters.

A possible conflict of interest arises if the offshore worker wants to use the liaison role as a base for starting a software business.

Due to the liaison's large influence in the project, the customer might be tempted to corrupt the liaison to gain undue advantages, apart from the "officially" negotiated ones.

6.8.1   Headhunting the Liaison

Many offshore scenarios require members of the vendor's team to work in the customer's office, at least for a limited time. Such liaisons are expensive investments due to the considerable travel costs. The liaison needs discussion partners and trainers from the customer's staff. Both the liaison and the trainers have to be paid according to the level of the industrialized country, as imposed by high cost of living and by visa legislation. Having offshore staff working in onshore sites is not cheap.

The liaisons have much responsibility both in the project and in the offshore company because on their return to the offshore country they will be project leads and take the role of multiplicators, which means that other colleagues will have to work under their guidance. Furthermore, they should leave a good impression about their company; this amplifies their role as representatives of the vendor's company. Given the expenditure and the crucial importance of these individuals to the success of the collaboration, they are usually selected carefully; no offshore company would send a washout employee. It does not come as a surprise that the people chosen for the role of liaison usually have outstanding technical and social skills, are multiculturally experienced, and are fluent in at least one foreign language.

office under careful surveillance. The customer has more than enough time to validate its opinion about their qualifications. Even customers with impressive office buildings might face problems in resisting the temptation of offering the young talent "attractive alternatives" — although the contract with the vendor excludes this option.

The issue of headhunting might be of minor importance when a large customer is cooperating with a large provider. Under such circumstances, the size of the cooperation involves a significant degree of importance for both sides, which guarantees a certain amount of fairness. Nevertheless, if a small customer works with a small provider, this issue should be seriously taken into account.

Rumors have it that some offshore companies try to get this problem under control by using illegal methods; the family of the software engineer who is sent abroad is kept hostage so that the engineer abroad behaves according the contract. Other companies try to solve the problem by offering the liaison part of the company's profits. Sometimes the liaison even owns part of the vendor's company.

6.8.2 Liaisons Who Want to Start Their Own Software Companies

From the liaison's point of view, the period of residence in the industrialized country is highly attractive: the liaison might have (secret) future plans to start a new company. During the stay, the liaison can make preparations for leaving the present position and taking the reins of a new, future company. Liaisons have the opportunity to establish business contacts with highly attractive partners, such as managers of software companies who are willing to work with offshore providers. They can make new friends among their colleagues, which might prove to be quite helpful in finding future projects insofar as they can provide the liaison with crucial contacts. A liaison's newly won friends form an important bridgehead once the liaison starts a small company: they can help the former liaison get the necessary visas and provide accommodations (for at least a few days in their guest room).

There are obvious reasons why the liaison may seize the chance of a lifetime and therefore might be tempted to use the time to the benefit of the liaison's own personal future — not necessarily to the benefit of the company who paid the liaison to go abroad.

and business culture that would not be disclosed otherwise. In addition, the customer's management might try to unfairly influence the liaison.

> An offshore engineer was sent to a Western customer for a week, during which he was supposed to learn about the requirements for a future fixed-price project. In accordance with the work plan, the software engineer returned to the offshore country and implemented the requirements with the help of some of his colleagues. During the next stage of the project, the software engineer spent about one week per month with the customer, installing the current version and discussing new requirements. It came to the ears of the offshore management that the software engineer was receiving valuable gifts while he was working at the customer's site in the offshore country.
>
> After a while the project reached a crisis due to considerable delays. It turned out that the project was much behind schedule, and this consequently brought about significantly higher costs on the part of the vendor. Because the contract between vendor and customer specified a fixed price, the vendor would not receive additional payment from the customer.
>
> Further investigation showed that the software team under guidance of the liaison had implemented many additional features that were not stipulated in the fixed-price contract. The customer's management asked the software engineer if he could not "by the way" be able to implement certain small features — i.e., without documentation and without payment made to his company. In fact, these "small features" were major extensions of the project that caused significant supplementary work and consequent delay in the schedule. They bought his "kind cooperation" with the expensive gifts they offered — to the disadvantage of the vendor's organization.

In the anecdote above, the customer bribed the liaison to implement an additional functionality that was not stipulated in the contract. Another illegitimate type of cooperation between customer and liaison occurs when the customer arranges business matters directly with the liaison, most probably at lower costs. The motivation is that establishing such contacts accounts for a significant part of the investment in an offshore cooperation. Having the key element of the cooperation at hand (that is, the liaison)

paying for the business trips, but the superior will not benefit from any future projects.

6.9   OFFSHORE ADVISERS

Establishing an offshore scenario requires much background information about the contributing countries and about IT outsourcing management. Some specialized consulting companies offer this know-how and can help the customer find a qualified vendor and establish the relationship

Some offshore scenarios enlist the help of specialized companies consisting of offshore professionals to establish the cooperation. The advisers working for these companies are experts in the offshore outsourcing of IT projects. They are well acquainted with the state of affairs in both countries, they are sufficiently knowledgeable on software technology and contracts, and they maintain excellent contacts, both onshore and offshore. These offshore advisers are frequently rather small organizations; sometimes they are in fact one-person companies where the offshore agent is self-employed. The agency can play various roles in an offshore scenario.

6.9.1   Consultant Role

These companies can act as advisers or consultants who take no legally binding role in the outsourcing partnership and bring no actual contribution to the project contract — i.e., the agency supports the customer in finding a qualified vendor and helps draft the contract, but the agency is not a signatory of the contract.

The agency can offer valuable support in setting up the offshore scenario, especially if the customer does not have the necessary experience in that country or in software outsourcing. The customer can enlist the support of the agency to set up the offshore scenario and carry through the first few projects. After the offshore scenario is established, the customer goes on without the agency.

6.9.2   Partner Role

between the onshore and the offshore partners is necessary. The agency enters the contract partnership and assumes all responsibility for software delivery. From the point of view of the vendor, the agency plays the role of the client.

Such agencies take the strain off outsourcing business for the customer, who will barely be affected by the disadvantages of offshore software production because it has a contract signed under the legal terms of the industrialized country and an onshore partner — i.e., the agency.

The only disadvantage is that offshore agencies are not exactly cheap. Working with an agency offers the client a level of comfort similar to that of working with an onshore vendor. The prices are comparable as well because in many cases choosing to contact an agency takes up most of the prospective savings within the offshore scenario. In many offshore projects the budget is simply too limited to afford employing an offshore agent.

6.10 SHADY BUSINESS AGENTS

Selecting a proper, suitable agency implies a certain degree of care and suspicion because not all offshore agents are creditable enough. The case study gives an example.

A small vendor in Romania received an e-mail from a new potential customer from Germany. The client was not an actual company but a private person, whom I will call "Fred Fender." The prospective customer communicated using the e-mail account of his wife, whom I will call "Fancy Fender." Fred asked for a small project offer. The vendor sent the offer and received an e-mailed acceptance. The vendor's manager knew that e-mail orders are not necessarily legally binding. For this reason he insisted on receiving at least a signed fax. Because it was a rather small project, the vendor drafted only a short contract and asked the customer to sign it.

The customer was not particularly keen on the idea of a signed contract. However, the vendor insisted and finally the customer sent a signed "paper" — a fax. The signed text was not in the form prepared by the vendor but a print-out of older e-mails where technical details of the project had been dis-cussed. The vendor did not want to upset the new customer

because he had maintained excellent contacts in Germany, where the customer was living, and he therefore had the necessary infrastructure to start litigation against Fred. The German lawyer confirmed that the legal situation was crystal clear. The only potential risk could be that the customer did not have any money at all and could not pay. The vendor's manager had some indications that this was not the case, however. So they started the lawsuit.

The plaintiff was confronted with an unpleasant surprise during the litigation: Fred Fender said he was not the contract partner and that in fact his wife had signed the contract. His wife, Fancy Fender, claimed that she was not the contract partner either because her husband had signed the fax. The truth was that the contract was signed "F. Fender," so either spouse could have signed it. Unfortunately, the fax transmission was not clear enough for a graphological evaluation.

The lawyer suggested initiating two lawsuits — one against Fred and the other against Fancy — so that the actual signer of the contract could be exposed. However, the vendor rejected this idea because one of the two litigations would definitely be lost because only one of the Fenders could be found guilty as charged. This would have entailed payment for the lawyers and court fees — which the vendor had to pay because it would lose at least one of the lawsuits. This meant a considerable amount of money down the drain. The other trial might be won by the plaintiff. However, even this was not certain: a business partner who had been able to conceive such a tricky legal architecture designed as a mischievous trap right from the start was quite likely to have additional lines of defense carefully prepared — and not at all obvious to the vendor's lawyers. For this reason there was a nonnegligible risk that even the second lawsuit might be lost, causing additional costs for lawyers and court.

In fact this was a small project. The price for the project would hardly be enough to cover the costs for one of the lawsuits — the one that would be lost for certain. The vendor's manager saw himself in a situation where he could only lose. For this reason, he decided to cancel all actions against Mr. and Mrs. Fender and accepted that this small project had been done for free.

"faraway" industrialized country because they lack contacts, funding, and know-how about the legal system of the industrialized country. Even if the German lawyer considered the situation "crystal clear," the final outcome was that the project remained unpaid-for.

There were also other indications that Mr. and Mrs. Fender were veterans in this legal architecture. This substantiated the suspicion that this couple had applied it many times before. I imagine that they occasionally ordered small projects that remained unpaid. In most cases the vendor would not even think of starting a lawsuit.

Among project managers in emerging countries, the saying goes that Internet-mediated projects are paid for only in exceptional situations — usually they remain unpaid. It seems that this kind of "shady business agent" is rather frequently encountered in offshore projects.

The Agent's Point of View

It often happens that the business culture gets harsher and thus more difficult to tolerate toward the end of the daisy chain. Each agent has to deal with even less reliable subcontractors. The prices are low and the margins are small. Crude management methods are particularly frequent at the borderline levels of the daisy chain — e.g., the last step before the order leaves the industrialized country. This level is attractive to underhanded agents; the subcontractors usually do not have enough funding and know-how to deal with the complicated legal situation of international business and laws. For this reason a lawsuit is rather unlikely. To a large extent the partners in emerging countries have to trust their "acquaintances" in the industrialized nation and often find themselves at their mercy.

Seeing it from the purely economic point of view, the position of offshore agent is not bad business; it does not require much know-how, nor does it imply IT skills or subject matter expertise. The vendor will contribute the software skills; the agent's customer will contribute the domain expertise. The agent is self-employed and thus the business does not require a lot of management skills, either. A carefully prepared legal architecture can be an advantage, as the anecdote shows. The necessary capital for entering the market is very limited, and once the contacts are established the agent can run the business with very limited time investment because the agent's main function is just forwarding e-mails. The payments made to offshore developers are low — if they are made at all. Thus, an agent can achieve a considerable income with very limited

of money. It is debatable to what extent these claims were justified. Anyway, the German partner refused to admit that there was any debt whatsoever.

The Russian "creditors" had little trust in the legal system of either country. For this reason, they confiscated assets of the German businessman's that were located at the Russian site. Because there was no hearing before the confiscation and no marshal was present, the German businessman claimed that the assets were simply stolen. The Russians declared that they were using them as a "safety measure" for the due payments. They even claimed that the "security" was not enough to cover the "debts." For this reason they expected additional payment. When the German refused to make any payment whatsoever, he received threats that were meant to intimidate him and to force him to pay off. If he did not, very "unpleasant things" were to happen to him.

Eventually, German law enforcement authorities solved the problem. This took a while, however. Meanwhile, the German businessman considered it wise to be whisked away to a secret location, and only his best friend knew where to find him.

These anecdotes are not meant to place all offshore agencies in an unfavorable light; the majority of them are serious and professional companies, even though the author has personally encountered a number of "fishy" agents.

6.11 PUBLIC OPINION IN INDUSTRIALIZED COUNTRIES: GLOBALISM

It is not only one company that goes offshore; the entire software industry in leading economies is on its way to foreign soil. This fact introduces a political dimension to the discussion.

6.11.1 Competition on Global Labor Markets

Ever since the beginnings of international trade, workers from different countries have been in steadily growing competition — basically on the

they achieved much higher productivity, which justified higher wages. The more efficient productivity in industrialized countries made their products cheaper and better, although salaries were orders of magnitude higher. The growing importance of multinational companies was a first step in turning indirect competition on labor markets into direct competition. In recent decades we have witnessed manufacturing industries being moved to offshore destinations. For the first time, globally active industrial corporations had the option of choosing between competing labor markets.

The labor markets in industrialized countries reacted to this process by producing workers who were better qualified and could therefore reach even higher productivity levels. The industrialized countries used their advantage over the developing nations to get another step ahead and transformed their low-paying manufacturing jobs into attractive high-tech and other white-collar jobs. What at first looked like a huge disaster for the workers in the leading economies turned out to be a major step toward a better standard of living.

Some economists think of the world economy as a ladder. At the bottom are countries producing low-tech goods such as textiles. At the top are the leading economies such as the United States, Japan, and Western Europe, which are producing expensive products — e.g., pharmaceuticals and software. At the middle of the hierarchy are countries with goods ranging from cars to consumer cameras. In terms of this analogy, the industrialized nations moved one rung up the ladder, leaving the rungs below open.

A number of analysts compare the current surge of offshore outsourcing of white-collar jobs with the process of moving manufacturing industries to developing countries. These analysts hope that the current boom in outsourcing will eventually display similar dynamics; innovation will produce new, more productive jobs in industrialized countries. The economy in the leading countries will adapt to the new opportunities, and the population in these countries will finally end up at least at the same level as they are now — probably even at a higher one.

Future prognosis has always been difficult, and it is not becoming easier. This is one reason why only some analysts believe that everything will turn out well for the population in the industrialized countries. The opponents of offshore outsourcing argue that there are significant differences between the process of moving manufacturing industries offshore and the current outsourcing of IT services.

In the current wave of offshore outsourcing the new rung is not as clear as it was decades ago. Some are even concerned that the industrialized nations have already reached the top of the ladder, and there is no such thing as a "next rung." The leading economies may be running out of rungs.

Decades ago, the result of the competition for the next rung on the ladder was rather clear even before it started: industrialized nations would be getting the best places. At that time the offshore workers in consumer electronics factories were being taught what a screwdriver was used for; they could not be considered serious competitors for high-tech jobs.

Things changed over time. Software engineers in offshore countries are as qualified as their Western colleagues, and they are learning from each outsourcing project and from each period of training they undergo in industrialized countries. In addition, many of the key scientific results are published and available worldwide. These resources put large emerging countries like India or China into the position to focus scientific brainpower on virtually any field they choose — e.g., biotechnology or telecommunication, which might be possible "next rungs" on the ladder. Such countries are quite likely to reach a leading position in any of these fields within a reasonable time frame. For these reasons some analysts doubt whether it will be as easy as it was before for the industrialized nations to take over the attractive next rung.

Jobs that do not require local presence — so-called "placeless" jobs — are particularly in danger. However, there are almost no types of white-collar jobs left that definitely *cannot* be outsourced to other countries. Only positions that require hands-on, face-to-face relationships are an exception — nurses and other healthcare personnel, for example. All other professions are potential candidates for outsourcing: designers, engineers, scientists — virtually everything.

Many published successful case studies of offshore outsourcing refer to large customers. This observation might lead to the conclusion that jobs in smaller organizations are safer. However, the example of the manufacturing industries a few decades ago teaches that this could be a fallacy; it was the large organizations that first initiated offshore outsourcing. The small companies did not have the necessary know-how and infrastructure to go abroad. The final effect was that the small companies lost their competitiveness and were taken over or simply closed down. Thus, jobs were lost in the small companies as well.

Transferring a factory to the other hemisphere is neither cheap nor

ladder. In addition, natural, demographic phenomena helped, too; during the rather long period of transition, many blue-collar workers in the old manufacturing industries retired, and the younger generation did not take up these jobs anymore; they received training suitable for the emerging new industries instead. Outsourcing information-based jobs to offshore countries is possible almost instantly. Building factories overseas required billions of dollars. Transfer of information-based jobs turns out to be much easier: on the hardware side it requires only a desk, a computer, and Internet access. The high speed of the process makes it more difficult for workers in industrialized countries to adapt to the new situation fast enough.

The effect of the so-called onsite offshoring is even faster than that of outsourcing: offshore staff work at the customer's site. Visa regulations provide that these workers have to be paid according to the local level. In this way, offshore workers should not be cheaper than the in-house staff. This is only the theoretical point of view, however. In practice, many companies have found ways around these regulations. An additional effect of having offshore workers in the customer's office is that they increase the supply of qualified workers in that region: when the supply of workers grows, salaries go down.

Thus, it is understandable that many people in industrialized countries are worried about their future and about the consequences of global outsourcing of white-collar jobs — in all areas, not only in the IT field. Especially in the United States, but also in some Western European countries, the political discussion of this topic is very heated and has reached groups outside professional IT. A central issue in the political discussion of the long-term consequences of offshore outsourcing is the question of whether this step will maintain the relative affluence among well-developed nations. Will offshore outsourcing lead to growing prosperity in all countries or will some countries lose and others win? That is, will countries like India and China draw closer and become first-class members of world economy? Perhaps leading economies such as the United States will even fall behind these former third-world countries.

The reason behind this concern is the global mobility of the core factors of productivity in our information age: education, training, technology, and capital. A few decades ago, it would have been considered rather risky to shift technology and capital to Asia or Eastern Europe. The United States, Japan, and Western Europe had similar labor costs. For this reason, no dramatic "offshore outsourcing" processes took place.

ones, but productivity is similar. For this reason an enormous transfer of capital — i.e., jobs — to developing countries is created.

Some analysts predict that wages in the United States and other leading economies will decrease under the pressure of the offshore surge. However, they are not expected to fall to the point where the onshore workers would enter direct competition with countries such as China or India. The higher cost of living, established standards of living, and existing contract mortgages form solid barriers preventing wages from falling below a certain level.

The salaries in developing countries, on the other hand, have been growing steadily throughout the years, in particular for the most attractive group: young engineers who are fluent in foreign languages, especially English. It is only a question of time until pay will reach a level where offshore outsourcing for pure financial reasons will no longer be attractive. As emerging countries become full-fledged members of the "first world," and the standard of living in these countries mounts towards the level in the industrialized countries, the cost difference will shrink, and outsourcing to these countries will become less attractive. Nevertheless, there are large and untapped pools of workers in third-world countries. This means that it will take awhile until cost differences diminish. Meanwhile, the developed nations will face irreversible changes to the outsourcing organizations and to the countries' IT professionals' structure.

It would be highly speculative to predict how long this will take and what life in industrialized countries will look like by then. Some analysts trust the unbridled power of innovation; that is where the United States and the other industrialized nations are strong. Nevertheless, most commentators expect that this trend will be irreversible: jobs that have been moved out of the industrialized countries will not return — even if the level of costs in countries like China and India adjusts to the level of the leading industrialized nations.

Other researchers expect offshore outsourcing to have an overwhelming impact on the whole lifestyle in the industrialized nations in the long run. These analysts are concerned for the following reasons.

As long as IT investment in industrialized countries is low, the process of offshore outsourcing will decrease the number of IT jobs in industrialized countries. A high percentage of dismissed IT workers will not obtain a similar-level position in their field. Sooner or later they will have to find other ways to earn a living, even though the process might be painful in

The new generation will carefully consider whether investing in IT training is worth the effort. It is difficult to predict what importance IT and other engineering disciplines will still have in the academic life of the next generation in industrialized nations. Some headlines already place the United States on the fast track to the third world unless the process is stopped and reverted. (See also Section 1.6 for some hard numbers.)

In the old economic system, factories, machines, and other fixed capital assets formed a precious part of a company's capital. The information society has altered these relations: the know-how of IT employees forms an important part of the intellectual assets of the organization. If software employees are lost to other companies, these intellectual assets will be lost as well. Perhaps management will be able to run the business even without them, at least for a while.

In the course of setting up the offshore relationship, IT know-how has been transferred to the offshore provider. After the offshore scenario had been established, the in-house IT team who had this know-how was no longer needed, and most of them were fired. If the executives decide, however, to bring this know-how back in house they will face serious obstacles — the same obstacles emerging nations faced when they tried to bring the know-how to their country: they needed the active and determined support of partners in industrialized nations.

> A few decades ago Germany had a strong position in the market for photo cameras. Then Japan tried to enter this market. When I was a child, I heard some adults joking that the Japanese were "students of the Germans" because they imitated German cameras — which looked similar but just had another label. We all knew, of course, that German cameras had much higher quality standards and could not be compared with these "Japanese toys."
>
> Far East wisdom, however, teaches, that "all things are quickly passing away" — and the German position in the market for cameras was no exception.
>
> Could something similar happen with the American dominance in the software business?

6.11.2 Public Opinion Regarding Offshore Outsourcing

Offshore outsourcing is increasingly unpopular among workers in some

The offshore surge further weakens the already-fragile relation between workers and employers. Even those employees who are not directly affected by a current offshore program witness what is happening to their colleagues. A few years ago many of them would not even in their wildest nightmares have dreamed that something like this could happen in their organizations.

> The managers of a large American organization called in an "all hands" meeting of the IT department. The workers were told that the IT department would be outsourced to an Indian partner. Those who were willing to train the replacement workers would get a contract for another three months. The others were asked to gather their belongings and leave the office building. Ten percent of the IT team chose the latter.

Some analysts emphasize that the angst is not justified; the economic numbers do not look so bad. Although there was a slight decrease in the number of IT jobs in the United States, the figures in 2004 are still much higher than in 1995.

Nevertheless, IT people and other outsourcing-prone employees in industrialized countries are deeply concerned about their future, and the topic has taken on a political dimension. Hence, organizations that envisage offshore activities might be well advised to take these issues into consideration. The managers have to decide whether they want to enter this politically hot area. There might be compelling reasons to do so, but the final decision has to be well considered.

6.11.3 Statements of Analysts and Experts

The highly respected Institute of Electrical and Electronics Engineers (IEEE) has said that offshoring "poses a very serious, long-term challenge to the nation's leadership in technology and innovation, its economic prosperity, and its military and homeland security."

McCarthy raised the issue of technological leadership: "If you don't have the entry-level programmers, how do you get people to become system architects — the high-level skills that we think are going to stay onshore?"

7

BUSINESS ARCHITECTURES

ABSTRACT

Analysis of offshore scenarios has shown that only a limited number of business architectures turn out to be successful in practice. Some business models that are successful on domestic markets may fail in an offshore scenario. Two aspects should be considered when establishing which business model is reasonable in a given offshore scenario: the projects' characteristics and the consequential damages if the project fails.

Costs for communication can be high in offshore scenarios, and management quality can seriously suffer as a consequence of lack of quality communication. Many analysts consider these facts among the prime reasons for failing offshore scenarios. For this reason, the business architecture has to address communication cost from the very onset. Following is a Business Models Overview.

7.1 BUSINESS ARCHITECTURE ADEQUATE TO PROJECTS AT HAND

The projects that should be carried out in an envisioned offshore scenario have a strong bearing on the business architecture. A scenario that includes many short and easy projects requires a completely different business model than a single large and technologically challenging project does. Consequential damages are of particular interest in case the project fails: if high damages are to be expected, the client will need additional

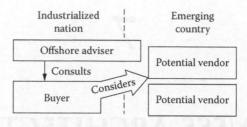

Figure 7.1 **The offshore adviser consults the buyer while it considers potential vendors and helps shape the business model. Frequently the offshore adviser has its headquarters in the industrialized country.**

7.1.1 Offshore Adviser

Offshore advisers are consultants or consulting companies. (See Figure 7.1.) They have (or should have) good contacts in the emerging country as well as broad experience in the software industry of the countries contributing to the envisioned offshore scenario. Good offshore advisers can greatly reduce the risk of failure by helping design the business model and finding an adequate partner. (See also Section 6.9 and Section 6.10.)

7.1.2 Project Characteristics

The characteristics of the software projects that are to be developed in the offshore scenario — e.g., the average project size and the applied technologies — are important parameters for suitable business architecture. A company that is producing various simple Web applications will need a completely different business architecture than will an organization that is developing a single large control system for a factory.

In the context of the control system, it might be reasonable that the offshore project manager pay periodic visits of a few days each to the customer's site — e.g., once in a month. The project lead installs the current version and discusses the next steps.

Of course it is more cost efficient if the projects can be carried through without travel expenses; the requirements are written at the customer's site, and the offshore team works according to these specifications. This might be a reasonable approach for the technologically less challenging Web pages. In many cases, however, the onshore staff needs additional training in requirements engineering if they want to apply this model; frequently, the onshore analysts are not used to the required level of

7.1.3 Consequential Damages of Project Failure

The project characteristics are only one influencing factor. The second aspect that should be considered when designing the business architecture is the consequential damage if the project fails. Projects that do not cause considerable losses for the customer in case of failure stand at the benign end of the range; if the foreign partner is not able to deliver, the project will not be paid for and that settles the problem. For such projects, the customer can definitely optimize the cost.

At the other end of the spectrum are projects that cause significant consequential damages for the customer if they fail. For such projects the customer needs additional means of influence. In many offshore scenarios, this goal is achieved by owning the vendor's entire organization or a portion thereof or by founding a foreign subsidiary.

7.2 OPTIONS FOR BUSINESS MODELS

When designing the blueprint for the business architecture, the customer has to decide whether it wants to work with an independent vendor or start its own foreign subsidiary. A subsidiary requires more know-how but provides the customer with strong control instruments.

In offshore business, several types of one-to-one relations are frequently applied — joint ventures, strategic alliances, etc. In practice, many of these business architectures are somewhere in between an independent vendor and a foreign subsidiary.

Another factor that influences the business model is the size of the contributing units: although most published case studies refer to large customers, small clients often have to find more creative solutions.

Important business models that are frequently applied in offshore outsourcing are onsite offshoring, body leasing agencies, and subcontracting (daisy chains). The so-called follow-the-sun model is used in help desk management where 24/7 availability is required.

7.2.1 Foreign Subsidiary vs. Independent Organizations of Customer and Vendor

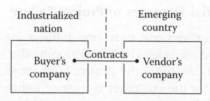

Figure 7.2 Two legally independent organizations — buyer and vendor — cooperating on the basis of civil contracts.

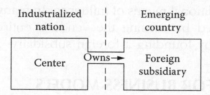

Figure 7.3 Foreign subsidiary. The center in the industrialized nation owns the organization in the emerging country.

interests of the customer — for example, selling the company to a competitor of the customer. Because establishing the offshore relationship constitutes a significant investment, losing the vendor to the other side generates losses for the customer. In addition, business secrets and competitive know-how may reach the hands of the new owner — i.e., the customer's competitor. This possibility is excluded in the case of a foreign subsidiary owned by the onshore customer.

Business architecture based on a foreign subsidiary allows the center (i.e., the customer) to gain extensive control. This makes fraudulent dealings of the foreign subsidiary's management less likely. In addition, greater understanding and good will are to be expected in an offshore scenario based on foreign subsidiaries because both companies have the same owners, and the profits eventually go to the same pocket. Mutual understanding is an important basis for efficient communication and successful offshore projects. Note, however, that a foreign subsidiary requires more background information about the country and about software management than cooperation with an independent vendor does, because an independent vendor contributes additional know-how.

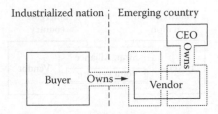

Figure 7.4   One-to-one relationship. The buyer orders only from one vendor, and the vendor works only for this client. Frequently, the onshore customer and offshore management share the ownership of the vendor's organization.

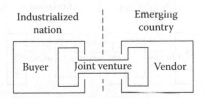

Figure 7.5   Joint venture. Both parties — buyer and vendor — provide staff or other resources for the joint venture, which becomes something like a "company within the company."

7.2.2   One-to-One Relations

On internal markets, many clients work with multiple vendors and in return, vendors work with multiple clients. In successful outsourcing scenarios, however, one-to-one relations are rather frequent — i.e., the customer orders from one vendor only, and the vendor works almost exclusively for this main customer. The management of such scenarios is rather similar to that of a foreign subsidiary, even if the two organizations are legally independent. This pattern stems from the strong economic dependence between vendor and customer. (See Figure 7.4.)

Patterns of one-to-one relations frequently used in practice include joint ventures and strategic alliances (Figure 7.5 and Figure 7.6). A joint venture is a cooperation of two companies that has been established to carry through a certain project. Usually, each side provides employees and other resources that are exclusively assigned to the joint venture. A joint venture is called "fully functional" if it can act on the market

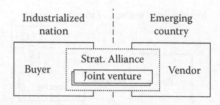

Figure 7.6 Strategic alliance. Although the joint venture is frequently limited to a certain project, the strategic alliance is designed for the long run. It may include one or more joint ventures.

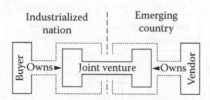

Figure 7.7 Fully functional joint venture. If the joint venture is a legally independent organization it is called "fully functional." Both sides share the ownership.

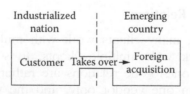

Figure 7.8 Foreign acquisition. The buyer in the industrialized country takes over the vendor's organization, which had previously been an independent organization.

Unlike a joint venture, which is limited to a specific project, a strategic alliance constitutes a long-term cooperation between the companies involved. Quite often, the strategic alliance includes one or more joint ventures.

There are countless alternatives for one-to-one relationship implementation in offshore business. In some cases the foreign customer owns a part

- The customer wants to have a high degree of control over the vendor's activities. Thus, the vendor is more like a foreign subsidiary than an independent organization.
- Even if the customer owns part the vendor's organization, the income of the vendor's management is closely related to the results and acts as a stimulus for high performance and loyalty. Frequently, this is achieved through a strategy that implies that the vendor's management owns a part of the organization and profits are consequently shared.
- The offshore management has to invest some assets (e.g., the existing company or their private savings). This way they can win something but they can also lose something — i.e., their investment.
- Owning and selling shares of the vendor's organization is subject to contractual restrictions. For example, an offshore manager who leaves the team is not allowed to keep shares anymore but has to sell them back. Shares can be sold only to the other partners of the joint venture, not to third parties.
- The customer provides continuity of project orders. The vendor's management is responsible for the day-by-day software production business.
- The strategic business decisions are in the hands of the customer.
- The working power of the offshore management is available exclusively to the vendor's organization. They are not allowed to do business outside the joint venture. They cannot start another company outside the customer's control, for example.

Many of these business architectures are somewhere in between a foreign subsidiary and an independent vendor.

An American customer wanted to establish an offshore relationship to Romania. In the long run the customer needed a high level of control over the vendor — something like a foreign subsidiary. However, the customer did not have enough knowhow to build up a foreign subsidiary from scratch. In addition, the offshore management was supposed to share profits as a sort of motivational guarantee.

The American customer selected a small vendor that offered high quality at reasonable prices. When the first small test

7.2.3 Working with Large vs. Small Vendors

A large vendor has already reached higher degrees of maturity, stability, and continuity in comparison to a small company. For this reason the cooperation will probably be smoother. More mature providers, on the other hand, are usually correspondingly expensive.

A small organization lacks the necessary capital to carry through larger projects and to provide the necessary compensation if something goes wrong. However, small vendors have more flexibility and can adapt their structures to the needs of a single customer.

In the extreme case when the vendor is an individual, the prices can be incredibly low. The professional quality is not necessarily bad; some of these one-person software companies are in fact talented programmers. However, the scenario may lack continuity and stability because as soon as the developer is presented with an attractive new offer — at home or abroad — the developer may close the "company" and take the new offer. The client can consider itself lucky if the project in progress is finished in a more-or-less civil manner. For these reasons, cooperating with individual developers is mainly applicable when the projects are rather short and failure of a project does not lead to serious consequential damages on the customer's side.

Working with a small vendor provides the customer with the option of buying the vendor's company. Thus, after a period of time dedicated to testing the cooperation, the independent vendor may be turned into a foreign subsidiary. The following anecdote gives an example of such a takeover.

A German software provider considered founding a foreign subsidiary in Romania. He contacted a small Romanian vendor and ordered few small projects of minor strategic importance to establish the cooperation and to test the professional level of the vendor. Because the customer was satisfied, he suggested using the vendor's existing infrastructure (employees, office, and computers) as a basis for a newly founded subsidiary.

The deal took the shape of a friendly takeover from the very beginning: The German customer owned about half of the organization. The other half was to remain in the hands of the existing management. Although the customer provided the orders, the near-shore management was responsible for the day-by-day business of software development. Hence, the cus-

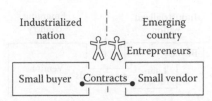

Figure 7.9   Small companies. The cooperation of the two independent organizations is based on civil contracts. However, there is a trustful and carefully managed relationship between the entrepreneurs.

7.2.4   Small Customers

Most published case studies refer to large customers. Small clients as well can have access to the advantages of offshore outsourcing but need more creative solutions. In some situations, small customers even have certain advantages because they can use models that do not have to scale up. For example, if the manager of a small company knows an appropriate project manager, this information can eliminate a significant part of the startup cost of the offshore scenario.

> A German company employed an immigrant software engineer from Poland. After several years the software engineer expressed his wish to go back to his country for family reasons. His superior said that this matched the company's plans very well because they wanted to set up a foreign subsidiary in Poland. They asked him to take an important position in this newly founded subsidiary. This way, they saved a lot of the expenses necessary for setting up the relationship: the manager of the newly founded subsidiary already had detailed know-how about the background of the projects, he was familiar with many types of requirements, he was adapted to the business culture of the respective organization — and, of course, he had comprehensive background information as well as reliable contacts in his native country, Poland.

In successful relationships between small companies, we frequently observe a trustful and carefully managed relationship between the entrepreneurs; perhaps this is what makes the scenario successful (Figure 7.9).

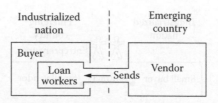

Figure 7.10 Onsite offshoring. The offshore vendor sends its employees to the customer. There they work under guidance of the onshore management.

work at the customer's site. Because the offshore workers must be paid just like onshore employees, the cost advantage of offshoring diminishes in onsite offshoring. Nevertheless, onsite offshoring has advantages:

- The scenario can be established very quickly. Provided that the offshore workers have the necessary language skills and visas, they can start working almost instantly as onshore workers.
- Onsite offshoring can help customers gain access to skills and talent that are not available in the in-house team.
- Sometimes the model is used in the early phase of an emerging offshore relationship. The vendor's employees work for a certain time at the customer's site. Once they have learned all the necessary skills, they return to their own country.
- The model is useful to balance a lack of qualified workers on the local labor market. A side effect is that onsite offshoring allows the company access to other labor markets. When the supply of workers grows, the prices decrease.

These observations explain why many companies consider onsite offshoring cheaper than onshore workers, even though the offshore workers have to be paid according to the wage standards in the industrialized country. In some countries this rule is not very efficiently enforced: the company decides what exactly the term "market level" means. In other cases, companies try to avoid paying the offshore workers on a par with local workers: if the offshore employees work long hours and overtime is not paid, the "imported" workers are considerably cheaper than onshore employees would be.

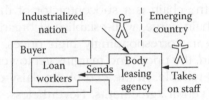

Figure 7.11   Body leasing agency. The agency hires staff in emerging or industrialized countries and sends them as loan workers to the customer.

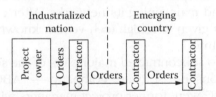

Figure 7.12   Daisy chain. The project owner orders the project from a contractor. The contractor subcontracts all or part of the work from another subcontractor, which in turn might use sub-subcontractors. In this way, the project may cross international borders one or more times.

fluctuations in demand. For this reason, they maintain a network of freelance employees whom they only access on demand. Many of the freelancers are small companies — quite often one-person companies. This network, together with the contacts to the clients, constitutes an important part of the working capital of such agencies.

Thus, protection of these contacts is of vital importance for the agency: under no circumstances should the freelancers and the customers do business directly. Even in the rather stable legal environment of the industrialized country, this requirement occasionally causes problems: the contracts disallow direct cooperation, but there are unfair people out there.

Offshore scenarios bring a completely new set of legal challenges into question: the offshore workers may seize the chance of a lifetime if they are working in the office of a well-off customer who is willing to cooperate with offshore staff. In many cases the contract is not reliable enough, and sooner or later the engineer will find a way to contact the customer directly — without the body leasing agency.

The lower rung in the chain is a subcontractor of the next higher rung. At the top of the chain, large, well-established organizations can usually be found, and so can correspondingly high prices. As work is passed down the daisy chain, the prices and margins get lower and the companies get smaller and less reliable. At the end of the daisy chain the "contracts" are frequently only verbal agreements. Nevertheless, most of the work is done at this end of the daisy chain — the so-called "ants' levels." The author does not want to speculate on how reliably confidential material is protected within these verbal agreements at the lower levels of the chain.

A large telecom provider decided to outsource software for controlling and maintaining its networks. After careful analysis, the order was given to a high-tech vendor known worldwide — say, "Global Info."

Global Info subcontracted major parts of the software system to a smaller onshore software company — "ABC." In fact, the owners of ABC were former project managers who had worked for Global Info. Years ago they started their own business, which almost exclusively offered services to their former boss. In time, ABC had grown and turned into a midsize business.

ABC often encountered problems employing a sufficient number of qualified staff at reasonable costs — particularly in times of high demand. So they decided to work with an offshore provider. They chose a small Eastern European vendor, "GoEast," which had a highly qualified staff. The prospective cost savings might have had their contribution. The new project from the telecom provider was well defined and did not require too much background information about existing "legacy systems." For this reason it was perfect for offshore outsourcing.

GoEast faced problems because of dramatic changes related to the workload: in times of high demand, the permanently employed team was not large enough. If there was less work to be done, the team had to be paid regardless of the circumstances. Given the low prices and small margins, it is obvious that the varying workload caused a cash flow problem for GoEast — especially because the vendor tried to avoid firing its highly qualified staff. The manager of GoEast was concerned about not being able to find qualified people again in case it needed them.

freelancers receive no pay at all. Most of the work for the telecom project was done by that freelance network.

Some of the freelancers even kept up a small network of their own; they worked with colleagues from a university, roommates in the students' hostel, or family members who have some software skills.

One of the most valuable parts of the business capital of agents involved in the daisy chain is the contacts to the upper levels. Such contacts are usually carefully maintained and not disclosed to the lower levels; as soon as the lower-level agents have access to some higher-positioned agents, they might try to bypass their immediate superiors and do business more directly. In this way they would achieve better margins and higher prices for the same work. For this reason, each agent in the daisy chain conceals the sources from which the order came. In addition, subcontractors do not inform their customers that they, in their turn, maintain a network of subcontractors — because the client might have (well-founded) doubts regarding the reliability of these sub-subcontractors. For this reason most members of the daisy chain are aware of only two or three levels. Few of them know about all levels of the chain.

7.2.8 Subcontractors

Some software projects are ordered from a customer that is a software company itself. The customer is subcontracting parts or the whole of a project to the offshore vendor. Such relationships between peer companies have some specific features:

- To some extent the cooperation is easier: both partners share the same field of action and thus speak a common professional language. The customer is experienced in the field and is familiar with the pitfalls of software projects. For this reason, it is sometimes easier to explain to the client some issues that are not obvious to partners in other fields.
- The software business undergoes strong economic cycles. This can be partly accounted for by the fact that software investment can be delayed, unlike other expenses such as fixed costs for office space. Thus, software projects are on top of the list of solutions

economic cycle. This explains why such relationships between a software vendor and a subcontractor are more important in times of IT boom when qualified software developers are urgently sought.

■ The partners are competitors on the market. They will probably not mention this explicitly, but it is true and they are aware of it. The offshore vendor is usually the junior partner in the cooperation, at least in the beginning. This can change, however, in time as the service provider gains experience and accumulates capital. In the long run the offshore vendor can become a serious competitor for the onshore buyer. This potential competition can cause tension in the relationship.

The aspect of competition becomes particularly obvious if the customer is not a genuine software producer but is in its turn a subcontractor. In this case they form a so-called daisy chain and the offshore provider might try to find a way to work directly for the initial buyer, the real owner of the project.

7.2.9 Follow the Sun

In most offshore scenarios, time zones are perceived as a strong obstacle because they hinder synchronous communication, such as telephone calls. In the case of certain models, however, the time shift is an advantage and the company places its sites intentionally in such a way that they cover many time zones: the working points are positioned so that at any time at least one office is always open during usual business hours. This model offers special advantages in help-desk management, which must provide 24/7 availability. All calls to the help desk are forwarded to the site that is currently open during regular business hours, irrespective of the location of the caller.

In software engineering this model is applied in extremely time-critical projects where time-to-market has highest priority. In this case three shifts of software teams work around the clock on the project. The shift in time zones has the advantage that none of the teams has to work during the night.

7.3 CONSTRAINTS FOR BUSINESS MODELS

Some specific factors have to be considered when designing the

professional background on software projects. For the customer,
it is wise to carefully analyze whether this know-how is available
in its organization.

7.3.1 High Startup Cost

The offshore activity requires rather high startup costs for acquiring know-how, finding partners, and establishing the infrastructure. A successful and smoothly running offshore scenario constitutes a precious resource that needs protection. For this reason, offshore cooperation is designed for the long run. This raises a number of important questions. How can key staff can be protected against headhunting? What can be done if a competitor plans a hostile takeover of crucial parts of the offshore scenario — e.g., a competitor wants to buy the vendor's organization or the bridgehead?

These problems can be solved more easily in some business architectures than in others. For example, an independent vendor is much less protected against a hostile takeover than a foreign subsidiary is. If the key personnel own part of the organization, they are not prone to headhunting to such a great extent.

7.3.2 Protection of Know-How

Successful offshore software development requires a lot of know-how: software technology, customer-specific domain expertise, management of offshore software projects, and background information on the countries involved. Acquiring this know-how constitutes a high investment. For this reason it has to be protected against losses — e.g., by natural attrition of staff. In addition, this know-how must be safeguarded against unauthorized access. The customer-specific know-how, for example, should not reach the hands of a competitor. If intellectual property and protected data play important roles in the particular scenario, business models that include two completely independent organizations — customer and vendor — might turn out to be inadequate.

7.3.3 Software Management Skills

A foreign subsidiary requires the customer to have a lot of know-how about software management. Software development is considered challenging for all kinds of software projects, not only for offshore scenarios

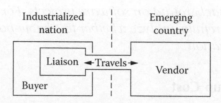

Figure 7.13 The liaison (aka straddler) is an employee of the offshore vendor. The liaison works either for a certain time or periodically at the buyer's site and travels back and forth between customer and vendor.

software projects and to already be knowledgeable in onshore software development.

7.4 COMMUNICATION AND CULTURAL DISTANCE

A major challenge for offshore software projects is the unavoidable long-distance communication. If this problem is not solved in a satisfactory manner, the communication costs are likely to take up most of the potential cost savings. For this reason the business architecture should be designed so that communication is minimized. (See Section 3.3.)

In general it is more cost efficient to outsource an entire project — not parts of a project, i.e., modules. In addition outsourcing only some phases (like implementation or test) causes higher costs than outsourcing the entire life cycle of the project. The staff at the offshore site should have enough competence and ownership to assume responsibility for the entire product — i.e., for the final result. Otherwise, the project may fail because no one is truly responsible for the outcome, i.e., for the success of the project in its entirety. A rule of thumb says: Outsource entire things (not parts) for their entire life span and make the offshore site accountable for the overall result. In many offshore scenarios this rule leads to acceptable costs of communication.

The following tactical approaches can help reduce the cost of communication as well as the cultural distance.

7.4.1 Straddler (Also Known as Liaison)

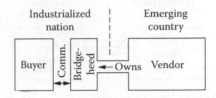

Figure 7.14 A bridgehead is a (usually small) office in the industrialized country owned by the offshore vendor. The bridgehead facilitates all communication with the customer, providing the buyer with the comfort of working with an onshore partner.

The straddler visits the customer periodically for several days, for example once in a month. In this period of time the straddler installs the current version and discusses new requirements. Straddlers can also visit the customer only once for a longer period at the beginning of the project. During their stay, they receive the necessary training for carrying out the project.

For many organizations the "straddler" business model is a reasonable starting point for an offshore activity. In fact the straddler gets not only the requirements, specifications, and technical details but also a lot of background information about the context of the project and the customer's business culture — "how things are done there." When the straddler returns, this information becomes accessible for the offshore software team. Hence, the straddler significantly reduces the cultural distance to both the customer's business culture and the industrialized country's culture.

7.4.2 Bridgehead

The vendor keeps a small office in the industrialized country that helps maintain contact with the customer and so that the customer gets the impression that it works with an onshore vendor (Figure 7.14). The long-distance communication is established only between the bridgehead and the vendor's offshore site and not directly between the customer and the offshore site. The fact that the software is actually developed far away in the offshore country is less visible to the customer.

Several years ago these bridgeheads had rather narrow competence; they were a kind of translation office. The client explained to the bridge-

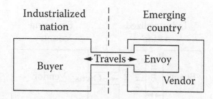

Figure 7.15 Envoys are employees of the buyer who travel between the industrialized country and the emerging country. During the periods of time when the envoy comes to the emerging country, the envoy is usually embedded into the vendor's team.

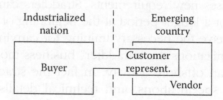

Figure 7.16 Customer representative. A person, trusted by the buyer, who lives in the emerging country on a permanent basis. This can be an employee of the customer or an independent company that runs an office geographically close to the vendor. The representative takes on surveillance tasks and makes decisions on the customer's behalf. This person can either be embedded into the vendor's team or visit the vendor's site only occasionally.

In the last few years, however, offshore business has become more mature. Recently, some of the large offshore vendors have reached a considerable size and have accumulated enough capital to allow them to buy well-established Western consulting companies, thus acquiring their staff and their know-how — a second generation of bridgeheads. These consulting companies are fully adapted to the Western business culture. Many of them have a high reputation on the market and in-depth know-how in their field of action. For the actual customer, it hardly makes any difference whether the work was done with a real onshore vendor or with such a bridgehead of the "second generation." Sometimes the onshore

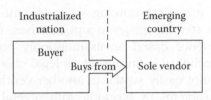

Figure 7.17   Single sourcing. The customer buys only from a single "exclusive" provider.

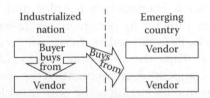

Figure 7.18   Multi-sourcing. The customer orders services from two or more vendors — which can be based in the industrialized nation or abroad.

7.4.3   Envoys and Customer's Representatives

A domain expert on the customer's part comes to the vendor's site and works there while the project is carried through (Figure 7.15 and Figure 7.16). The representative is accessible on a permanent basis to the software team and makes all necessary decisions on behalf of the customer.

Another perk of having a customer representative is that it is less likely that the vendor will report an incorrect number of working hours in unit-price projects, although this alone is usually not enough justification to send a representative offshore.

7.5   MULTI-SOURCING

The customer can try to avoid dependency on a single vendor by working with multiple vendors in parallel — so-called multi-

In the course of many outsourcing scenarios, the customer's dependency on the vendor steadily grows to a point where the service provider achieves strong influence based on its monopoly position, especially if the customer faces technical, commercial, or legal obstacles to terminating the contract and cannot easily switch to another vendor. Some customers try to solve these problems by working with several outsourcers at the same time — called "multi-sourcing" in contrast to "single-sourcing" (or "sole-sourcing") — see Figure 7.17 and Figure 7.18. This way a certain degree of competition is incorporated into the scenario, and the competing vendors are controlling each other. Price and scope mismatches are more likely to be identified. The customer has the opportunity to crosscheck the suggestions of one outsourcer by asking the opinion of another of its providers. By exposing itself to alternative technical and commercial solutions, the customer is continuously learning and has access to information that might be difficult to obtain in a sole-sourcing scenario. In addition, it can gradually shift orders from one vendor to another to express dissatisfaction. Thus, the monopoly position of the unique vendor is broken, and some competition arises between the customer's outsourcers.

In some situations multi-sourcing is the only feasible option. A leading-edge project, for example, may need the contribution of a multitude of specialized high-tech vendors. No single provider has enough know-how in all relevant fields to carry through the project alone. Such cases where single-sourcing is simply not possible occur in practice, but other reasons for multi-sourcing are more frequent — e.g., the customer wants to include competition into the scenario.

Multi-sourcing does not offer only advantages, however. The competitive situation that is desired in this business architecture might cause tensions that could have a detrimental influence on projects. A vendor could unduly criticize the contributions of the other outsourcers with a view to destroying their reputation with the customer because, of course, failure of one outsourcer can be to the advantage of the others; if one outsourcer's project fails then the relative standing of the other outsourcers who were not involved in the project is improved. For this reason some outsourcers might be tempted to disturb the projects of other vendors (their competitors) in a subversive way.

Such architectures of "mutual control" can turn out to be very fragile. The tensions between competing vendors become particularly noticeable if the competing vendors have to cooperate and contribute to the same

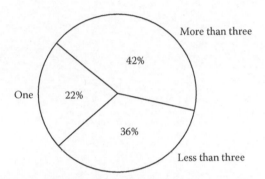

Figure 7.19 In February 2005, www.cio.com conducted a poll among its readership studying the question of single-sourcing vs. multi-sourcing. The readers were asked: "How many IT outsourcing providers do you have?"

"trusted individuals" in a central role in the project. In the context of multi-sourcing, the project may need an arbitration committee to coordinate the contributions of the various vendors. The buyer can take this role, but it might turn out to be not only rather time-consuming but also quite unpleasant if the customer does not possess the necessary IT know-how to take the role of a really qualified arbitrator in a situation where technically knowledgeable vendors are in contradiction. In such cases, the customer's representatives find themselves in a very confusing situation, where the customer might be unable to discern the conflicting points of view and cannot therefore trust any of the parts involved. The only report they can put forward could simply include mentions of a serious crisis and the imminent threat of terrible technical mistakes. In this case the customer's management needs access to a trusted engineer of high professional qualification and an incontrovertible record of loyalty.

An alternative is that one of the vendors is assigned the task of coordinating the work of the other vendors. Notice, however, that the coordinator is in competition with the other vendors and might abuse its position as arbitrator to gain competitive advantages.

The issue of managing competing vendors is more frequent if these providers contribute to the same project. If each of these vendors has its own project, multi-sourcing might be the best solution, providing the customer with a real market test. Even if the customer works mainly with a favorite provider, occasionally outsourcing smaller projects to other vendors can offer the buyer important experiences. In many scenarios

8

SELECTING SUITABLE PROJECTS

ABSTRACT

Certain types of projects can be transferred offshore more easily than others can. For this reason, the selection of suitable projects is a crucial success factor for an offshore scenario. The category of projects that can be outsourced advantageously includes short projects and routine-work-based projects. In projects that require very specific know-how, outsourcing can lead to considerable advantages. It is generally easier to outsource entire projects than parts. Highly iterative processes such as "eXtreme Programming" require specific business architectures to be accessible for offshore outsourcing. More obstacles have been reported within projects that fall into one of these categories:

- *Projects with high risks of consequential damages in case of failure*
- *Projects that include confidential intellectual property or technologies that are covered by export restrictions — e.g., military projects*
- *Innovative products that require much interaction between the software team and domain experts or management*
- *Projects that require a high degree of security*

8.1 LESS CHALLENGING PROJECTS

Less challenging projects, routine work, and short projects are

8.1.1 Short Projects

Most software projects require a certain continuity of staff to be carried through successfully. Whenever a developer leaves the team, a part of the know-how is lost to the project. The replacement worker needs training to be able to contribute to the project. Therefore, software managers are especially keen on ensuring that all software engineers complete their work and carry out their set tasks within the project before leaving the team.

High attrition causes fewer problems in short-period running projects because management has a good chance to keep the developer within the team for the short time until work is finished.

Offshore vendors encounter more problems with high attrition of staff than companies in industrialized countries do, especially if the vendor offers services or products at lower prices. In such cases, the vendor can only pay low salaries. This causes instability because of the risk that some of the employees will at one point take more attractive offers.

> An American organization offered small Web applications at affordable prices. These simple applications did not impose any particular technological challenges. Their development consisted mostly of routine work, and most of the projects required less than one month of development time for three developers at the most. The American company started cooperating with an Eastern European provider. The vendor did not need to worry too much about attrition of staff. Even if an engineer wanted to leave the company, due to the short time needed to complete these small projects the engineer could usually finish work in progress before leaving. In addition, the vendor did not encounter any problems in taking on new staff for these rather undemanding tasks.

8.1.2 Routine Work

An important problem related to staff attrition is the training needed by the replacement workers. Projects that consist mainly of routine work, with few challenging aspects, require less training and are thus less threatened by high attrition. In addition, even junior programmers can do the work. It is easier and cheaper to find assistant programmers with limited qualifications than highly skilled senior developers.

Simpler projects require not only less training and experience but also less specific project know-how. This makes it easier to set up the offshore cooperation because less know-how needs to be transferred from the customer's in-house team to the vendor. As an experienced project manager once said, "Low-tech means high margins; high-tech means low margins." Maintenance of legacy software is an example of typical routine work that has been successfully outsourced in many scenarios.

A western vendor specialized in producing software for glass industries. Even though the software was rather well-rated on the market, the applied technology had become out-of-date. The management decided to develop a completely new version of their software, but their in-house software team was busy maintaining the legacy software. For this reason the development of the new framework progressed more slowly than expected. So, after reevaluating their priorities, they decided to outsource the maintenance of the legacy software to an offshore vendor. One of the senior developers of the in-house team assumed responsibility for conducting the maintenance reassignment. Thus, the other in-house developers were freed to work on the development of the new system.

8.2 PROJECTS REQUIRING VERY SPECIFIC TECHNOLOGICAL KNOW-HOW

Some specific technical problems can be very easy to solve for someone who already did this work but extremely time-consuming for someone who is green in the field and who must first learn the technology. Therefore, outsourcing the solution to specific technological problems can be a major advantage.

The following is an example of a project that requires very specific know-how about a certain technological aspect.

A customer ordered a project that included diskless Linux workstations. The project was designed for a low-price segment of the consumer market. For this reason the workstations should use only memory, thus eliminating the cost of a hard disk. The

The most challenging technological part of the project was the configuration and recompiling of the Linux kernel in such a way that it would boot not from a hard disk but via the Internet. For an expert in Linux systems who had already done this kind of work, it would be a rather easy task and could be finished without investing too much time. For someone who was not so savvy in the inner workings of the Linux system, it would be a rather challenging task that could take up several weeks. Notice that most of this time is needed to learn the specific details of the applied Linux technology — i.e., the time is not used for productive work but mainly for learning. The vendor's organization rarely needed these details, so they worked with a freelance expert who had mastered all facets of Linux installations.

In projects that require knowledge of rarely used details of a certain technology, outsourcing can lead to considerable savings, sometimes 90 percent or even more. In such cases most investment consists of acquiring the necessary technological knowledge. Once the solution is understood, the actual productive work is rather easily and quickly done. In some cases, investments made in technological qualifications might be justified. In other cases, however, this know-how is rarely used and does not justify the high investment.

Large IT providers rarely face this problem because they have many permanently employed experts in various fields. This problem is more likely to occur in small organizations. For this reason, some small vendors maintain a network of freelance IT experts who have know-how in a broad diversity of technologies.

8.3 VIRTUAL TEAMS

In some scenarios there might be compelling reasons to outsource only a part of a project or only certain phases of the development. In many cases, however, outsourcing an entire project for its entire life cycle is more cost efficient.

8.3.1 Collocated Teams vs. Distributed Teams

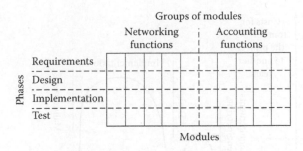

Figure 8.1 Splitting a project into modules or phases. A project can be split into smaller chunks of work by dividing it into modules or phases. A module is a group of functions that belongs together logically. Phases are tasks that are done in certain stages of the project, across all modules.

scenarios work has to be shared between the contributing sites. This can be done in at least two ways: through modules or phases (see Figure 8.1). A module encapsulates a group of functions that belong together somehow — e.g., the features for a certain dialog box could be grouped together in a module. The phases, on the other hand, are stages in the developing cycle of a software project. Some companies decide to out-source only certain phases. In this case usually the early phases (e.g., requirements engineering and architectural design) are done in house because these phases require more domain expertise, but the ensuing phases (e.g., implementation and test) are outsourced.

Some customers may want to outsource only certain modules for a project. The reasons for this decision might include:

- *Buy-in of specific know-how.* The outsourced modules might require specific know-how that is not available in house.
- *Keeping confidential modules in house.* In some projects strong motivations, such as concerns about intellectual property or secret know-how, may hinder the outsourcing of certain modules.
- *Outsourcing of routine work.* In these cases the part based on routine work is outsourced, and modules that require specific domain expertise are done in house.

In some projects there might be compelling reasons for distributed

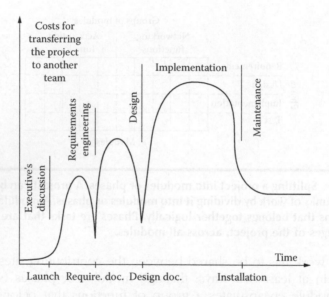

Figure 8.2 Costs for transferring a project. The diagram shows how the efforts necessary to transfer a project to another team may evolve over time.

vendors that have much experience dealing with both the management of huge software projects and globally distributed software development across multiple time zones. In such organizations distributed software projects may be possible because the organizations have already reached a high level of maturity (CMM) and necessary expertise in projects of this kind.

Figure 8.2 explains what is necessary to transfer a project from one team to another (e.g., from the in-house team to the offshore vendor). The diagram shows that the costs for transferring the project dramatically change with time. In the very beginning, the envisioned project is just an idea in the minds of some top executives. At this time, the project does not include much detail, and it is quite easy to transfer it to a new team. In fact, in most companies this is routinely done; after the executives decide to launch the project, the responsibility (in jargon, "ownership") is transferred to a new team, which elicits the requirements. During requirements engineering, a considerable increase of detail and complexity occurs: the requirements team collects and merges opinions of various interest groups. Thus it is not desirable to transfer the project to another

AU7017_book.fm Page 161 Thursday, March 16, 2006 5:07 PM

is the corresponding down-spark — i.e., the lower are the costs for transferring the project at this time. In many organizations, the designers come into the project at this time and the requirements analysts leave the team; thus, the project is transferred to a (more or less) "new team."

During the design phase a similar curve occurs: complexity grows in the beginning of the design phase. The end of the design is marked by the design documentation, which is another carefully engineered document. In large organizations, it is not uncommon for most or all of the designers to leave the team at this point and for the programmers to come in to implement the project.

Usually, the implementing team has to deal with so many details that the costs for transferring the project to a completely different team are prohibitively high. To be honest, the author has not yet seen a project that has been successfully transferred to another team while the programmers were in the middle of their work.

When the implementation is finished, the project will be installed and the maintenance phase starts. It is still difficult to transfer a project during maintenance. However, it is much easier than during implementation. A common-sense example makes clear where this difference stems from: repairing a car requires knowledge about many details of the car. However, constructing a completely new car requires much more in-depth understanding than maintenance does.

Figure 8.2 gives a rough and qualitative idea of how the costs may evolve during the various phases of a certain project. However, it cannot be used to derive quantitative results. The diagram suggests several points when it might be reasonable to transfer the project to another team: after the requirements are elicited, when the design is finished, or during maintenance. All these options are applied in practice.

Another idea is to transfer the project offshore in the very beginning, when it is launched. In many instances, the costs for transferring the project will never again be as low as at the very beginning — even if requirements and design documents are prepared with due care. Thus an interesting option might be to transfer the entire project, not just some phases.

A rule of thumb says: Outsource entire projects for their entire life cycle and make the offshore site accountable for the overall result.

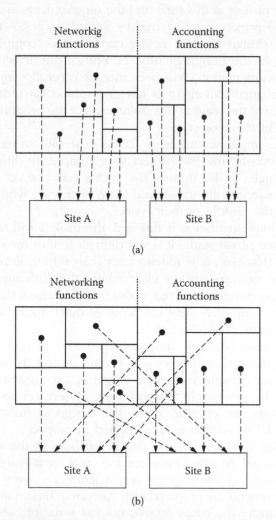

Figure 8.3   Coherent (a) vs. noncoherent (b) task assignment. An example project
consists of two groups of functions: networking and accounting. These groups
have been split into subtasks. Figure 8.3a shows the coherent approach to task
assignment: the tasks that belong together are assigned to developers on the same
site. In Figure 8.3b both sites are managed as one united team: the tasks are

- *Coherent task assignment:* The software developers at one site are assigned tasks according to the feature content: each site is responsible for a certain functionality chunk. For example, one site implements the networking function although another site is responsible for the accounting function.
- *Noncoherent task assignment:* The distributed groups are managed as one united software team. Assigning tasks to software developers is done irrespective of the actual location of the respective developer.

Sometimes the term "virtual team" is used if the task assignment is done in a noncoherent way and advanced communication technology, such as video conferencing, is applied to establish the team structure.

There is some evidence against noncoherent task assignment and virtual teams: it seems that collocated teams that are assigned coherent tasks perform at more time-efficient standards. Christof Ebert (IEEE Software, March 2001) reported that a coherent team at Alcatel took only half the time to carry through certain tasks compared to a virtual team. This observation turned out to be applicable even in the extremely professional environment of a global high-tech organization like Alcatel. Organizations with less experience in global software development might face even more insurmountable obstacles when they try to use "virtual teams." This evidence supports the general observation that splitting a project into parts and outsourcing only some of these parts causes additional overhead.

8.4 HIGHLY ITERATIVE DEVELOPMENT PROCESSES

In some projects where time-to-market is extremely critical — e.g., Web applications — eXtreme Programming and other highly iterative software processes have reported impressive successes. In such software management processes no (or very few) requirements are written in advance. Instead, one or more user-representatives are permanently working with the software team and specify new requirements just as the project is being implemented. Integrating highly iterative processes into the widely used outsourcing frameworks — like the fixed-price contract — is difficult. For this reason eXtreme Programming requires a specific business architecture to be successfully outsourced. The anecdote is an example of such a situation.

months. All members of the core team were expected to have at least conversational German skills. The language abilities were further polished while they were in Germany.

The e-commerce system was to be implemented by the newly founded foreign subsidiary in Romania. The members of the core team returned to their country and became team leaders of the now-established development teams.

The software team was supported by a German middle manager who was a domain expert in all accounting matters. This customer's representative stayed on a permanent basis with the development team in Romania and helped clarify questions that appeared in the course of the project. In addition he made the necessary decisions about options and alternatives. The middle manager was thus responsible for most day-to-day decisions. Only the most fundamental decisions were made after consultation with his top management.

Thus, the mail-order company outsourced an "entire project"; the entire e-commerce system was under the responsibility of the Romanian team that was under guidance of the straddlers and the customer's representative. In this way the company greatly reduced long-distance communication.

8.5 UNSUITABLE PROJECTS

Some projects are less accessible to offshore outsourcing. This class includes:

- *Projects with high consequential damages due to project failure*
- *Projects that include valuable intellectual property, confidential data, or technologies subject to export regulations*
- *Projects that lack clear written specifications*
- *Innovative projects for which complete requirements are hard to specify in advance*
- *In some organizations, anticipated cost savings are limited and do not justify the investments and risks of the transition period*

the customer has probably already contributed certain vested interests to the project — e.g., writing specifications, training the vendor's team.

Important risks of failing projects include lost opportunities and damaged reputation on the market. Other departments within the customer's organization might have relied on the project and will have to change their plans if the project fails. In extreme cases the consequential damages of the failed project can be even higher than the negotiated price for the project.

Not all projects include these types of risks, however. In some cases the harm done to the customer's interests is very limited: if the vendor cannot deliver, payment is not made. That is the end of the story. Nothing worse happens.

An Internet company produced tiny Web applications and other software tools for the public domain. They used these applications to direct traffic to their Web site and to harvest e-mail addresses for their Internet advertisement business. The customer was rather skilled in writing specifications, which were then posted on the Internet where potential providers could make an offer. Usually, the projects were assigned to one of the cheapest bidders. Occasionally, one of these inexpensive providers turned out to be rather unprofessional and could not deliver the contracted software. In this case, the project was simply not paid for, and the order was given to another provider. The undelivered project did not entail any financial damage to the customer; the only inconvenience was that the tool simply appeared a few weeks later in the public domain.

A German software company decided to develop a new software project. The project was still at an early stage, and the company considered the possibility of using some open-source software instead of developing all the functions from scratch. This option had the sole disadvantage that the code had to be ported from Linux to Windows, the target operating system of the new project. The port was expected to include significant technological risks and a lot of routine work, which constituted a major argument against using the open-source software. For this reason the team was about to decide against the open-source option and wanted to develop the functionality from scratch.

project of the German company was still at an early stage and therefore potential failure on the part of the vendor would not cause any delay; thus, using the vendor entailed little risk for the planned project. If the ported code was not produced successfully, the company would simply have to develop the functionality from scratch. Without the near-shore vendor, they would have decided for this option anyway. Because the contract had a fixed price, the customer would not have to pay any money in case the project failed. So the risk for the German company was very limited.

The vendor's team was already accustomed to carrying through projects of this kind, so they were rather confident that they would not encounter major technological problems when attempting to port the code. If successful, they would receive rather advantageous payment for their work and would open a good gateway to potential additional orders from this customer in the future.

8.5.2 Intellectual Property, Confidential Data, and Technologies Subject to Export Regulations

All kinds of outsourcing activities raise the question of how intellectual property and confidential data are protected against disclosure. Offshore projects include the additional problem that in most emerging countries intellectual property does not benefit from the same legal protection as in industrialized countries. This stems from the less reliable legal system in developing countries and the insufficient steps taken to deter industrial espionage. For this reason, projects that include confidential material might undergo strict assessment before they can be outsourced. The result of these investigations might well be that it is not possible to outsource a specific project to an offshore country because the risk regarding confidential material is too high. This is true especially if the confidential data is protected by legal regulations. (See Chapter 10.)

A Western software company considered outsourcing the maintenance of legacy software for hospitals. This step was considered so that the internal team would be free to develop a completely new version of this software system. The maintenance task should have included correcting faults in the code

AU7017_book.fm Page 167 Thursday, March 16, 2006 5:07 PM

user's failure report, there were a few cases that required that a service engineer operate from the user's site (the hospital) and analyze the problem on the computer system there. During this intervention, the service engineer might have access to confidential medical data — i.e., data concerning the patients of that hospital. This data would not be sufficiently protected in the offshore country.

The problems outlined in the anecdote can arise in many organizations that are responsible for managing confidential information such as medical data. In various situations, it might be necessary for the developers to be provided with access to original data — for example, when constructing test cases. It might be difficult to construct realistic test cases for something like the software system of a hospital without any access to real data.

Similar problems appear in projects that include important intellectual property or materials covered by export regulations — e.g., technology that can be used for military purposes. In such cases the obstacles can be so compelling that the organization decides that this kind of project cannot be outsourced.

8.5.3 Lack of Reliable Specifications in Written Form

Offshore projects require a higher quality of specifications than in-house development does (see Section 9.1). Efficiently elaborated and detailed specifications are an advantage for all kinds of software projects, not only those taken offshore. Although weak specifications are a nuisance even for an in-house team, their detrimental effect is much stronger when the software is outsourced: it is simply much easier to clarify issues in the specification if the developers work in the same office building and frequently meet the domain experts for lunch. If the development team and the customers are separated by long distances and many time zones, communication is much more difficult. High-quality specifications involve specific skills and a certain type of business culture. This might require training and a dramatic shift in the organization's working culture insofar as requirements documents are concerned. If management does not get written requirements specifications of satisfactory quality from its IT departments, it might be difficult to successfully set up an offshore scenario.

innovative in the first place. The users have no clear image of how the entirety of software features and hardware devices will work together with nontechnical business processes. For this reason it is difficult to pinpoint the features of innovative products in advance — i.e., at the beginning of the development cycle. Thus, many innovative products have inherently weak specifications.

8.5.5 Unacceptable Risks during the Transition Period

A medical software vendor considered outsourcing its software from an offshore provider. Developing and selling this software was the company's main business. For this reason the software was of crucial importance to that company. Nevertheless, the actual software development constituted only a small fraction of its costs. Most of the expenses pertained to other areas of activity — user support, help desk, sales, marketing, and research. Only about 10 percent of the employees were full-time software developers.

Further analysis of the outsourcing plans revealed that transferring the know-how to the offshore vendor would require significant investment. In addition, serious resistance from the onshore staff was expected; they were concerned about their jobs. Yet another obstacle was the fact that offshore projects are prone to higher risks of failure than onshore projects — at least the first few projects at the beginning of the offshore relationship. A steady production of software, however, was of vital importance to the organization.

Finally, the management decided to cancel the offshore plans. The in-house software team was rather small; for this reason, the budget for software development was limited. Also, the company could not close down its in-house team completely. Even after the software production was moved offshore, the company would need several project managers at home. Thus, the expected savings were rather limited and did not justify the investments and risks of the offshore activity.

For some organizations, offshore outsourcing is simply not the answer. This is especially true if there are high consequential risks attached to this

9

CONTRACTS: PROJECT CONTRACTS AND SERVICE AGREEMENTS

ABSTRACT

The contracts used in outsourcing business can be roughly grouped in three categories.

- *Fixed-price contracts. An estimate of the workload is prepared in advance, and the contract partners agree on a fixed amount of money for the entire project.*
- *Unit-price contracts. The contract sets a certain sum to be paid per hour of actual working time (i.e., payment for "time" and "material").*
- *Service agreements. The provider substitutes for the customer's internal IT department for a certain period of time. The contract specifies the vendor's duties and the monthly fees.*

Project contracts involve more-or-less detailed written requirements determined before the implementation can start. When the implementation is finished, the product must be officially accepted by the customer. In most projects, the implementation is followed by a guarantee period during which reported failures must be repaired without additional payment.

9.1 REQUIREMENTS

Software Requirements Specifications (SRS). Before the CONOPS is agreed upon, the project is considered to be in the "brainstorming phase." In this phase many projects are likely to undergo fundamental changes regarding the feature set and the volume of investments. Quite a number of projects are cancelled before they reach the phase of detailed specification.

Frequently, the vendor has to contribute in one way or another to the requirements phase. In some outsourcing scenarios, the partners start discussing technical aspects even before the contract is completely negotiated and signed. This practice raises two important issues:

1. *How is the vendor's precontractual investment protected?*
2. *How is the confidentiality of the requirements ensured?*

9.1.1 Requirements Documents

The requirements documents include the following:

■ *Product Vision Statement.* The Product Vision Statement offers a rough idea about how the software product should look and which business goals are to be achieved. The customer usually does most of the work for the product vision — without or with only limited support on the part of the vendor. The final outcome of this phase might be a document, it might be a few handwritten pages and diagrams, or it might simply be an idea that some managers have about the product. In any case, this "Product Vision Statement" is a rather informal stage in product development.

■ *Concept of Operations.* Based on the Product Vision Statement, the so-called Concept of Operations (CONOPS) document is developed. This is the central document for discussions at the managerial level. The CONOPS summarizes the main features of the new project and includes the business goals that should be achieved with the aid of the new software. It also constitutes the basis for a first rough estimation of costs. This way, the CONOPS document allows for an analysis of the returns on investment (ROI) and a first study of technological feasibility. The audience of the CONOPS document includes top management, the marketing department, and software leads. For this reason, using overly technical language in a CONOPS document is generally avoided.

- *Software Requirements Specification.* When the CONOPS reaches a degree of maturity, another document, the Software Requirements Specification (SRS), will be developed on the basis of the CONOPS. Unlike the CONOPS, which is a short, concise management paper addressed to nontechnical readers, the SRS describes the features of the new software project in considerable detail, using significantly more specialized technical language. The SRS will be an appendix of the project's contract. For this reason it is not only a technical but also a legal document. In addition, it forms the basis for the detailed estimate.

  Sometimes the SRS is split into two parts: an informal description of the project using plain language and a more formal document using diagrams and other structured forms of specification. The formal part of the SRS is exclusively addressed to the members of the software team. However, even the informal part of the SRS might be difficult for nontechnical readers to penetrate.

  The SRS is frequently a rather lengthy document: for a medium-to-large project, the SRS can cover thousands of pages. Thus, developing a high-quality SRS requires rigorous training of the analysts and constitutes a significant investment.

Two important issues have to be considered in this phase of the project:

- The primary readership of the SRS is the software team. However, the SRS is also part of the contract and thus it must be signed under legal terms. This puts the top management in the difficult position of signing a lengthy document including many important details of which they have only superficial understanding. In many cases, management has to rely on trustworthy software engineers who understand the text, verify it, and translate the core statements so that they become intelligible to the executives.
- In a fixed-price project, the project contract can be signed only after the requirements phase is completed. Thus, even before a signed contract is ready, significant efforts flow into the project. The SRS constitutes a major investment and takes up a nonnegligible part of the project's budget: a rule of thumb is around eight percent for smaller projects and up to twenty percent for large, innovative, and conceptually challenging projects. If the customer

9.1.2 The Vendor's Precontractual Investment in the Requirements

Many customers expect some contribution on the vendor's part even before a contract is signed. The customer wants to discuss what is possible according to the state of the art in software technology and the limits of the budget. In addition, the client wants to verify the qualifications of the particular vendor and whether it is suitable for the planned project. Some customers are unwilling to pay separately for these efforts, and many vendors accept this practice. When the contract is to be signed, the vendor demands a proportionally higher payment for the project, which also covers these precontractual investments.

This calculation fails, however, if the customer changes its mind and does not sign an order. Perhaps the customer orders the project from another vendor or completely cancels the project. In this case the vendor cannot recuperate its precontractual investment because there simply will not be any project contract.

In some projects, the customer outlines verbally the scope of the new project and asks the vendor for a detailed written offer, which will be the basis for the future contract. In fact, the customer expects a document that is approximately at the level of maturity of a CONOPS. Frequently, this document is not paid for separately. From the vendor's point of view, this situation is difficult: providing technical suggestions is costly in terms of time and is done before actually signing the contract. For this reason, it is uncertain whether the precontractual investment will ever lead to an order.

Another issue is the technical aspects included in the offer — which is de facto a CONOPS document: in the course of writing the offer, the vendor might have to provide some technical ideas. The offer contains many details that are quite valuable because they bring into discussion certain problems and solutions. They may indicate issues and risks of which the client had not been aware. The customer, on the other hand, is free to disclose the information contained in this document to other vendors, which can use the technical suggestions included in the offer, improve them, and add their own ideas. This way the customer can benefit from the vendor's investment even if an order is never given. An unfair customer can use this practice to benefit from a technically improved suggestion, even though it is usually considered in poor taste to act in this fashion in the bidding process.

A customer had developed accounting software based on mod-

up on modern software technologies. However, they did not
apply the underlying paradigms of state-of-the-art GUI design.
They still used the GUI models of the COBOL era.

The customer's top management was concerned about its
competitiveness on the market and decided to bring its software
to a modern look and feel, although trying to avoid the necessary investment. So they sent Requests for Proposals (RFPs)
to various vendors with the announcement that they were
intending to outsource a new version of their accounting software that should apply modern GUI design. The primary condition for the outsourcing project to be implemented was that
the vendor could provide strong evidence that the GUI could
be clearly improved. So the customer alleged that it was unsure
whether the GUI could be improved at all, claiming that it did
not want to invest in a newly designed GUI if the final result
would not be significantly better than the old interface. For this
reason, the customer said that it was open to suggestions on
the part of the vendors concerning potential improvements of
the GUI.

These invitations were sent to quite a number of vendors
who were well known for excellent GUI designs. Some vendors
ignored the invitation and did not send any suggestions. However, quite a few of the addressees had idle resources and
suggested some carefully prepared ideas — hoping that these
suggestions might lead to an order.

The truth was that the customer had never intended to
outsource the project. By using this subterfuge, the customer
received quite a number of suggestions regarding possible
improvements that could be made to the GUI. The customer
selected some of these proposals and implemented them with
the help of its in-house team. This way the customer received
consultancy for GUI design for free.

In quite a number of projects this precontractual investment made by
the vendor is necessary to obtain the order — although the size of the
investment depends on the maturity of the relationship and the balance
of power. In a long-term relationship where mutual trust has been established, the vendor will be more generous with precontractual investments.
On the other hand, a well-known large vendor working with a small

9.1.3 Confidential Requirements

The vendor is not the only one in a difficult situation before a contract is signed; the customer too might encounter risks. Requirements documents for most software projects are strictly confidential because they may contain unpublished technology, technical secrets, and intellectual property. They may also reveal the customer's business plans. The customer would not like to see them in the hands of a competitor. For this reason, provisions are necessary regarding confidentiality of this type of material. This conclusion seems to be a truism but in practice it is quite often ignored. The reason is that at the time when the client and the vendor discuss the requirements, they do not always have a project contract yet. Unless the partners have another kind of outline contract, the legal basis for the requirement's confidentiality might be uncertain.

Although even without a contract there are some legal restrictions regarding business secrets of prospective partners, these provisions might turn out to be insufficient if it comes to a trial. What is more, the legal situation of international cooperation might be complicated, as the following incident shows.

> A customer from the United States invited a Romania-based vendor to bid for a new project. At this point, no contract existed between the partners. The vendor worked with some subcontractors and freelance developers, one of whom was a Moldavian citizen who lived in Romania. This person broke confidentiality by disclosing parts of the requirements to a competitor of the customer, without knowledge of the vendor. This raised a number of questions: Who would go to court against whom? Because the vendor had not done anything illegal, the customer could not easily bring an action against the vendor; after all, the vendor had not even signed a contract. Would the Romanian vendor be the plaintiff, defendant, or witness — or none of these? Would it be a civil action or a criminal case? Which country's laws would be applied — Romanian, Moldavian, or American laws? In which country would be the venue?

Even this case of obvious breach of confidentiality raises difficult legal questions; a situation where things are more complicated and the line

however, the author has seen a number of projects where the confidentiality of the requirements was not adequately protected.

9.2 FIXED-PRICE CONTRACTS

In a fixed-price contract, the partners agree in advance on a certain price for a specified project. The requirements must be rather well specified in advance and in written form because they form the basis of cost estimation. For customers, the fixed-price contract has the advantage that it provides prior information on how much the project will cost. In practice, however, this apparently firm base of calculation must be questioned because most software projects require changes and extensions even before the first version is delivered. These changes add to the price. In extreme cases the final price can be double the initially agreed-on fixed price — or even higher.

The "acceptance" is an important milestone in the life cycle of a software project because it triggers the start of the guarantee period. In addition, the payment for the project must be made at this stage — at least a significant part of it.

A specific problem that might arise in fixed-price contracts is cancellation. Unless the contract includes a carefully drafted clause, the customer can only cancel the project with high losses.

A fixed-price project includes the following steps:

- *Product vision:* A first rough idea of the new software's purposes.
- *Specification:* In one or (usually) more steps, an increasingly detailed requirements document is engineered.
- *Estimation:* Based on the specification, the efforts are calculated and a price is set.
- *Project budget:* The project budget is an alternative to the estimate. At the beginning of the project, the customer's management establishes the level of investments. The specifications are developed in light of these figures.
- *Implementation:* The software team implements the specified project.
- *Acceptance:* The customer agrees that the delivered software conforms to the contract.
- *Payment schedule:* The customer pays for the project in one or

9.2.1 Cost Estimation

Several published methods may be used to estimate the costs of a software project. Some of them are rather simple, such as the method of analogy — comparing the size of the new project to those of older ones. This relationship and past cost information on older projects is used to estimate the costs for the new project. Other methods, like Function-Point and COCOMO (COnstructive COst MOdel), are rather complicated and require significant training. Most of these methods include subjective factors and entail a significant degree of experience. This contributes to discrepancy between the estimates of two different analysts, even if the same estimation method is applied.

Experienced analysts combine several different estimation methods. The motivation behind this approach is that the various methods have different flaws as well as strong points. It often happens that two different estimation methods have very different results — e.g., one method estimates twice as much as the other. The results are compared in a review meeting and merged together into a single estimate, which is usually more reliable than each individual estimate. Despite the care of the analysts involved, the result remains an "estimation" — not a "calculation." Even if the analysts are extremely thorough, the estimate may turn out to be wrong by at least 10 or 20 percent, except perhaps in the case of projects that include a large amount of routine work or that are very similar to older projects (for which reliable data exist).

Some case studies report much more dramatic errors of estimation: the project needed 50 or 100 percent more than estimated — and even more extreme cases have been reported. In most instances, the estimate turns out to be too low — rarely too high. Some of these software disasters have been carefully analyzed, and case studies on them have been published. In many cases, these are not actual estimation failures. Frequently, the requirements were changed while the project was in progress. In this case, the estimate was made against the initial set of requirements — i.e., for a different project. In other cases technological or other risks were not considered adequately: the analysts assumed that everything would "go smoothly." Experience shows, however, that in the course of most projects unexpected risks and problems appear.

In fixed-price contracts, the risk of wrong estimation is on the side of the vendor. Many vendors take this into account by including a kind of "risk reserve" in their estimates. Anyway, technical estimation is not very exact because it is a process that includes a good deal of subjective

rather straightforward: they should simply multiply the estimated number of working hours by the price per hour. In practice, however, quite a number of strategic and political considerations influence the final price.

One factor is whether the vendor was involved in developing the requirements documents. A vendor who had some responsibility during requirements engineering is in a somewhat privileged position: the vendor knows much more about the background of the project than its potential competitors do. In addition, the customer has already confirmed its trust in this vendor by including it in the requirements process. To some extent the customer has already decided for this vendor. Under these circumstances, the vendor is not really bidding against other competing vendors but negotiating the price with the customer.

Sometimes the customer and the vendor prepare independent estimates. These two numbers are compared and discussed. The fact that the estimate is closely related to real money is the reason why these "independent estimates" are frequently biased: the customer tends to underestimate; the vendor tends to overestimate (see however the upcoming paragraph on inadequate resources). To some extent the vendor might try to "guess" how much money the customer is willing to pay, and the customer tries to find out how much has to be spent so that the vendor will be willing to carry through with the project.

Even if the vendor was not included in the preparation of the requirements, it will take other factors besides the technical estimate into consideration: how tough the competition for this project is, whether technological difficulties or other risk factors can be anticipated, how important this customer is for the future, how good the customer's credit rating is. Last but not least, the chance for future extensions might have an influence; most project changes and future extensions are carried out by the vendor who developed the first version. Other vendors usually cannot make a competitive offer for changes and extensions. A new price is negotiated for these extensions and so, even if the vendor makes only a small profit (or no profit at all) with the first version, the company might be expecting to make profits with the maintenance.

For the customer, on the other hand, it is not easy to validate the estimate. A sound estimate requires a good understanding of software technologies; it needs time, training, and experience. Not all customers have these skills, and some who have them are not willing to spend the time needed for a professional estimate. For this reason, some managers

time comes to discuss the price for a project. In many cases the technical estimation is only a minor factor in the negotiation of prices, even if the meeting has "discussion of the estimates" written on the agenda.

9.2.3 Project Budget

The explanations above have shown that technical estimates include experience and also some subjective factors. Moreover, the calculation of the price based on these estimates is strongly influenced by negotiation and other political factors. Only in rare cases is the cost of a fixed-price project calculated in a mechanical way, as the term "price calculation" may suggest.

In some outsourcing scenarios, this observation is taken into account and the customer decides on a budget for the project. This budget can be established even before the requirements engineering process starts, i.e., "We are willing to invest this amount of money. Now what software we can produce that fits into this sum?" The requirements are developed with one eye on the budget.

In addition, many requirements are somehow flexible. In many respects, there are various options for the software developers, some of which are more comfortable for the user and others that are easier and cheaper to implement. This observation provides a new line of reasoning for a project budget other than estimation. If the project works on a small budget, the developers have to constantly implement the cheapest alternatives; a larger budget would allow for more expensive alternatives.

9.2.4 Inadequate Resources

Many projects start with an inadequate budget. This is particularly applicable in government-sponsored projects, but it also occurs in private industry. In some cases there are political reasons behind this: it would be politically unacceptable to be fully realistic about the needed budget because decision makers on the buyer's side would conclude that the project should not even be started. Once the project has started and has made some progress, it is less likely that it will be canceled because cancellation would mean throwing away all the money already invested. In this phase some useful functionality is already available and can be used (or at least demonstrated), and thus it is much easier to obtain

9.2.5 Weak Requirements Documents

Fixed-price projects rely heavily on high-quality written requirements. This poses the question of what happens if the fixed-price project is carried through without a requirements document that reaches the necessary quality. The answer is that in many projects a weak and unclear requirements document is to the disadvantage of the customer. This is especially true in the case of a vendor who was not involved in the requirements engineering process and thus bears no responsibility whatsoever for the elaboration of the requirements. If the customer is not content with the final project, the customer must support its dissatisfaction with solid evidence and prove that the project is noncompliant to the specification — evidence that might be difficult to provide considering the unclear or ambiguous requirements.

The following situation shows a less obvious effect of weak requirements that works to the disadvantage of the customer. The vendor might follow from the beginning the strategy of making gross profits on account of changes and extensions and not on the basis of the initial project. A weak requirements document is a strong indication that the customer does not yet have a very clear image of what kind of software it really needs. For this reason, many changes or extensions are to be expected in the long run. Because the price for the extensions is negotiated separately, an unfair vendor could try to make undue profits on account of these extensions, which might be much more expensive as compared to the initial set price.

9.2.6 Necessary Changes

In the course of most software projects, modifications of the initial requirements document are necessary regardless of the quality of the requirements document. Even if a fair calculation of additional costs for the extensions is made, the result might look surprisingly high, at least for customers who are lacking in software business experience. Although in other fields it goes without saying that requirements changes are expensive, in the software business some customers have problems understanding this issue.

A family makes arrangements for a four-bedroom house to be built for them. When the construction is structurally complete, the building owners visit the construction site and decide that

For many customers, evaluation of expenses for necessary requirements modifications is rather challenging, especially if the client does not have know-how in software projects. Sometimes changes that appear to be a simple matter to the customer are in fact expensive new features.

Occasionally, the customer simply refuses to understand that an apparently small change can be rather costly. Because most vendors want to maintain a trustful relationship, they try to avoid cold-shouldering the customer. In some cases the vendor consequently applies a kind of calculation that misguides the client into believing that it is pulling a bargain; the vendor offers the requested feature rather cheaply. Original losses, however, are in fact balanced by future extensions that might seem to be major supplementary features but actually represent only minor changes, i.e., the vendor calculates the price for a change request according to "how much work it looks like" — not how much work it really is.

9.2.7 Budget for Necessary Adaptations

Changing the specification requires adapted estimates of prices and schedules. The modified contract needs to be signed by authorized persons — i.e., executives. In most cases, top management is not directly involved in the details of the project; the project lead on the customer's side is usually a middle manager who is not authorized to sign contracts. Whenever changes are necessary, the customer's project lead has to suggest changes in the contract to the executives. Because the middle manager has been responsible for engineering the requirements, frequent changes could leave the impression that the initial design of the requirements was carried through superficially and inadequately. For this reason, middle managers on the customer's side try to avoid changes in the contract.

This is only one side of the coin, however — the client's point of view. In virtually all cases, changes of the requirements generate additional work on the vendor's side and thus additional costs. In addition, an adaptation of the schedule is required, which means that the project will be delayed. The vendor will insist on these matters. From a purely technical point of view, customer's representatives usually understand this necessity. However, representatives find themselves in a difficult situation; on the one hand, they are aware of the fact that changes of the contract are necessary for technical reasons, but on the other hand, they do not want to risk their reputations in front of top management. The situation of the project lead on the vendor's side is not much better. It is usually difficult

As a result, the customer's middle manager might be tempted to insist that this is the vendor's fault and has to be corrected without additional payment and without alteration of the schedule. The vendor's project lead is responsible for finishing the project within budget and schedule. So project leads cannot easily give in to customers' pressure even if they are (secretly) aware that the blame for the changes can be attributed at least partially to their teams. Otherwise, they would risk their reputations in front of their own top management. Notice that top managers are usually not qualified to evaluate the situation without support of technical staff. Therefore, the top managers on both sides (customer and vendor) have to rely on the statements of their middle managers — each of whom is placing the blame on the other side.

In some projects this problem is solved by including a certain "risk reserve" in the initial cost estimation. The partners agree that these funds should be used for necessary changes and adaptations of the requirements.

The customer's top management does not always agree to include this kind of "buffer" in the price estimate, however, especially if the company is not very experienced in outsourcing fixed-price projects or if the project has a tight budget. Notice that the risk reserve makes the project more expensive. The customer's management might fear that an adequate countervalue for the money will not be received.

Even the vendor's top management might not be very enthusiastic about this idea; they could be concerned that the customer may expand changes beyond the payment made. Middle managers are aware of this type of reticence. I have seen projects where this matter was settled as a "gentlemen's agreement" between the middle managers. The middle managers are aware that the estimation contains some "space" for maneuvers, but they report that the estimate is tight. Because most top managers do not have technical qualifications, they have no other option than to trust their engineers. This reserve gives the middle managers some space and flexibility in negotiations done "in the backstreet" — away from the main lane of top management negotiations.

9.2.8 Acceptance

The *acceptance* is an important milestone in the life cycle of a fixed-price project; the customer confirms that the implementation is compliant with the specification and that the project has reached the necessary level of maturity to be used in practice. This way the acceptance indicates that

or no contractual obligations anymore. For these reasons, the customer tends to delay the acceptance step while the vendor tries to accelerate it. Thus the acceptance meeting sometimes takes place in a rather tense atmosphere, particularly if the project is in crisis and the partners do not intend to continue their cooperation further.

The central issue of the acceptance meeting is pinpointing as objectively as possible whether or not a project is mature enough to be accepted. Many projects still contain small defects at the time of acceptance; these defects will be corrected during the guarantee period. It might happen that even during the acceptance meeting some defects are discovered. The question is which defects in the project justify the customer's refusal to accept the project. Everyone will agree that a project with serious flaws that make it impossible even to test entire parts of the project cannot be accepted. A spelling error in a message, on the other hand, does not usually justify refusing the acceptance. Unfortunately, many real projects are somewhere between these two extremes.

A customer ordered an automatic warehouse for storing and processing steel beams and pipes. The company already had a steel depot, which was managed using human-operated cranes. Now it wanted to switch to automatic processing based on computers and robots.

The vendor was rather experienced with automatic warehouses. However, this specific warehouse had several new features. For this reason, the project required developing a great deal of demanding new software. During the development of the project, the vendor ran into serious technological troubles. Because the customer was rather inexperienced in software outsourcing, it was not fully aware of the imminent fiasco. The vendor delivered a first version of the project that was in a really poor condition. A colleague with extraordinarily good social skills accompanied the vendor's engineers when they installed it. A demonstration of some features was carefully prepared in advance and presented more-or-less successfully. However, most of the other features that were not included in the demonstration could hardly be used at all. The vendor's employees asked the customer to sign a paper that confirmed software delivery. In fact the customers signed the "acceptance" — a step that was not really given proper consideration. This ill-considered action was

sort of routine document certifying that the software had been installed. The vendor's employees did their best to cushion the actual situation, claiming that it was just a paper that they needed for their accounting department as evidence for hotel bills, transportation costs, and the like. Another reason why the customers signed this paper, without carefully studying it, might have been the presence of the colleague with strong social skills who managed to establish a friendly and trust-filled atmosphere.

Very soon the customer ran into serious trouble with the new software, which was not at all surprising to the provider. The customer reported the problems, and the vendor tried to solve them. However, the entire software structure was in very poor condition and so by the time the software team solved a few problems, other new defects were appearing as a consequence of the changes made. The vendor occasionally delivered a new version of the software, which was not much better than the last. So the software remained in a state where it could hardly be used for actual work.

The contract offered a guarantee period of one year, which was triggered by the acceptance. By the time the period of guarantee ended, the customer had never seen a version that could be reasonably used in practice. After the guarantee period, the vendor had fewer legal obligations.

The customer's naiveté played a key role here, but it should be borne in mind that they were mechanical engineers and very inexperienced in software outsourcing; this was in fact their first software project. Because mechanical engineering is a rather old, established field, they had not encountered such an experience before. They simply could not imagine that such things can happen.

A rather large customer made an order for a new database application. The project had an attractive budget, and the small vendor accepted the order. The contract provided that an acceptance meeting was to take place and once the project was accepted, payment was due and the guarantee period was triggered. However, the acceptance procedure was not specified in detail.

about the delay. At the meeting, the customer refused to give
acceptance because of minor faults — e.g., spelling errors in
messages. The vendor fixed the reported problems very quickly.
However, the customer asked for another extremely long period
of testing before the next acceptance meeting.

This situation was repeated several times, and the customer
succeeded in generating a significant delay of the acceptance.
The advantage was that this would delay payment for the
project; thus, the customer could use the liquidity for other
purposes. In addition, delaying the acceptance in fact added to
the period of guarantee; the customer could use the software
without the period of guarantee having even started.

The anecdotes above show two extremes, neither of which can be
considered fair.

Because the acceptance is an important step with extensive legal
consequences, it is wise to specify the acceptance conditions in the
contract instead of relying on the "subjective impression" concerning
maturity. One way to clarify the procedure of acceptance is an "acceptance
test" that is specified in advance (i.e., when the contract is signed). For
each requirement in the Software Requirements Specification (SRS), a short
test is defined. Example: The requirements of a certain project may include
the feature of a printable list of all users. A possible acceptance test for
this feature could be: input some users into the system and print the list
of all users. If the list is correct, this feature is accepted.

Only the prior-specified tests are considered for acceptance. If all these
tests are passed, the project is accepted. If any of them fails — even on
account of a tiny detail — acceptance is declined.

The acceptance test is an appendix of the contract and thus signed
and legally binding. In this way, acceptance tests are reliable tools to
avoid disputes regarding the acceptance. The prespecified acceptance test
has the additional advantage that it also improves the quality of the
requirements document: while constructing the acceptance test, the analyst
is forced to look at the requirements from another point of view. In this
way many omissions, errors, and ambiguities are exposed. One obstacle
is that acceptance tests require a rather detailed and mature SRS in written
form, which might not be available for the project at hand.

For projects where acceptance tests are not possible, other ways of
obtaining a fair and reliable acceptance procedure must be found. In some

9.2.9 Payment Schedule

Establishing a payment deadline for a fixed-price project requires careful consideration. One possible solution is that the project is paid for in several steps: for example one third when the order is signed, one third when the first beta-version is delivered, and one third when the project is accepted. In some projects, the customer keeps back a certain amount of money (e.g., 10 percent) until the guarantee period is over.

Another obvious course of action is to pay for the entire project only after it has been accepted. However, this solution has its own shortcomings:

- Many software projects span a long period of time. There will be a considerable delay between when the order is made and when the acceptance is given. The vendor invests in the project by paying salaries and covering other costs, but it will receive payment for the project only after the acceptance — which might be years later. This way the vendor has to cover development costs for the time until acceptance is given. Most offshore vendors and even some onshore providers do not have enough liquidity to bridge this gap.
- In addition, covering development costs is a kind of "hidden credit" granted to the customer by the vendor. This requires further consideration. Is the credit rating of the customer good enough? Will the customer be able to pay at all for the project once it has been accepted? Many of the smaller offshore vendors do not have the necessary skills to evaluate the credit rating of a customer and do not know how to contract consultation in industrialized countries that could provide reliable credit ratings.
- If the development costs are covered by the vendor some interest rate must be calculated, which implicitly increases the price to be paid for the project.

A French software company developed controlling software for glass industries. In fact, they worked almost exclusively for one main customer, a major producer of glass bottles. The French provider encountered problems in finding qualified developers under reasonable conditions. So they worked with an Eastern European vendor. The cooperation started off promisingly, and several projects were carried through successfully and were paid in due time. In time there was a growing feeling of trust.

business and invested in the production of plastic bottles. The entire software infrastructure had to be reconsidered, and no new orders were given to the French software producer. Even some pending projects were cancelled. As a consequence, the French software producer faced serious financial problems.

The contract with the Eastern European vendor stipulated that projects are paid at delivery. However, at the time when the project was finished and payment was due, the French software producer was already in crisis and was no longer solvent. In addition, they did not need the software anymore. The French company wanted to avoid bankruptcy and announced that it would take legal action against the validity of the invoice. It would try to question whether the delivered project matched the requirements.

From a common-sense point of view, the situation was rather easy: the delivered software was all right and thus had to be paid for. However, because many of the requirements had been established by e-mails or by phone calls, it would be difficult for the Eastern European vendor to provide legally valid evidence that the delivered project really matched the requirements. Hence, from a purely legal point of view, it was unclear how the trial would end. In any event, international litigation would be difficult and take quite a while.

Finally, the partners avoided litigation and negotiated a settlement. The French software company only paid for a fraction of the project — as much as it could pay without facing bankruptcy. The Eastern European vendor received some money to cover part of its costs and gave up the litigation.

As a result, the Eastern European vendor lost a substantial amount of money because the contract provided that projects would be paid in full only after they were completed.

The problems outlined above show that paying for the entire project after acceptance usually requires the involvement of a bank — except perhaps in the case of very small projects. Only a bank has the necessary funding, know-how, and experience to solve these issues.

9.2.10 Cancelled Projects

department. The customer's organization might have been sold or might have merged with another company. Business contexts might have changed and the project is not useful to the customer anymore, or business has just evolved worse than expected and the customer needs the money for other purposes.

Fixed-price projects are difficult to cancel. One reason is that contracts for most fixed-price projects are not designed for canceling the project just as it is being developed. Even if the contract includes a side-rider stipulating that the customer can cancel the project for strong reasons, in practice the cancellation of the project frequently leads to high losses for the customer. This observation motivates the customer's management to search for other ways of getting out of the contract.

Obviously, the best solution for a customer in this situation is that the vendor agrees to cancel the project by applying only small penalties or even no penalties at all. One step in this direction is to make the project as unpleasant and risky as possible for the vendor: the customer sends signals pointing at the fact that it does not have any interest in continuing the project anymore, behaving in an extremely uncooperative way, and escalating even the smallest mistakes of the vendor. In this situation the vendor might be concerned whether the project can be finished success-fully at all and if it will be paid once it is completed. The vendor might worry that the customer will fight with all technical and legal means against accepting and paying for the project, especially if the project is to be completely paid for only after it is finished. The possibility of project cancellation constitutes another reason why many vendors disagree with the provision stipulating that the entire project should be paid upon acceptance. Hence, many vendors ask for part of the money in advance.

9.2.11 Superior Performance

Some fixed-price projects include two prices: a fixed price for delivered performance and a so-called "incentive fee" for higher performance. It is important, of course, that the contract include details regarding superiority standards. In projects where the time-to-market constitutes a high priority, the customer can offer a reward if the project is delivered before the scheduled deadline.

9.3 UNIT-PRICE CONTRACTS

form) does not limit the budget for the contract. Because a limited project budget is of vital importance for most buyers, unit-price contracts frequently include upper limits, ensuring that the project will be finished within this budget.

Unless the contract provides something else, the maintenance of a unit-price project is paid for separately. This is at the very least a nuisance for the customer because it has to pay the vendor for repairing its own faults. In some cases the maintenance can significantly increase the costs of the project.

Because the customer has to pay for each working hour, it has an interest in making sure that the reported hours have really been used for its project. Verification of the reported hours is a particular issue if the vendor is offshore.

9.3.1 Unit-Price vs. Fixed-Price Contracts

In the ideal situation of a project with reliable specifications and precise estimation, the final payment should be about the same regardless of whether the payment was set at a unit price per hour or a fixed price for the entire project. If the project encounters unexpected technical problems, the unit-price contract entails higher costs on the customer's part and, of course, an unexpectedly easy project (which is rare in practice) implies paying a lower price.

In many situations customers prefer a fixed-price to a unit-price contract because the customer knows beforehand the price to be paid and can compare the costs to the expected benefits. In addition, the risk of technological problems and mistaken estimates is on the side of the vendor.

Ideal situations, however, are rare in practice, and ideal fixed-price projects are no exception. One of the most important reasons is that the customers change their requirements as the project is being carried through, which leads to reestimation of schedules and budgets.

Scenarios where unit-price contracts have considerable advantages over fixed-price contracts include projects with high technological risks. The vendor has to protect its own company and includes some risk reserves in the contingency budget. In such cases the provider might come up with a surprisingly high estimate because it has to be prepared for the worst to avoid losses on its side. Thus, a unit-price contract might be to the advantage of both sides; it limits the risk for the vendor, and the

- The project team is not experienced enough to write reliable specifications in advance. This is frequently the case when the software had until then been developed by an in-house team because this scenario does not require specifications on a very high level of quality.
- Some projects have inherently unclear requirements — for example, innovative products. In the course of the project all participants will learn a great deal about the new product. For this reason, the requirements are expected to undergo substantial changes.
- In some small projects, detailed requirements are not written in advance. In such cases the vendor has an excellent understanding of the background of the project, and there is a strong feeling of trust between customer and vendor. The customer outlines what its expectations are regarding the final product, and the vendor does its best — perhaps occasionally requiring that further decisions be made as the project is developed.

In all these cases where no detailed requirements exist in advance, a fixed-price contract is almost impossible because the fixed price is based on an estimate that relies on detailed specification. A fixed-price contract without detailed specification is prone to disputes at the time of acceptance.

9.3.2 Limiting the Budget

With a contract that stipulates payment per hour, the level of investment into the project should be limited somehow. Simply cutting back on the budget (i.e., the working time) is not always the best solution for this problem because it is not certain that there will be a finished project at all. If costs exceed the planned budget while the project is still in progress, it will remain unfinished forever.

This problem can obviously be solved by a contractual provision: the project has to be finished within the limits of a maximum budget. This solution has another disadvantage, however. In practice it frequently turns out that these maximum margins of the budget are finally met. That is, if a maximum amount of hours is given, the project is quite likely to use up this budget. Given that the vendor has to deliver a certain set of functionality and the customer will finally have to cover the maximum

on payment per working day (instead of payment per working hour), which might be a way to avoid paying overtime. In any case the customer's investment will be within a certain controlled range.

Note, however, that this contract architecture requires rather mature requirements specifications that are written before the contract is signed. Thus, the provision of limiting the budget in a unit-price contract constitutes a combination of a fixed-price contract and a unit-price contract.

9.3.3 Fixing Defects

In most projects, defects after installation (i.e., "in the field") are a nuisance for users and badly damage the vendor's reputation. In a unit-price contract, the customer even has to pay for maintenance unless the contract includes other stipulations.

> A software producer of an automatic warehouse software system outsourced some modules of a new project to a freelance consultant. The contract set a unit price per working hour and a deadline for delivery of the project. In this way, the client intended to limit the investment. In the course of the project, the consultant became aware that he could hardly finish the task in time. One reason was that he had additional duties concerning other customers. So he was lax and superficial because he wanted to accelerate the project. Finally, he had "something" to deliver. However the quality of the delivered project was unacceptably low. Many defects were reported, and the consultant had to fix them. Because there was no other provision in the contract, each working hour spent correcting the defects had to be paid for by the customer.
>
> In addition to the problem of poor quality and supplementary costs, the customer was uncertain whether the consultant was interested at all in improving the product quality: the more defects reported, the more money he received.

The anecdote shows that maintenance costs can seriously undermine the idea of limiting the investment. In some projects, maintenance costs can be even higher than the investment for the initial project development. In extreme cases when the quality is very low, the maintenance can be a multiple of the first-version costs.

site, in which case they are under surveillance. However, the problem can arise when the engineers work at a different site, especially if they work offshore.

> An offshore vendor carried through a project for an American customer. In the beginning, the specifications were rather unclear. In addition, the project involved new technology that had previously been unfamiliar to the software team. For these reasons, the partners agreed on a contract per working hour. They established a team size of nine persons, who were to work full time.
>
> The offshore vendor's management decided to assign one of these nine developers to another (secret) project without informing the customer. In fact there were only eight developers working on the project for the American customer who, unaware of this fraud, covered salary costs for all nine engineers.
>
> The secret project's customer was a friend of the offshore manager. This project was carried out without accounting papers and was based on a cash-payment agreement. Even in the unlikely case that the customer suspected that something was wrong with its project, it would be rather difficult to provide legal evidence if it went to fraud trial.

One possible way to forestall this kind of fraud is to provide in the contract for the customer's right to make unannounced check-up visits at the vendor's site. The check-up visits' efficiency might be limited by the long distances between the onshore customer and the offshore vendor. In this case the visits have to be rather few and far between unless the customer has a reliable and trustworthy representative in the offshore country. Another obstacle in the way of efficient check-up visits might be access control to the vendor's office building; the doorkeeper will probably be instructed to inform management whenever the customer's representative enters the building. The time between the representative entering the office building and arriving at the particular software lab might be enough for the corrupt manager on the vendor's side to tamper with the results of the control visit.

A customer representative who has solid domain expertise and is permanently working with the team can efficiently replace standard check-ups. Simply controlling reported working hours will probably not justify

Another possibility to maintain control over the project could be for the customer to have remote access to the system of video surveillance in the vendor's office — although this possibility has scarcely been given practical consideration so far. In addition, it might be in conflict with the privacy laws of the particular country.

9.4 GUARANTEE PERIOD

The purpose of the guarantee period is to provide the customer with the right to free-of-charge repair of defects discovered after the project has been delivered. Although the guarantee period is an important part of most contracts, some issues require further in-depth consideration.

There will usually be a delay between the error report and the corrected version. The customer would like to obtain the corrections as fast as possible. In practice, however, this is not always possible.

Some defects require that a service engineer come to the user's site and analyze the problem there. The costs for travel are usually much higher than the few working hours spent correcting the error. If this is an issue, the contract should provide how such costs are handled.

Repairing reported faults is much more efficient if the failure is reproducible on the developer's computer — i.e., if the developer has a known procedure that always shows the reported wrong behavior. Mature defect reports, however, require additional efforts on the side of the user. A particularly challenging class of defects is "transient defects" — i.e., failures that occur only sporadically, even if the same sequence of operations is performed on the same computer. Resolving defects of this class can be very costly. Thus, the contract should include stipulations in case the project is prone to this class of errors.

In some cases it may be debatable whether a reported behavior is in fact a failure or if it is a desirable feature. Many of these potential disputes are clarified in style guides, which specify in detail the "look and feel" of the applications of a certain operating system. In practice, however, it may prove costly for the vendor to stick to each tiny detail of the style guide that is

Software does not wear out over time. All failures that are identified afterwards are already present in the software at the time of delivery. In some countries, legislation does not cover this case adequately, and it might be necessary to make clear that these are not "latent defects" — otherwise, the guarantee period for software would never end.

9.4.1 Delay between Failure Report and New Version

Deadlines are important when technical problems must be resolved. How much time is granted to the vendor to repair a reported defect? From the customer's point of view, it is preferable that the problem be solved as soon as it is reported. In practice this is usually impossible, however; the vendor has to appoint one or more developers to take responsibility for this defect report. Because this engineer will probably have other responsibilities, there will be a time gap between the error report dispatch and the actual problem analysis. This delay can range from a few seconds' time in the case of highly important projects where human lives are at risk to several months for customers who have accepted a lower service level. The maximum delay should be specified in the contract — shorter delays usually entail higher costs.

Analyzing software defects is a challenging issue. Repair time may range from just a few seconds or a few hours to several weeks, especially if is very difficult to analyze the defect. In other cases an apparently easy error report reveals a deeply rooted conceptual problem with the software; the reported error shows only the tip of the iceberg. Thus it is difficult to specify a maximum period of time necessary for the repairs because this approximation may be either unreasonably long for the vast majority of minor defects or too short for a few challenging problems.

Some contracts specify that the vendor has to solve the reported problem by relying on certain amount of working time continuously. For example, until up to three working days after the failure has been reported the vendor has to assign at least one engineer to work toward the solution of the reported defect for at least seven hours per day continuously until the problem is resolved.

The response time is often calculated in working days. Weekends and holidays are usually not considered for the deadline. This may become an issue if urgent problems have to be solved during legal holidays in the vendor's country

report. However, in a few exceptional situations it is necessary that an engineer visit the user's site and analyze the defect there. One reason can be that the particular failure only appears on a certain computer or in a certain environment. Solving this kind of defect can imply high costs for transportation and accommodation, which are much higher than the engineer's few hours' work at the customer's site. If such problems can appear in a project, the contract should specify how the costs are to be handled.

9.4.3 Transient Errors

A small but important class of failures is particularly difficult to handle: transient errors. A "transient error" only occurs occasionally. Even if the user gives the same input and makes the same operative steps, the error may or may not appear. For this reason, this type of failures is also called "nondeterministic" errors. These are among the most challenging defects in software projects.

> A software project was developed to control a group of cooperating robots. The software worked well for a while and the robots did their jobs. Suddenly one of the robots stopped working, as though it were frozen. A few minutes later a second robot was blocked. After a while all the robots in the group had stopped working. Both the vendor and the user were very confused and could not find a solution other than restarting the entire system — which caused significant losses because the half finished work-parts of the robots had to be thrown away.
>
> This unpleasant and costly scenario recurred occasionally — once every few weeks. The users could not see any pattern that caused the failure: it seemed that the robots followed exactly the same steps every time. Suddenly they stopped in the middle of an operation that they had performed successfully many times before. It was not even clear whether the robots were causing the problem or whether the controlling software was responsible.
>
> The engineers were eventually able to solve the problem. However, it took several months of intensive work and a great deal of cooperation and mutual understanding on the parts of both the vendor and the customer.

Not only high-tech robot control software, but even rather unpretentious projects such as common database applications can include transient errors; this is why contracts should include provisions on how these problems should be handled, especially if the project is prone to this kind of nondeterministic error. Contractual provisions gain particular importance if the cooperation comes into a crisis and the partners have no intention of continuing their relationship after the contract expires. In this tense atmosphere, the goodwill necessary to solve transient errors does not exist anymore, especially in light of the high costs related to transient errors.

9.4.4 Maturity of Defect Reports

An important step in finding a solution to a reported failure is the developer's ability to reproduce the problem. Once the software engineer can replicate the error in a controlled way on the engineer's own development computer, it is frequently only a matter of minutes until the problem is solved. The ideal error report is a short sequence of operations: whenever the developer executes this exact sequence the reported failure occurs. The developer now has the optimum conditions to analyze the problem.

This introduction makes it clear that efficient software maintenance depends crucially on the quality of the error reports forwarded by the users. Finding a software failure based on an excellent error report can be ten times faster than finding the same defect using a cloudy and obscure error report because in the first case the developer needs much less time to reproduce the reported failure.

Unfortunately, in practice many error reports cannot easily be reproduced. Some classes of errors are really nondeterministic. One example of a transient error was given in the anecdote above of the robot control system: despite all efforts the users could not find a pattern corresponding with the defect occurrence. Even though this kind of problem can appear in software projects, other kinds of nonreproducible defects are more frequent; the user may report a failure but may not remember the steps of operation prior to the time of the failure — at least not to the degree of detail and precision necessary for the software engineers to reproduce the problem.

The engineer has some technical options for analyzing the problem

Basically it is a conflict of cost distribution between customer and vendor; if the user has to garner more information concerning the failure pattern, the customer has the costs for this additional investigation. If the vendor, on the other hand, has to analyze the problem based on a cloudy defect report, this will take up more time and the vendor's costs will be correspondingly higher. Two fictitious examples illustrate this conflict.

> The entire error report is "The software was blocked. The user was forced to cease work and had to reboot the computer." The user could not remember what steps were followed before the failure appeared or which windows appeared on the screen when the software was blocked.

This error report obviously does not include any detail that could help the developer find the cause of the software failure. At the opposite pole of the problem, there is the case of vendors who do not make enough efforts to solve the problem.

> The user reported a sequence of steps that always led to a certain error message on the user's computer. The developer tried this sequence on his own computer. No error message appeared; the reported sequence was carried through successfully. The responsible programmer's response to this was: "What can I do? It works!" Thus the vendor rejected the defect report and claimed that the software functions properly. They said it was obviously a mistake of the user who did not use the software correctly because the software in itself was obviously all right.
>
> This is not necessarily true, however; the failure may occur only on a certain computer. Developers frequently use rather strong hardware. This particular user might have an older computer. Another possible explanation could be that the failure appears only when a certain version of the operating system is used, which might differ on the developers' computer.
>
> The developer had the complete sequence of the steps and the exact text of the error message. This alone should be a good starting point for analyzing the problem, even if the error

The examples show two extreme scenarios: the former involving an uncooperative client and the latter an unqualified vendor. Such extremes happen occasionally in practice; it depends on the balance of power between vendor and customer. In any case, the anecdotes prove that both extremes are not at all appropriate. To avoid future disputes, the contract should specify what level of maturity is required for a failure report.

In many projects it is reasonable for the user to report a reproducible defect: i.e., a sequence of steps that leads to the failure of the software system on a certain computer, at least in a reasonable number of cases (e.g., in one out of ten trials).

9.4.5 "It's Not a Bug; It's a Feature"

The user reports a defect (in jargon "a bug") to the software team: the program does not behave in the way the user expected it to. The software engineer analyzes the situation and rejects the defect report because the program behaves in the exact way it should to according to opinion of the software engineers. That is, the developers claim that the reported program behavior is in fact a desirable program feature — not a "bug," as the user says. Sometimes the program behavior for this particular situation is specified in the requirements document. In this case the solution of the conflict is simple and can be found by merely checking against the requirements documents. In many cases, however, the requirements are not detailed enough and leave the program's behavior unspecified for this special case. There might be a number of reasons why such details are omitted:

- Writing detailed requirements is a rather expensive and time-consuming task. Some projects might lack time or budget for a detailed requirements document. Software engineering books warn against shortening the requirements phase. In practice, however, such cases are rather frequent.
- Even if the requirements are carefully engineered, the analyst might have inadvertently left aside certain important details. The requirements might be ambiguous or include contradictions. In practice, requirements documents that fulfill the three big "C"s of Requirements Engineering (Correct, Complete, and Consistent) are rare.
- The requirements might have been changed in an informal way

might be given straightforward consideration, and the problem is solved without paperwork. In this way, the requirements document may not reflect the currently valid requirements.

Most software projects involve many user groups and stakeholders, each of whom usually has an at least slightly different opinion on what the program should do. Usually, all groups have to make compromises that should be somehow documented — this is what software engineering books recommend. In practice, however, this kind of compromise is frequently forgotten in time. This is not necessarily done with bad intentions; there are many details to be discussed and negotiated in the course of a software project. It is difficult to keep track of all these problems. Other colleagues might enter the project — colleagues who were not involved in the negotiations at that time and who might be unaware of these compromises. From a certain user's point of view it would be much better if the program behaved differently. This, however, is only the isolated point of view of that specific user group, ignoring the needs of other stakeholders.

Thus far, this discussion has focused on reasons why a certain user and the software team might have different opinions on whether a reported behavior is in fact a failure (a "bug") or a useful functionality (a "feature"). These reasons might even appear in projects that have a fair balance of power between customer and vendor and that do not include any illegitimate motivations. In some cases, either the customer or the vendor tries to take advantage of omissions in the requirements documents for illegitimate purposes.

A vendor had to provide a graphical user interface (GUI) for a certain special hardware environment. Due to the project's specific hardware the software team had to write a considerable part of the basic input/output (I/O) functions (e.g., keyboard input) from scratch — a task that turned out to be unexpectedly challenging.

When the project was delivered, the users complained about the inappropriate performance of the Insert key. The key inserted a single blank character (a "spacebar") instead of toggling the mode between the insert mode and the overwrite mode, as it is handled in most modern GUIs.

any clear statement about the Insert key in the requirements document, the vendor's programmers implemented the latter one.

This was not true, however. The vendor was well aware that toggling the mode is the standard behavior for Insert keys. When the vendor's programmers tried to implement this feature, they encountered technological problems with the innovative hardware. For this reason, they decided to implement a rather exotic behavior for the Insert key, which turned out to be easier. Because this behavior was not in clear contradiction to the requirements, the customer could hardly reject it.

9.4.6 Style Guides

Many experienced users know in a general way how programs of a given operating system usually behave. When it comes to details, however, this approximate knowledge might turn out to be imprecise. To clarify the details, so-called style guides have been published for all popular operating systems. Style guides are documents maintained by the provider of the particular operating system; they clarify details such as what happens if the Insert key is pressed, thus avoiding unpleasant surprises on the customer's side, as in the anecdote above.

It is hardly possible to specify each detail of program performance applied to each particular situation — such as the behavior of the Insert key in the anecdote above. This is particularly important because omissions and ambiguities in the specification frequently turn out to be to the disadvantage of the customer. For this reason, many contracts include style guides specifying the look and feel of the software used with a certain operating system.

Style guides are not only advantageous, however, especially for the vendor. In fact, style guides are lengthy documents that specify a huge number of implementation details. For this reason it is difficult for software developers to penetrate them fully, keep them in mind, and implement each detail according to the guides. Even a programmer who is skilled and experienced in developing software for a certain operating system does not know each detail of the style guide by heart. In most projects this is not a problem: the users are content if the project has the subjective

200 ■ The Insider's Guide to Outsourcing Risks and Rewards

If the project reaches a crisis, however, and the partners consider litigation, the reference to the style guides might turn out to be a dangerous weapon against the vendor. Reviewing the lengthy guides and verifying the numerous details line by line against the delivered software might reveal a large number of small differences. The guides are stipulated in the contract; thus, they are part of the legally binding agreement, and all these small differences could be considered programming defects that are to be solved. The costs necessary for making the software fully compliant with the agreed-on guides might even exceed the price for the entire project. Hence, if it comes to a conflict, any reference to the guides might provide the customer with a strong negotiating position that most vendors are not aware of: "Either you (the vendor) will make serious compromises in other respects or we (the customer) will cause you a lot of trouble with this style guide — no matter whether we benefit from this or not."

Some vendors do not even know the details of the style guides because they have never bothered leafing through them. What is more, they might not even know exactly where to find them. The vendor accepts the contractual reference to the guides because it thinks that this provision is more-or-less equivalent to the statement "the software should be in line with the look and feel of this operating system." This is not true, however. A manager who signs this reference implicitly signs a lengthy document. Most management books advise against signing unknown documents before reading them.

The almost infinite number of details that are mentioned in a typical style guide is only one issue. Another risk stems from the fact that it is usually written and maintained by the owner of the particular operating system, who might have other specific interests.

> The owner of a popular operating system (say, "XY-Soft") followed the strategy of trying to persuade as many other vendors as possible to adopt the proprietary technology "XY-Tech" in their applications. If XY-Soft's proprietary technology was employed by as many applications as possible, the company expected strategic advantages against vendors of competing operating systems. To achieve this goal, the operating system's style guide included the stipulation that each application has to use XY-Tech. In this way XY-Soft pursued its strategic goal of widespread distribution of its proprietary technology.

was implemented. For some applications, it constituted even a disadvantage because it generated unnecessary overhead. In any event, implementing this technology required considerable work and represented a major new feature. If this functionality was really necessary, it should have been considered in terms of the costs and schedule estimation.

The anecdote shows that some style guides include provisions that are far beyond the intuitive meaning of style — i.e., the look and feel of the programs of a certain operating system. Sometimes the managers on both sides — customer and vendor — are not even aware of these new features mentioned in the style guide. These new features take a backdoor way into the contract.

The customer is usually unwilling to pay extra money for the provision that the software has to be compliant to the standards of the specific operating system. This kind of provision is usually taken for granted when a professional vendor is involved in the working relationship. It is similar to the provision that partners will not disclose business secrets. Provisions of this kind are usually not paid for separately because they are not considered to be additional features but are part of the very basis of the cooperation.

Referencing a style guide in the contract is similar: in most cases the customer simply wants to be sure that the final product is compliant with the standards of the operating system. The customer does not want to exceed the project's budget by including major expenses for this provision. From the vendor's point of view, however, it is necessary to analyze the referred-to style guide very carefully to discover any new features that go beyond the intuitive meaning of "style." It should also make sure that the wording of the style guide can be established with no additional costs, particularly if the customer has a reputation for being litigious. In most cases both vendor and customer are not aware of these aspects of style guides — usually because they have never read the style guide. For this reason, risks associated with guides reference rarely manifest in practice.

9.4.7 Delivery

Once the defect is fixed, the new version must be delivered. In many cases the delivery of a new version causes higher costs than fixing a single

9.4.8 Latent Defects

Software does not wear out in time. This makes it utterly different from other products such as cameras, for example; the camera might have been all right at purchase time, but it becomes damaged during the guarantee period — a scenario that can never occur in the case of software. Software might already have been damaged at the time of delivery, but it cannot become damaged during the period of guarantee — except in some special cases where the media is damaged (e.g., the CD becomes scratched).

For this reason, the guarantee period for software has a different meaning than in the case of other products: all defects discovered and reported during the guarantee period have to be repaired without additional payment. Nevertheless, even a defect discovered after the guarantee period was already in the software from the very beginning. In the case of other products it would be considered a "latent defect." The legislation in many countries includes latent defects in the guarantee period: the vendor is obliged to fix them with no extra payment even if they are discovered after the guarantee period. From this point of view, the guarantee period for software would in fact be never-ending because all errors would fall into the "latent defects" category.

Another variation on the same theme is the vendor's rejection of the existence of a guarantee period at all. Most providers of standard software (in jargon, "shrink-wrap" software) use this practice in their licensing agreements; the guarantee period only refers to the media. If the CD is damaged, it will be replaced, but the vendor does not guarantee that the functionality of the software is correct.

Even if legislation covers the problem of the period of guarantee for software adequately, the issues outlined above can still cause disputes if the order includes not only software but also hardware or other components. In this case the client could bring up as an argument the fact that the order was issued for a complete system and not just the software component. The existing legislation might cover the issue of latent defects only in the case of software and not that of complete systems, including hardware and other components. The customer might argue that this complete system has latent defects that have to be solved without additional payment even if the guarantee period has expired. If the legislation of the countries involved does not cover this problem adequately, the contract should stipulate the exact meaning of guarantee period.

a software project. Prior to a certain date, a certain team "owns" the source code; after that date, another team is responsible for it. Notice that in this context "ownership" is equivalent to responsibility and does not hint at the notion of ownership in a legal sense.

One example where transfer of ownership is necessary is the guarantee period: before the guarantee period ends, the vendor is accountable; afterward the customer is responsible (unless the contract provides otherwise). Transfer of ownership can entail difficult defect responsibility issues.

Another example of transfer of "ownership" is that of maintenance contracts — e.g., the so-called Y2K maintenance of the anecdote below.

On January 1, 2000, many software products faced an important problem: in numerous programs the internal representation of the year used only two digits. At the moment when the year is switched from 99 to 00 a problem could appear because 00 is smaller than 99. Notice that many programs compare the arithmetic value to find out if a date is more or less recent. This issue was known as "year 2000 problem" — in jargon "Y2K" — and attracted quite a lot of public attention, even outside the software community.

From the point of view of software technology, this problem requires a large number of routine changes in the source code: all occurrences of the two-digit representation of the year must be replaced by the correct four-digit representation. After this step the entire program has to be tested in detail to exclude possible errors caused by inadvertent side effects due to the numerous changes. The so-called "Y2K maintenance" was not a particularly difficult task, but the large number of changes required quite a lot of time. In addition, it was a clearly defined and well structured task. For this reason many companies considered Y2K maintenance an ideal project for offshore outsourcing: a time consuming, clearly defined routine project.

In the course of this task, the project's entire source code had to be transferred offshore, and to a large extent the customer had to trust the vendor's team's assurance that all changes were being been made with due care. The customer could not check each of the thousands and tens of thousands of changes;

customer delivered the new software to its clients. Later on, it turned out that the software contained a defect that caused high damages. The customer tried to blame the offshore vendor for this defect, saying that the problems were included in the software during the Y2K maintenance, and wanted to make the vendor liable. The vendor defended itself and said it was not its fault — the defects were already in the code version that it had received. Because the onshore customer did not have a backup of the old version of the software it handed over to the offshore vendor, it could not provide legal evidence that the faults were actually added during the Y2K maintenance.

9.5.1 Legally Evident Copies of Source Code

The anecdote highlights an important problem. Whenever responsibility for source code is transferred, the partners should keep a legally valid copy of the source code at the moment of the transfer. It is not even enough for the partners to copy the source code onto a CD and safe-keep it; the copy must constitute legal evidence. Otherwise, there is a risk of modifications afterward. For this reason, the copy must be protected by digital signature or other technical mechanisms unless it is deposited at a trusted neutral organization.

9.5.2 Masked Defects and Inadvertent Side Effects

If it comes to litigation, the meaning of the phrase "a new defect has been included in the program" could turn out to be unexpectedly ambiguous. The common-sense meaning is quite obvious: before responsibility for the source code was transferred, the software failure was not present. When it came back, the code was erroneous. There is an important class of errors, however, that is not covered by this straightforward definition: masked errors. These are defects that exist in the source code but do not occur on the screen for one reason or another. Small changes in a completely different part of the program might have unexpected side effects that cause the failure to manifest. The source code was wrong from the very beginning, but this defect had never been seen. After the changes were completed, the failure appeared on the screen.

An everyday life example should explain the concept of

"masked" — the car has a problem but the defect is never apparent.

After a while the car is sold, and the new owner removes the advertising material. Now the masked problem becomes apparent: a small change causes a completely unexpected problem and raises the question of whether or not the person who removed the advertisement material is responsible for the flaw.

For people who are green in the software business, the concept of "masked errors" might seem rather artificial or more of an academic problem. In practice, however, this kind of error is not at all rare.

An even more frequent type of problem related to masked errors is the class of "inadvertent side effects." One module is modified, and a completely different module (which remains unmodified) changes its behavior — in most cases, changed behavior means that it exposes "new" defects. Assessment of masked defects is comparatively easy: a software engineer who analyzes the source code sees that there was in fact something wrong in the particular module and can find out why this problem did not manifest so far. The car in the example above had in fact a production problem, which did not manifest because of the plastic films. Legally valid assessment of inadvertent side effects is more difficult; usually, none of the parts involved is really wrong. An engineer who analyzes each part separately reaches the conclusion that the unmodified module is all right but the changes are not wrong either. The problem stems from the details concerning the interaction of these parts.

Perfectly designed software should include only a small number of possibilities for inadvertent side effects. Perfection, however, is hard to attain. In practice a rule of the thumb can be stated: each major modification of source code is quite likely to lead to some unexpected problems — be they masked errors or inadvertent side effects.

9.5.3 Faults in Source Code and Failures in Executable Files

The analysis above pinpoints the fact that the contract should stipulate the exact meaning of "a new defect has been introduced into the source code." The evidence for a "new defect" can be based either on source code or on executable files — i.e., files that can be executed on computers (so-called EXEs). This subtle difference may cause significantly different

206 ■ The Insider's Guide to Outsourcing Risks and Rewards

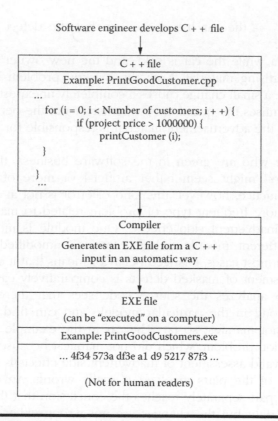

Software engineer develops C + + file

```
C + + file
Example: PrintGoodCustomer.cpp

...
for (i = 0; i < Number of customers; i + +) {
    if (project price > 1000000) {
        printCustomer (i);
    }
}
...
```

```
Compiler
Generates an EXE file form a C + +
input in an automatic way
```

```
EXE file
(can be "executed" on a comptuer)
Example: PrintGoodCustomers.exe

... 4f34 573a df3e a1 d9 5217 87f3 ...

(Not for human readers)
```

Figure 9.1   Relationship between source code, compiler, and executable file. The software engineers are writing so-called source code — e.g., in C++. This source code is highly structured but is still comprehensible to humans. It constitutes the input for a computer program called the "compiler," which automatically translates the source code into an executable file — "EXE." The executable consists of machine language that is optimized for the target processor. It is not intended for a human reader (although a few specialized programmers know how to deal with it). Most end users deal only with executables, not with source code and compilers.

Source code, on the other hand, is a quite challenging asset. Its development and maintenance are demanding, and it is difficult to understand. In fact, "source code" is a text that is written by software developers in a certain programming language (e.g., C++ or Java) and serves as an input for a program called a "compiler." The compiler produces the

single line can have dramatic effects. One special aspect of this "contract" is that it has millions of lines — i.e., tens of thousands of pages, each of which is important. That is why grasping it is a challenge even for experts.

9.5.4 Assessment Based on Source Code

A provision regarding "new defects" based on source code has its pitfalls; lawyers and judges have to understand the source code (e.g., C++ text). It may be difficult to explain the inner workings of a complex source code to a judge who is not even using the Internet and who can hardly plug in the cables of stereo equipment.

The court can enlist the help of an independent expert witness. In some instances, however, even software engineers might have problems in understanding source code well enough. The independent expert has to grasp millions of lines — an effort that results in high cost.

The practical important error-class of "inadvertent side effects" deserves special attention. The key problem is that no part is intrinsically wrong: the extant "old" part was not wrong, and the new changes are not wrong, either; the interference between them is the cause of the problems. For this reason, even an independent expert's analysis might remain inconclusive.

9.5.5 Assessment Based on Executable Files

Executable files cause fewer problems when establishing whether the defect was preextant in the program before responsibility was transferred; the court can simply try the old version and test whether it was erroneous. However, a provision based on executable files introduces other problems. The most obvious is that "masked defects" fall under the sphere of influence of modifications — i.e., they are considered "new" defects because they did not appear in the old version. From a common-sense point of view, this might be considered unfair. In the previous anecdote, the person who removed the advertisement material could be considered responsible for the production problem: "Before you removed the films the car was dry; now it is wet. Thus you are responsible."

Another, less conspicuous problem is the necessary availability of executables at the time when the court wants to see them. This condition sounds obvious, but there might be cases when it is problematic; there

starts. In most countries legal institutions are quite infamous for their slow, bureaucratic system. In this way it might well happen that several years pass between the time when changes in the source code are made and the moment when evidence has to be presented in court.

Meanwhile, IT technology development goes on. When the moment comes for the lawyers to take the precious source code CD out from their safes, they might be unpleasantly surprised: the old source code does not compile and the old EXE cannot be executed anymore. The old versions of the executable run only on old hardware. The old compiler version (which might still be available) requires an old version of the operating system, which requires (perhaps different) old hardware. The current version of the compiler cannot deal with the old software, and thus adaptations are necessary. These adaptations might be rather easy, routine work; however, even the smallest change in the source code destroys legal evidence. Even if it is possible to run the old program on new hardware, it might behave slightly differently. Experience shows that if any of the components (compiler, operating system, or hardware) has significantly changed, then the behavior of the software will change as well. In practice, this modified behavior might be either serious or negligible. In the case of litigation, however, even the smallest modifications are more than enough to destroy legal evidence; the behavior of the program that is presented in court is simply not the same as the behavior to which the plaintiff refers.

For this reason it is not enough to merely safekeep the program at the moment when responsibility is transferred. In fact, a complete development environment has to be preserved, including hardware, operating system, compiler libraries, and technical documentation on how to use this old equipment. Note that it might be difficult to find somebody who knows how to use a five-year-old compiler and who knows all the details by heart.

The necessity of maintaining a complete development environment is quite obvious in light of the analysis above. In practice, however, it is rarely considered. The real situation is more like this. IT staff is enthusiastic about the advantages of new technology. The system administrators are worried about the workload necessary for installing it and the risks of the transition period. When everything is finished, all participants are happy and nobody is thinking anymore about old CDs that have been handed to an attorney years ago. As time goes by, even newer versions of hardware

9.6 SERVICE AGREEMENTS: OUTSOURCING THE IT FOR A CERTAIN TIME

A service level agreement usually includes the following parts (among others):

- *Contract terms — How long is the contract valid?*
- *Scope of services. What exactly are the vendor's duties?*
- *Service Level Agreement (SLA). A detailed specification of the quality of provider services (e.g., response time).*

9.6.1 Contract Terms

Contract terms are frequently negotiated for a rather long time, generally ranging from three to ten years. The vendors usually try to negotiate rather long terms for the following reasons:

- Setting up the relationship implies high costs. The cooperation may need significant investments in terms of new technology.
- Many contracts are "back-loaded." Most of the upfront costs are charged to the customer in later years. In such scenarios, the vendor needs some time to recover from the financial engineering made at the beginning of the cooperation.
- Longer contracts imply higher investment volume, which usually means higher profits.

It is quite likely that things will change during the service agreement; most businesses undergo several rounds of strategic changes over the ten-year term of a service agreement. For this reason, the customer is highly interested in ensuring some flexibility of the contract. The customer should make sure that the following items are possible:

- The contract must be flexible enough to ensure that adjustments to it can be made in a predictable and controlled way and to realistically foresee business changes.
- If the adaptation is not possible, the customer should have a clearly conceived plan to exit the cooperation. Sometimes the contract is quite unbalanced in favor of the vendor and does not include an

important for ending the relationship with a vendor but they are not enough; they must be supported by day-by-day business decisions (see Chapter 11).

9.6.2 Scope of Services

The services that are provided in the scope of the contract should be clearly defined. In general, vendors prefer a narrow and "crisp" definition of the scope because all services outside the scope are paid extra. Thus, vendors suggest lists of strictly defined (and well-paying) services.

The customer, on the other hand, would like to sign a contract that has a rather broad definition of its scope and that includes all of the former employees' activities — e.g., "Vendor provides all services of the former IT department unless expressly excluded."

9.6.3 Service Level Agreement (SLA)

Purpose

The SLA specifies the quality of services and the level of the provider's performance. SLAs are used to serve several purposes. The customer states its expectations. The vendor has an authorized statement of the customer's priorities from the onset. The vendor can pay the necessary attention to the stated qualities. If the specified service standards are met, there is no basis for complaint. If the vendor temporarily or permanently fails to reach some of the service standards, the partners can identify incidents and take counteracting actions. In this case, the clause includes a scheme of compensation that the customer receives for failed service levels.

Objective Measurement of the Service Level

Typical provisions of SLAs are availability of maintenance of systems and networks, usability of software products, and user satisfaction. Other common measures (in jargon, "metrics") include bandwidth of networks, response times of applications, system capacity (e.g., transaction rate), and reaction time for solving problems.

To avoid further disputes, the definition of the service level should be based on objective measures. Some measures, such as availability of networks, are intrinsically objective. Other service levels — e.g., usability —

More problems arise with metrics that can be manipulated to some extent by the customer, e.g., "user satisfaction." The users (i.e., employees of the customer) can at any time say that they are not satisfied. As these examples show, definitions of service levels require careful formulations.

9.6.4 Data Elicitation Costs

Collecting and processing the necessary data to evaluate the service levels is not cheap, especially if the data is compiled over a long period of time or even permanently. Some issues require careful consideration:

- It should be easy to elicit the necessary data. If possible, the data should be collected automatically or as a byproduct of other business processes. Otherwise, the costs for providing the data can outweigh the benefits of the SLA.
- The relevance of each requested service level requires careful assessment. A common mistake is to specify too many service levels.
- The selection of the metric requires careful consideration as well. The metrics should measure the customer's real priorities — not something where the vendor knows how to excel. For example, the vendor might have a team that is well qualified in network maintenance. In this case the network reliability will be rather high. However, the customer might not need extremely high network reliability. Other service levels might be more important.

Collecting and processing metrics is the subject of ongoing scientific discussion. For this reason, the customer may want to enlist the help of an expert.

9.6.5 Exclusions

Most SLAs contain an exclusion list — i.e., times that are not considered when the achieved service level is calculated. For example, the times for "scheduled maintenance windows" or "periodic reboots" are usually not taken into consideration when network availability is computed. Service providers that offer high availability frequently have lengthy lists of exclusions. Particular attention is indicated if the vendor can influence the

9.6.6 Compensation Scheme

If some service levels are not met, the vendor's fees are reduced accordingly. Consequential damages are usually excluded. In case of permanent underachievement, the customer has the right to terminate the contract. Some contracts include the possibility of "service bonuses," where the vendor can recuperate lost fees by overperforming.

10

INDUSTRIAL ESPIONAGE

ABSTRACT

Confidential assets benefit from little legal protection in emerging countries. In this chapter, an introductory case study shows how easy it was for a Pakistani clerical worker to threaten a prestigious American hospital with publishing their confidential patient files on the Internet. Ultimately, the Pakistani worker could not even be sentenced for what she had done.

Potential targets of industrial espionage include data, source code, and business secrets, each of which has different dynamics and is thus analyzed separately in this chapter. There are a number of ways that confidential material can fall into the wrong hands, including server access, test data, access of the offshore liaison to the customer's networks, an unreliable subcontractor of the vendor, professional industrial spies, criminal attacks against the vendor (e.g., forced entry into the office building), and vendors who are also working for the customer's competitors.

Protection against espionage includes tight monitoring of human resources and understanding of the legal systems of the countries involved — to provide the necessary deterrence of adequate punishment in case the attacker is caught. Despite all precautions, watertight protection of confidential material in developing countries has been difficult, at least so far. For this reason, the customer has to assess carefully which risks its organization can afford and whether the cost advantage justifies the risk.

10.1 ESPIONAGE: AN INTRODUCTORY CASE STUDY

claimed that her client owed her money and threatened to make the patients' files public through the Internet unless she was paid the money she believed was due to her.

A highly prestigious medical institution in California received an e-mail from a woman in Karachi, Pakistan. In this message the woman threatened to release the hospital's confidential patient files on the Internet unless she was paid a certain amount of money (about $500). She claimed that this money was lawfully owed to her by a Texas-based U.S. national for transcribing the files: "Your patient records are out in the open, so you'd better track that person and make him pay the money due to me or otherwise I will expose all the voice files and patient records." To prove that her intentions were serious, she attached two authentic patient records to the e-mail. At that time, the hospital had no information on the existence of either the woman in Pakistan (we will call her "Lubna") or of the man in Texas ("Tom"). This raised the question of how the files could arrive in the hands this person in far-off Karachi. Urgent investigation revealed that the transcription of those files had been outsourced to a well-established company in California that specialized in transcribing medical records from voice files. This is a widely used practice in hospitals; many medical institutions outsource at least part of their transcription work to specialized companies. The hospital knew that the California company maintained a network of about 15 subcontractors throughout the country to handle the hundreds of files received by their office every day but assumed that was as far as it went. One of these subcontractors — a Florida-based woman — worked with Tom from Texas, who in turn subcontracted the work to Lubna in Pakistan — even though the agreement with the Florida woman excluded outsourcing outside the borders of the United States. The hospital paid about 18 cents per line to the California company. Out of this, about three cents reached the Pakistani clerical worker. In the beginning, the Pakistani woman was paid in due time. Eventually, however, payment was increasingly delayed. Thus, an increasing amount of debts accumulated. Finally, she asked Tom to stop sending her work

From the very beginning, Tom had refused to give Lubna any phone number or postal address, so she no longer had a way to contact him. Her only possibility was to write to the hospital; this is what Lubna said. Finally things went well: Lubna received her money and she retracted her previous threats. She claimed she had destroyed all confidential data from the hospital. Nevertheless, the case stirred up considerable public interest.

What happened afterwards? A few weeks later, Lubna was still in Karachi, still free and still working for doctors in the United States. In fact, one doctor in California, who was not aware of the details of that case, was still sending her files for transcription.

This case study includes a number of important details that justify a closer look.

The Daisy Chain

The business architecture of the case study includes a chain of outsourcing relationships. In management jargon it is called a "daisy chain" — a structure that is quite frequent in outsourcing. At the top of the chain are large and well-known organizations, high prices, and polished manners. At the bottom, as prices decrease, the organizations become smaller and less reliable. In the case study above, it would not come as a surprise if Lubna maintained in Karachi her own network of subcontractors. One could imagine some medical students with fluency in English and quick fingers at the keyboard working for Lubna.

The Hospital

From the point of view of the hospital, it was an egregious breach — something between a crime and a terrorist action. Only the rather modest sum of $500 might justify doubts that the threatening e-mail was not part of a criminal blackmail scheme. Before this happened, the hospital considered itself to be in a safe situation: they were working with a well-established transcription company within the borders of the United States. For many years, they maintained smooth cooperation and paid fair prices.

go wrong in this scenario. U.S. laws, however, are virtually unenforceable
if foreign nationals are acting outside the borders of the United States.

The Agent "Tom" from Texas

The role of the outsourcing agent does not require very much know-how
nor does it entail management skills and subject matter expertise. In
addition, very limited capital is necessary to enter this market. It is easy
to establish the business relationships, and once the ball is rolling, the
agent does little more than forward files and manage contracts (i.e., writing
invoices). The prices are low but it is a "volume business." In this way a
person with very limited professional skills can earn an income per
working-hour that is not much lower than the salary of managers of a
reputable company. Thus, these positions in outsourcing business are
rather attractive for disloyal business agents.

From the beginning, Tom built his business architecture so that the
possibility of litigation being started against him was remote; he refused
to provide phone numbers and postal addresses. It seems that he had
foreseen from the very beginning that his Pakistani business partner might
consider filing a lawsuit against him sooner or later, and he wanted to
make this as difficult as possible. The clerical worker might even become
so angry and desperate that she would consider courses of action that
were worse than a lawsuit. In this case it might have been an advantage
for Tom not to be found.

At the beginning of the cooperation, Tom was paying in due time to
instill a feeling of trust. In time, however, debts grew. This put the Pakistani
partner in a difficult position; if she continued to work for Tom she was
risking a growing amount of outstanding payment. If she dared to insist
on timely payment, she ran the risk of making her Texas partner cancel
the cooperation and not pay the already accumulated debts; this is what
finally happened.

Tom's business architecture included a number of carefully prepared
lines of defense. First, the Pakistani woman had to be daring enough to
insist on a timely payment, risking the accumulated debts and the allegedly
"precious" business contact to the United States. Then she had to find the
owner of an e-mail address — the real person — a task that is not easy.
Once she found him, she would have to start litigation against him, which
would require know-how and funding. Last but not least, she had to win

"business model." For this reason it would not come as a surprise if Tom had done this kind of cheating before. This time, however, an "accident" occurred; for one reason or another, the Pakistani woman knew the name of the hospital where the files came from. Otherwise, she would not have stood any chance of contacting anyone relevant in the United States.

The Clerical Worker from Pakistan

Although $500 is a rather modest amount in the everyday business records of a U.S. hospital's management, it constitutes a large sum for a private individual in Karachi. In 2004, the per capita income in Pakistan was around $700 per year. If someone is going to be cheated out of $500, that person might consider aggressive and energetic steps of defense necessary. The clerical worker in Pakistan might not have foreseen the huge implications for the hospital and the considerable public interest that she caused with her threat. Anyway, later she said that she "was the real victim in this case" and she had never truly intended to make the records public; she was just asking for her due payment to pay her debts. At least, that was what she declared afterwards. If she had been aware of the serious consequences of her e-mail she might have considered a less spectacular first step — e.g., writing an e-mail to the hospital in which she explained her situation and asked for help without threatening the hospital. If this first step failed, she still could consider a harsher course of action.

Perhaps some of her colleagues in Karachi were not even able to grasp the reasons behind all the excitement: rich clients in a rich country did not want to pay their debt of $500, which was a substantial sum for Lubna and a small amount for the clients. Anyway, the payment she demanded was next to nothing by comparison. So she "scared them a little" — much ado about nothing, isn't it? This is what some of her colleagues in Karachi might have thought. Anyway, two weeks after all this happened she was still free. This means according to Pakistani law that what she did was not considered a serious crime.

The Patients

Even before this happened, the hospital had a number of security mechanisms in place that were meant to protect confidential patient information. For this reason, the voice files that the clerical worker from Pakistan could

with too much inconvenience. They simply went on with their lives; perhaps some of them have never heard of this case.

10.2 TARGETS OF ESPIONAGE

In this section three targets of espionage are addressed: confidential data, source code, and business secrets. Data is the most systemized and easiest item to protect. Source code and the related technical documentation are more difficult to protect because they have to be handed over to offshore staff who need to work with them. Business know-how has a rather unstructured meaning; even a handwritten page of paper on which an executive outlined a new business idea can be top secret. Background information about the business is usually not considered "secret." Nevertheless, on some narrow markets it can constitute a precious resource that is managed like a secret.

10.2.1 Confidential Data

There are at least two reasons why foreign nationals gain access to confidential data:

1. The data is processed by offshore staff (as in the case study above of the Pakistani clerical worker).
2. Offshore developers have access to a server, for example for maintenance purposes, and this server hosts confidential material.

Below, an anecdote involving a military aircraft manufacturer where this issue was of core importance will be presented. In particular, data in regulated industries (like financial and health services) requires strict confidentiality policies. Data from the military–industrial complex demands even greater consideration because it is subject to export regulations. Violating them can cause high fines, some of them exceeding $10 million. However, even rather common business data, such as contracts and accounting numbers, requires protection lest it be unwarrantedly accessed — e.g., by competitors of the owner.

Throughout the offshore cooperation, disloyal individuals can gain access to confidential data. From the moment when the data reaches the offshore country, it is prone to less strict protection than in industrialized countries because of underdeveloped legal systems and unreliable indi-

offshore scenarios, matters are worse. The hospital already had some lines of defense so that no patient names reached Karachi. Nevertheless, the offshore worker could threaten the hospital and cause considerable public interest. She did not encounter any obstacles in accessing confidential material even though she did not have any special skills or training in breaking data security. She was just a clerical worker, not a whiz hacker. At least in the beginning, she did not even have the intention of gaining access to important business secrets; she entered the offshore cooperation to earn money from transcription.

Many offshore scenarios are even less protected than the hospital in the case study. Quite a number of them do not benefit from any protection at all. What will happen if experts in breaking security perimeters (i.e., spies) enter an offshore scenario from the very beginning with the clear intention to access confidential data? They will find open doors.

The following anecdote provides another example where confidential data constituted a major obstacle to offshore outsourcing.

> An American aircraft manufacturer, a U.S. national defense contractor, resorted to outsourcing to cut costs, to have access to skilled workers, and to make its business processes more efficient. The aircraft manufacturer (we will call it "Mil-Aircraft") was outsourcing extensions of its management information system (MIS) to a well-known onshore provider (we will call it "Global-Tech"). In fact, Global-Tech was a U.S.-based high-tech vendor with global activity and high reputation. It followed a policy of disclosing its intention to use subcontractors to the client. Thus, Global-Tech announced that it intended to enlist the help of an Indian partner for the maintenance of the system.
>
> To some extent Mil-Aircraft welcomed the potential reduction of cost because it felt pushed by its shareholders, who benchmarked its IT cost against that of other Fortune 500 companies — which were not restricted by export regulations and could benefit from the cost reductions of offshore outsourcing. However, Mil-Aircraft was concerned with the security of its data. For technical reasons the software team had to have access to the production server, at least for the time of the project. This server, however, hosted not only sensitive data that was subject to export regulations but also classified infor-

■ Indian nationals could access confidential data hosted on the server.
■ Engineers with the right skills could use the SAP production server as a bridgehead to gain unauthorized access to other areas of Mil-Aircraft's network. Notice that it is easier to intrude into a network once the attacker has access to a system inside the network. An attack from outside is usually more difficult.

To solve these problems, Mil-Aircraft designed a security plan:

1. The first step was to identify which data the Indian engineers were allowed to see. In fact, the server hosted some confidential data. However, there was also much material on the server that was less sensitive and could be accessed by the workers.
2. The confidential material was isolated from the nonconfidential material.
3. Mil-Aircraft installed additional security facilities that ensured that each worker could only access the data he or she was allowed to see. In addition, the company implemented a network security perimeter lest Indian developers should leave the SAP server and gain unauthorized access to other areas of the Mil-Aircraft network.
4. Once this work was finished, the company hired an outside security company to try to break the new system. If this failed, the system would be considered "secure" and Global-Tech and its Indian partners would be allowed to access the production server.

In this example the security problem stemmed from the server being accessed by foreign nationals, not from the actual processing of sensitive data, as in the case of the Pakistani clerical worker who threatened the hospital.

Because a possible attack against Mil-Aircraft had potentially far-reaching consequences, the case caused considerable public interest.

AU7017_book.fm Page 221 Thursday, March 16, 2006 5:07 PM

task of the Indian vendor was finding and correcting faults in the source code of the existing CAD system. In jargon, this is called "debugging." To finish this task, India-Geo was granted access to the complete source code of the CAD system. Source code for such a large system constitutes precious intellectual property; in this case the owner estimated its value at about U.S. $70 million.

The partners had cooperated successfully for six years when one of India-Geo's former employees wrote e-mails to competitors of US-CAD and offered them the source code for the CAD system for a fraction of its real value. US-CAD was lucky: one of the addressees of these e-mails announced to US-CAD that its source code was for sale.

US-CAD informed U.S. authorities, who put together a set-up scenario; an agent traveled to New Delhi and arranged a meeting with the disloyal software engineer (we will call him "Shekhar"). The agent posed as a buyer ready to pay $200,000 for the source code. In a joint action of the American and Indian law enforcement authorities, Shekhar was apprehended and imprisoned.

However, India does not have special laws against theft of intellectual property and trade secrets. For this reason, the prosecutors filed charges under a general civil theft law. Although the situation was crystal-clear, and the police had every piece of evidence needed against Shekhar, the prosecution turned out to be more difficult than expected. One important legal detail was that India-Geo was not the owner of the source code. The company worked with the source code, but the legal owner of the source code was US-CAD. This detail constituted a major obstacle against India-Geo bringing an action against Shekhar. In fact, Shekhar could not steal from India-Geo something that they did not own, and how could something be stolen when the company still has it?

Shekhar was finally granted bail by the court a few weeks after all this happened. When this book was written, the case was still pending. However, the agent who nabbed Shekhar suspects that the odds are good that he will avoid doing prison time. She also said that Shekhar "made two small mistakes

new defense mechanisms in place. The policies for copying source code are much stricter now; in particular, employees are no longer allowed to take source code home and work there.

Ironically, India is among the offshore countries where intellectual property is taken relatively seriously. There are other countries where it is possible to buy cracked shrink-wrap software at a corner in the marketplace.

Source code is the life blood of a software company. Source code not only constitutes a precious investment with a high value; it also includes the company's condensed IT know-how. For this reason source code is usually kept highly confidential. Even in onshore relations, source code is handed out only if an established relationship based on trust exists. It often happens that offshore countries do not have enough laws protecting intellectual property and rarely enforce whatever laws are present. This explains how situations similar to the anecdote above can occur. As time goes by, the offshore countries will enact the necessary laws; this, however, will take time. Until then, customers will try to protect their precious source code by means of civil contracts and by using technical defense perimeters, both of which are not easy.

10.2.2.1   Civil Contracts

In the anecdote above both companies, the U.S. customer and the Indian vendor, were large organizations. This suggests that they had access to qualified legal consultation. Nevertheless, accusing and sentencing the disloyal software developer turned out to be difficult. This incident demonstrates that an outsourcing business requires an excellent business attorney who has insight into the difficult terrain of offshore software projects. Such lawyers, however, are few and far between because there are few precedents and not much material is published, so documentation is scarce.

10.2.2.2   Technical Access Protection

Offshore developers have to access source code because processing it constitutes the very object of their work. More often than not, they even produce it. Source code is an asset that is per se in the hands of the offshore team. This makes source code different from sensitive data;

digital media out of the office. In some cases it might prove rather difficult to enforce this policy, particularly if the developer's computer has access to the Internet (the developer can send source code by e-mail) or if the developer's computer has a CD writer (the developer can burn the code onto a CD and put it in a pocket). Nevertheless, the developer is doing something forbidden and could be caught — a risk that may act as a deterrent. Anyway, these methods require additional support regarding network access and control of the material that leaves the office, which is sometimes not very efficient. Personally, the author has worked on quite a number of sites with access control. However, the author does not remember having his pockets checked when leaving the office.

Another possible idea for protection is that each developer has access to only a small fraction of the source code, the part on which work is currently in progress. If access control is reliable (i.e., cannot be hacked), this step greatly diminishes the risk of losing source code because source code loses most of its value if it is not complete. If a disloyal employee steals only a small fraction (a few modules) of source code, it might be almost worthless, unless these few modules alone feature important technological know-how. It is as if one page of a large encyclopedia were torn out; it will be of no use at all. Either you have all 20 volumes or you have next to nothing.

If each potential thief has access to only a fraction of the source code, stealing the complete source code requires a more advanced level of criminal activity — a conspiracy. It is not as easy as in the anecdote above, where "Shekhar" was officially allowed to take source code with him and work at home.

An important feature of the technical defense is a log-track. All access to protected material (i.e., source code) is recorded. These records are kept for a long time. Even several years later, information about who copied which modules and at what time can be accessed. Systematic collection of data is usually noticeable in the log-track: in the records it looks quite different from accesses generated by legitimate day-by-day business.

In most scenarios, it is wise to keep the implemented lines of defense secret. Almost all technical defense mechanisms can be broken one way or another, and many software developers know how to do this; that is precisely why they are software developers. However, it is rather difficult to break all lines of defense without raising suspicion if the attacker does

even he (the executive) did not know was that all these accesses were carefully recorded in a log-file.

He brought the stolen material to his new organization and included it in their knowledge management system. Meanwhile, his former organization analyzed the log-files, which contained clear traces of systematic data collection. They informed law enforcement authorizations, who were able to provide the necessary evidence of industrial espionage.

The manager's new organization was threatened with litigation and high indemnities, plus legal fees. To avert these consequences, the organization had to agree to a settlement that included a multimillion dollar payment to the manager's former organization.

This anecdote shows that "in-depth defense" occasionally leads to catching the "big fish" of industrial espionage. This is particularly valid if protection mechanisms are concealed — i.e., potential attackers do not know which pitfalls are to be avoided. In this case, the secret log-file provided the necessary evidence.

Nevertheless, all security mechanisms cause inconvenience. If the protection is overly restrictive, even productivity can suffer. For this reason, a balance of priorities is necessary.

10.2.2.3 *Legal Protection of Source Code*

Even if source code takes an illegal route — via industrial espionage — to the hands of a competitor in an industrialized country, the competitor cannot easily use the source code. If the unfair competitor just compiles the source code and sells the software, it is breaking copyright laws in its country. In this way stolen source code is different from a stolen camcorder, for example, which the thief uses or sells as if it were his legitimate property.

Nevertheless, source code and the related technical documentation represent important ideas that a competitor might use to improve its own products. These ideas are not necessarily protected by copyright laws. It is like the case of a math book: it is much easier to write a book on, say, algebra if the author has access to published books on algebra. Writing the math book "from scratch" is much more difficult. In this way, the legitimate owner of the source code loses competitive advantage. How-

espionage activity. The unfair competitor will be accused of industrial espionage. If both companies are located in industrialized countries with stable legal systems, legal action against the thief will probably be successful. In offshore countries, however, awareness regarding confidential source code is instilled into the minds of some developers to a lesser extent, as the following anecdote illustrates.

> An offshore developer copied the source codes of all projects he had developed throughout his career on his private laptop. Whenever he received an invitation for a job interview, he would take some selected projects with him and demonstrate them during the interview as evidence of his professional skills. If the person conducting the interview expressed doubts regarding his actually developing those projects, he would show the source code and explain it.
>
> This software developer did not even feel guilty about this practice. He said that he simply came forward with the projects he had developed, and not the code pertaining to other colleagues. He considered it his right to take pride in his accomplishments and use these projects to get future assignments. It did not cross his mind that the source code constituted the intellectual property of the respective organizations or that he was breaking the law when he disclosed it to third parties.

10.2.3 Business Secrets

> A well-established hospital software provider considered extending his business activity and developing a pharmaceutical database, specialized on hospitals. This kind of application requires detailed knowledge of the country's legislation on drugs and health insurance as well as in-depth background on hospital software. Although there already were some pharmaceutical databases in that country, the market for these specific applications was rather narrow — only a few vendors were active in this business.
>
> The fact that a large vendor with strong software experience and sufficient funding wanted to enter the market would be extremely interesting for competitors. Obviously, the new ven-

This anecdote illustrates how stolen business secrets are more difficult to define than stolen data. If data is stolen from a database — e.g., a medical record of a certain patient — things are rather clear. It is easy to establish whether the stolen item is a data record or a rumor. Stolen data can frequently be traced back. Witnesses are subpoenaed to court. Technical methods, such as a database's access logs, can help clear up cyber crimes. Such facilities help to record who accessed the disclosed data during a particular period of time.

Business secrets have a less definite border. This fact has a number of consequences:

■ A data record can either be "stolen" or not. This is always a clear yes or no situation, and it makes a data record different from a business secret: a business secret can "leak out." First, a competitor picks up a rumor. Then someone asks a carefully prepared question to this or that stakeholder at one or another occasion. The answers are corroborated with published facts. Some rumors can be confirmed; others are refuted. By committing themselves to detective work, competitors might finally obtain a rather clear picture of the business secret.

■ If the business secret leaks out, it might be very difficult to provide any legally valid evidence of criminal activity, espionage, or unauthorized disclosure of business secrets.

■ In legal terms, it might even be difficult to define what exactly the content of the business secret is. Is something still a secret when it is widely known within the customer's organization and when it is officially unveiled to dozens of software engineers? The court might have doubts. Nevertheless, the customer will definitely dislike it if the plans concerning a new software project reach competitors.

This problem can be solved, of course: the customer can explicitly state that everything pertaining to a certain document is "classified." Some contracts even stipulate that "everything" is secret. The author has doubts as to how valid these kinds of provisions are if it comes to litigation because sometimes even the customer itself does not handle the "secret" material with the necessary care. Some customers allow the allegedly secret material to be made widely known within their organizations. In some cases, the customer even publishes parts of the "secret" material

The unclear definition of the term "business secret" and the limited legal evidence cause particular problems if competitors gain access to the vendor's staff by headhunting key personnel, by natural turnover, or by the vendor's company being taken over by a competitor of the customer. In such instances, the customer might be able to prevent the competitor from having access to source code and data. However, it would be difficult to decline access to business secrets. It would be particularly difficult to forestall access to the grey area between business secrets and background information, i.e., information that is not officially a business secret, but that the customer would not want to fall into the "wrong hands."

Protecting this kind of information requires that a whole regime be put in place — something like the system of "classified information" in military projects. The skills required to establish and maintain such a system are beyond the possibilities of most offshore scenarios, not to mention budgets.

10.2.4 General Business Know-How and Domain Expertise

Domain expertise is usually not considered particularly secret because all companies active in a field possess it; thus, at least in legal terms, it is not "secret." Nevertheless, on some narrow markets it might be difficult to acquire this know-how. This obstacle may prevent potential competitors from entering the market.

> A vendor produces software for cameras that are used for surveillance of the production process in glass industries. This business requires a lot of rather specific know-how about optics, electronic cameras, the production processes in glass industries, and how software interacts with these items.
>
> Most of this know-how is published "somewhere"; no part is considered "secret" in a legal sense. Nevertheless, the vendor will handle it as such. In fact, this know-how is difficult to acquire. Finding all the necessary information might turn out to be so expensive that the necessary investment constitutes a prohibitive obstacle for potential competitors who might otherwise enter the market.

Domain expertise and business know-how are very difficult to protect

The other reason emerges from the fact that this kind of know-how is not secret in a legal sense. It is published somewhere, and industry experts in that field share most of it. For this reason, it enjoys very limited legal protection. If litigation takes place, it might turn out that it is not protected at all.

Even if it is usually not considered secret in a legal sense, this know-how can constitute a valuable asset, especially on narrow markets dealing with very specific applications (as in the anecdote above). In some fields of activity, this know-how constitutes a major part of the organization's capital. This raises the question of how the customer in the industrialized country intends to prevent the vendor from turning into a competitor; the vendor has an excellent cost structure (i.e., low salaries), specific and extensive know-how, and insight into the software that is applied to the field. Why does the vendor need the customer anyway? Why can the vendor not carry out its business alone?

The customer might foresee this possibility and forestall it by resorting to contractual provisions that restrict the vendor's attempts to enter the market as a competitor. It is doubtful whether this strategy would be successful. Once the business know-how is in the offshore country, it can be passed along paths that are inscrutable and unexpected from the point of view of the onshore client. To mention just a few possibilities:

■ Employees might leave the vendor's organization and start a business of their own.
■ Developers might have relatives who work in that field or who would consider starting such an activity. In developing countries, loyalty to relatives might be more important than loyalty to the company, even if the company offers good pay and the relatives are distant.
■ Software engineers might be headhunted by an organization that wants to enter that particular business.

After all, one must keep in mind that this kind of know-how is virtually unprotected from a legal point of view. Even if the customer has legally valid evidence showing that a software engineer has given information to, for example, his brother-in-law about the background of the business — even in this unlikely case, chances are that the software engineer will not be accused of having done something illegal.

10.3 POTENTIAL SECURITY VULNERABILITIES IN OFFSHORE SCENARIOS

There are a number of ways for potentially unreliable offshore workers to access confidential information:

- ▪ *The protected data is placed on a server that can be accessed by offshore staff, either foreign engineers who gain access to the server password in an unauthorized way or developers who have legitimate access to the server because they have to carry through maintenance tasks.*

- ▪ *Test data frequently contains information that can be traced back to real persons or real customers. This is true especially if the test data is used in the context of analyzing a reported defect that only occurs in very specific conditions.*

- ▪ *Workers in emerging countries are rather poor and thus more tempted to take up illegal offers. Although many customers have some lines of defense in place against external attacks, the defense against attacks from inside is frequently rather poor. Throughout the offshore cooperation, foreign staff can gain the status of insiders. In this case it may be ridiculously easy for the offshore developer to break the lines of defense that were supposed to protect against "attacks from inside."*

- ▪ *Some offshore vendors subcontract part of the work to other countries where the salaries are even lower — and so is the reliability of workers.*

- ▪ *Another category of unreliable workers is spies in software teams who get employed from the very beginning for the main purpose of stealing confidential information.*

- ▪ *A special kind of espionage strategy is that of "intentional security vulnerabilities" — fragments of code that are included in legitimate software allowing unauthorized access to classified information (e.g., "backdoors" and "Trojan horses").*

- ▪ *Security in emerging countries frequently fails to meet the standards of industrialized nations. Unless the ven-*

> ■ *Vendors who are also working for competitors constitute*
> *a particular danger for confidential information. In*
> *extreme cases, the competitor could even buy the vendor's*
> *organization.*

10.3.1 Server Access

Server Password

In a number of ways, offshore staff can gain access to servers that host
sensitive data:

■ The most obvious way is that the offshore staff officially gains
access to server passwords in the course of the cooperation. They
may really need the password, for example, to do some work on
the server that requires access to it.

■ Another possibility is that the password is widely available and
not very well protected within the customer's onshore site. In this
case, it is quite likely that offshore staff visiting the customer on
a regular basis sooner or later gain access to the server password.
The password is neither stolen nor officially transferred. Perhaps
the offshore engineer sees it written on a small sticky note at the
edge of an onshore operator's screen. In the context of an offshore
cooperation involving countries with limited political stability and
unreliable legal systems, password availability can prove to be
quite risky.

■ Some kinds of activities performed on the server are easier to carry
out if the operator knows the administrator password (in jargon,
called the "root password"). Quite a large part of this work could
be done without full access rights. However, work is easier and
more efficient if the engineer has the administrator password. In
other cases the engineers might not know a solution for the
problem at hand without the root password, although there might
be a solution that the engineer just does not see.

Security systems generally make daily operations more difficult and
cause inconvenience. This increases the likelihood of the root password
sooner or later "finding its way" to the offshore staff, especially if the
offshore staff is responsible for some system administration tasks. This
happens even if the management decided at the beginning of the coop-

forward the password to some offshore colleagues. Perhaps the management will never find out that the password is in the hands off offshore staff, against the corporation's policy.

Server access is particularly dangerous if the server hosts data that is protected by laws — financial or health services data or military information that is subject to export regulations. However, even "common" business secrets can cause damage if they reach the wrong people.

Illegitimate Server Access

Even if the password has never been transferred officially, offshore staff can gain access to sensitive servers illegitimately: they might be able to "crack" the server. The following observations explain how this can happen:

- It is easier to crack a network from the inside than from the outside. An attacker is more likely to be successful with access to at least one computer within the network — a so-called bridgehead. Even if offshore staff is not granted access to the server, they might have access to other computers that are in the same network as the server. These computers can constitute a bridgehead for the attacker.
- It is easier to crack the network if the attacker knows details about the structure of the network and its defense lines. If the customer is outsourcing the entire IT department, the client will not employ much technical staff after the outsourcing relationship is established. In this case the vendor is quite likely to know almost all relevant details about the network. In many cases the provider will even know more about the customer's network than the customer itself does.

Irrespective of how the offshore staff gained their way in to the server, once the attackers have access to the sensitive server, they can read and even modify or delete whatever data they want.

10.3.2 Abuse of Test Data

Access to Sensitive Data during Implementation

Whenever software is implemented and maintained, the developers need data to test the features they are working on. It is often possible to generate "synthetic" test data, and frequently this kind of data is used for the first

infrastructure for keying in data must be provided, or an existing infrastructure must be adapted.

■ It is difficult to generate synthetic datasets that include all details and exceptions belonging to real production data. Usually, software that has been exclusively tested with synthetic data is not fully reliable. If this software runs against production data, new defects are usually discovered. Production data includes special cases that had been left out of the test data, and the software is not tested taking these exceptions into account.

■ Misunderstandings between the project team and the users might occur. The project team implements the software as they envision it. However, users may expect something different. If synthetic test data is provided, the project team is usually responsible for producing it — because providing the test data is part of their job and is paid for from the project budget. Thus it is rather likely that the test data includes the same misunderstandings as the actual implementation. Real production data, however, should reveal these misunderstandings.

For these reasons, in many projects the software team has access to production data. Security experts advise against this practice. In real software projects, however, it is quite widespread. In some cases the data is somehow made "anonymous"; the names of real patients or real customers are replaced by fictitious names — the so-called dummies. This method is already a big step towards protection of the real data. In some cases, however, it might not be enough:

■ The clerical worker from Pakistan who processed medical voice files only had access to this kind of anonymous data. Nevertheless, she threatened the hospital and created a scandal of considerable public interest.

■ The step of making the data anonymous might not have been fully successful. The data might still include some "traitorous" fragments that can be combined and used in an unexpected way. Hence, the data may still be traced back to real persons and customers in a way that is not apparent to the people who tried to make the data anonymous. The following fictitious example explains how it can be unexpectedly difficult to make a database anonymous.

All data pertaining to a fictitious insurance company is based

ID. However, the person who obtains the information does not know to which person this client's ID belongs. At least, so it seemed to those who tried to make the database anonymous.

The database also includes a file with all letters from customers. These letters are scanned and saved completely, and many include the name and address of the customer. Frequently, the letters refer also to the client's internal ID and to an insurance case. A potential hacker can link a client's name and internal ID from these letters. Thus, it is possible to break the anonymity.

Even if the data does not contain such hidden relationships that offer the possibility of tracing them back, there might be other ways of breaking the anonymity by combining the data with other, apparently innocent, information from sources outside the database. Two fictitious examples show how this can happen:

A provider of financial services makes its data anonymous by deleting the name, address, and birth date of each client. An attacker knows that a client drew money from a certain ATM at 12:15 on November 7. This information might be enough to retrieve this client's entire record because only one person accessed this ATM at the given time.

Data from a healthcare provider has been made anonymous by deleting the names and addresses of patients and doctors. Somebody knows that a certain person has broken his right leg on August 12 and has been treated for flu in the week after Christmas. It is rather likely that the database contains only one patient for whom this data fits. This way, the patient's full medical record can be retrieved.

The examples above show that it might be more difficult than expected to make a database really anonymous and secure it against a well-prepared, determined attack.

Access to Test Data during Maintenance

So far we have analyzed the problem of test data for software that is in

- Maintenance engineers at the user's site

    Most faults can be solved at the developer's site based on the error report. Experience shows, however, that there remains a small fraction of errors that requires an engineer to travel to the user's site and analyze the problem there. Such is the case with defects that only appear on a certain computer or only with a certain data set. The maintenance engineer at the user's site frequently has at least partial access to the user's database, which may constitute a security vulnerability.

- Maintenance channels

    If users and developers are separated by large geographical distances, or if the project has a small budget, these maintenance trips can be too costly. Consequently, the partners might agree to establish a protected channel that enables the engineers to solve a problem by using remote access and thus avoiding expensive business trips. Such maintenance channels open a big gate to disloyal maintenance engineers' unauthorized access to sensitive data.

- Automatically generated error reports

    Some software products generate an automatic error report. This report includes all the necessary information that maintenance engineers need to analyze the problem. In fact this kind of error report is very comfortable for both sides — users and software team. The users simply have to send an e-mail with an automatically prepared attachment. The engineers get a perfect error report containing all the necessary information. However, this kind of error report might include real production data. There are some classes of errors where this method can barely be avoided. For some types of so-called nondeterministic errors (which occur only sometimes — not always) this might be the only solution. However, owners of sensitive data have to carefully evaluate the advantages and risks of this approach.

Watertight Protection of Test Data Is Difficult

Thus, it is not easy to prevent developers from having any access to "real" production data for test purposes. In some cases, this means that a carefully prepared infrastructure needs to be established.

Organizations that are responsible for sensitive data have to decide

to maintain it, and to ensure its reliability in the long run. Notice that a protection system that includes security vulnerabilities is even worse than no protection system at all because it gives the users a false impression of security.

10.3.3   Reliability of Security Systems

Software Developers Know Numerous Vulnerabilities of Security Systems

Some people like to find out secrets. Many of them are in elementary school. Quite a few, however, are older.

The customer should not underestimate the skills of the developers: many developers know more about software and IT security than most of their clients do. What is more, some younger software developers know a great deal about security vulnerabilities and so-called exploits of various systems. They keep it up as a kind of hobby even if they do not use their know-how in a contraventional way. It is like collecting stamps: the philatelist has no intention of using the collected stamps for letters. Nevertheless, an IT engineer who maintains an interest in exploits for a while is rather likely to be able to break a security system if a desire to do so arises.

Tens of thousands of security vulnerabilities are published in books and on the Internet. Tools can be readily downloaded from the Internet to exploit these vulnerabilities. Vendors of standard software publish so-called "patches" and "service packs," which are resistant against these known vulnerabilities. However, if there is software on the network that is older than, say, a few months, it is quite likely that this software contains known vulnerabilities. By investing only a few days' time, an interested high school student can learn enough to exploit it (e.g., by reading a book like *Hacking Exposed* or studying the published material on the Internet).

Security Systems Are Unpopular among Software Engineers

Security systems for data protection are quite bothersome for the staff that has to work with them. Managers are frequently not aware of this fact. It is not just a matter of loss of time due to these forms of protection — say, 20 × 3 minutes = 1 hour per working day. The organization pays for

IT work is frequently difficult and demanding enough, especially when the team is pressed for time (which is almost always the case). In many situations, the security system makes the work even more difficult. This contributes to the unpopularity of security systems that limit the access of the software engineer within certain developers' groups. Some developers might think that access control is unjustified and makes their already rather hard work even more difficult. Particularly when the project falls behind schedule and the developers have to work long hours, perhaps at night and during the weekend, it may happen that passwords are forwarded between colleagues without the knowledge or agreement of the responsible management. For this reason, it might be reasonable to invest some political work into convincing the software team to reach a broad consensus concerning the necessity of access control.

Reliability of the Customer's Security System

Many customers do not have any mature security concept against a determined attack from insiders. An *inside attack* means that an employee of the customer or someone who has legitimate access to at least one computer of the customer's network wants to attack the customer. The term "determined" indicates that the attacker has advanced skills regarding security vulnerabilities. In the rare cases where the customer has a security system against insiders at all, the defense lines are ridiculously easy to break. Nevertheless, so far many customers have not encountered problems with attacks from the inside.

Part of the basis of this observation is that industrialized nations have a rather mature legal system and onshore employees are not bitterly poor. For this reason they are usually unwilling to take the risks of engaging in criminal actions. They do not want to risk their personal and professional futures for a limited amount of money by stealing business secrets — the money they might get if a swindle turns out well.

As soon as a customer inaugurates an offshore relationship and staff from emerging countries enter the scene, a completely new situation has to be considered. Throughout the cooperation, some members of the offshore team can gain a trusted status "like in-house employees." They have the same access to the network as the in-house team does. In some cases this means that they enjoy a rather unrestricted access. From the technical point of view and for the sake of an easier workflow, this status might be more than justified. Nevertheless, they are foreigners. As soon

10.3.4 Unreliable Workers

> A study was conducted at a university concerning which librar-
> ies reported the most stolen books. The results: theology and
> law. Engineering was ranked among the most honest departments.

Confidential Material in Poor Countries

In general, software engineers are rather honest folks. However, rotten
apples are to be found everywhere. Some offshore developers might be
in a difficult economic situation and might be tempted to solve their
problems by stealing customer intellectual property (IP). The value of
confidential material is very high in comparison to their salaries. The
money that can be earned by stealing intellectual property can be far
beyond the legal income that software developers can earn in a bitterly
poor country during their entire careers. A few thousand U.S. dollars is
a huge amount of money to them. For this reason, they might be vulnerable
to disloyal offers.

Low Awareness of Intellectual Property Criminality

Persons with different cultural backgrounds may have different outlooks
on business secrets and intellectual property — which are sometimes
difficult for the onshore management to understand. "Intellectual property"
is a rather new term for many developing countries. In some offshore
countries, stealing intellectual property has not been considered a serious
crime so far. Perhaps only persons who worked with a publisher had
even known that there is such a thing as intellectual property. For this
reason, the perception of "crimes" related to intellectual property is not
very deeply rooted in the culture of some offshore countries. This applies
especially to owners of the intellectual property who are not individuals
but organizations — organizations that earn so much money that it is
beyond the imagination of most inhabitants of developing countries. The
owners of such organizations are in turn organizations. This gives "crimes"
regarding intellectual property a degree of abstraction in the minds of
certain offshore citizens: "What has been stolen anyway if they still have
their source code? And who has lost something — i.e., who exactly is
now poorer than before?"

So far only few cases of espionage have been reported. However,

Reliability of Subcontractors

It often happens that offshore vendors maintain their own network of freelancers — casual workers, students, and experts with special knowledge of a certain technology. This network helps them solve specific technical problems, cover peaks of high demand on the work force, and reduce costs. In many cases, these relationships are not based on something equivalent to a contract. Nevertheless, these freelancers might have access to confidential material. It might well happen that a CD with precious source code is left unprotected on a desk in a four-bed room in a students' dorm because one of the four roommates has a summer job with an outsourcing vendor.

In most cases the subcontractor is smaller and less reliable than the primary vendor is. Subcontractors might lack reliable staff, tight screening of human resources, well-protected networks, and access control to office buildings even if the vendor has these measures in place; thus, the customer is lulled into a false sense of security. A potential attacker might consider it easier to attack the subcontractor and access the confidential material than to attack the primary vendor. A chain is only as strong as its weakest link.

The importance of subcontractors for the security concept depends on the level of the subcontractor's contribution to the projects. One extreme is that the subcontractor makes only some marginal contributions and does routine work, thus not having access to confidential material. In this case, the danger from the subcontractor is rather limited. The other extreme is that the subcontractor does almost all the work. The customer's direct partner does little more than forward e-mails and write invoices. In this case, the subcontractor's reliability requires careful analysis. However, the customer might not even know of the existence of subcontractors. The customer might think that all the work is done in the office of its partner, the primary offshore vendor.

In such a scenario the customer may not know who has access to confidential material. The subcontractors might be quite illegal — even if the primary vendor looks rather reliable. This is why most organizations that are responsible for confidential material exclude from their contracts the possibility that their outsourcing vendors subcontract work to other partners, hoping that their far-away partner will observe this contract provision.

is outsourced to a provider in another country. For example: a large IT vendor in India might subcontract work to Vietnam or China, where the prices are even cheaper than in India. In this case the assessment of the situation is even more difficult because the laws of more countries are involved. In addition, the reliability of the subcontractor and the legal system of its country might be even lower.

10.3.5 Well-Prepared Attacks

Spies in Software Teams

In the few published cases where offshore staff was reported to have stolen confidential material, the workers did not enter the organization with the intention to do so. They were employed to develop software or to transcribe voice files, so in the beginning they wanted to earn good, honest money. They ended up stealing the material because it was easy to steal it, because the legal situation in their country was foggy in this respect, and because the risk was low and the prospective profits high. They were not professional spies getting employed to steal confidential material; rather, they were a sort of "casual spies." From the point of view of professional spies, their actions were just dilettantism:

- They did not consider legal advice before getting involved in this action. They did not build up lines of defense in case they were caught, but even without legal advice a number of them could not be prosecuted.
- They did not have a backup organization to forward the stolen material to its final destination in roundabout ways. They did not have well-established contacts to circles of organized crime, which were to receive the confidential data. They did not even make special efforts to cover up their traces: actually they even made the fact that they had some confidential material public and sent unsolicited e-mails to potential buyers. Even so, they were caught only by accident.
- They did not have special skills in security systems or in breaking them. They were mere workers, not hackers. No special training or particular efforts were necessary to access the confidential material; they just took a CD that somebody put on their desk or downloaded their e-mail. Despite this limited effort, they obtained

benefited from professional training on how to break security systems and would have secretly forwarded the stolen material.

The author is not aware of published cases of professional spies attacking an offshore cooperation. The case studies show that even "amateur spies" are hardly ever captured and sent to court. It is hard to conceive of a scenario where a professional spy is caught and finally sentenced. For this reason, the author could imagine that there are a number of undiscovered cases.

Intentional Security Vulnerabilities

The following fictitious example illustrates the concept of intentional security vulnerabilities.

> A company orders a business information system to provide their executives with the necessary data. The system should be accessible via the Internet to support managers who are not on location and for those who have to take business trips. For testing purposes, the software team uses a database with fictitious data — i.e., a synthetic database without any relation to the real situation. After work is finished the database is filled in with real data. From this moment on, the developers do not have access to the database any longer because their passwords are no longer valid.
>
> A disloyal engineer develops code for the password system. This code should allow access to the database only if a correct password is provided. However, the engineer develops the code in a way that access is allowed either if a correct password is provided or if someone uses the password "t?z55&c$8k9H" This "hard-to-guess" password is known only by the developer. In this way a backdoor is installed, allowing the engineer unauthorized access to the database. Whenever he wants he can connect to the system via the Internet and use his secret password to access confidential information, even after the real business data has been introduced.

In real-life situations, security vulnerabilities — like Trojan horses — are usually much more involved, technically speaking. Nevertheless, this fictitious example pinpoints the core idea of intentional security weak-

access to source code. In this case, the customer hardly has any possibility at all to find out whether the software contains intentional security vulnerabilities. Even if customers have access to source code, this helps them only if they have the necessary skills to understand the source code and are willing to invest time and effort in analyzing it.

"Malignant" (i.e., illegal) code in software projects is not a problem specific to offshore outsourcing. Even if the software is developed in house, it might contain such security problems. What is more, software that was "clean" at the time of installation can get "infected" in time — e.g., by "Trojan horses" or "backdoors." In industrialized countries, introducing intentional security vulnerabilities into software projects would be considered a serious offense and would entail corresponding legal consequences. In emerging countries, it might prove difficult to accuse and sentence those responsible, not to mention the challenging problems of obtaining adequate compensation after the offender has been sentenced; the offender may not have enough assets.

10.3.6 Attacks against the Vendor

So far we have analyzed security breaches for which the vendor or its subcontractors could be made accountable. In addition to this possibility, the vendor can be attacked from outside without the knowledge or contribution of any of the vendor's employees.

Access to Office Building

Unless the vendor ensures permanent surveillance of its office, it is quite possible that the building can be broken into. The burglars are most likely to steal only hardware and other valuable equipment. However, there is some risk that the thieves maintain the necessary contacts to criminal circles and try to sell the confidential material found on the hard disks as well.

The possibility of criminal attacks also exists in industrialized countries, of course. Offshore vendors, however, usually work on tight budgets. For this reason, it might be tempting to save some expenses for network protection and surveillance of the office building.

The Vendor Also Works for Competitors

In an extreme case one of the customer's competitors might manage to take over the vendor. In this case the vendor has broad access to key staff and documentation.

10.3.7 Network Security

An obvious security problem is caused by the vendor's networks because they can be attacked from outside. Hence, it is advisable that the client send someone to inspect the networks.

There are plenty of published anecdotes about systems and networks that have been attacked. I have selected two that shed an interesting light on various issues. They show how difficult it is to protect a network against hackers, to provide legal evidence against the attackers, and finally to ensure that they are sentenced for what they have done.

> Two Russian hackers (both 21 years old) evaded the networks of a prestigious U.S. institution and stole tens of thousands of credit card numbers. When they started abusing this data for fraudulent transactions, U.S. law enforcement authorities analyzed the case. By studying log-files and other digital resources from various Internet Service Providers (ISPs), the authorities could identify these persons. Because they were Russian citizens who were living and acting outside the borders of the United States, American laws were hardly enforceable in this case. So the authorities used a trick to lure them into the United States; they started a bogus company that had the sole purpose of promising these hackers an attractive consulting contract. So the hackers came to California to interview and negotiate. However, on the computer that they used to demonstrate their skills, a certain software had been installed that can be used to spy passwords (a so-called "keyboard locker") without the knowledge of the hackers, of course. Using this software, the authorities found out the passwords and used them to break into the hackers' systems at home in Russia. In this way, they could gather the necessary evidence and bring an action against the attackers.
>
> Later, Russian authorities complained about the practices of the American police and said the Russian citizens had been hacked themselves; only Russian authorities were allowed to

■ This all happened to renewed, prestigious organizations.

They have access to a lot of resources — many excellent people who know a lot about network security. At least their security budget is far larger than most companies'. If they could not make their networks safe against hackers, what about "usual" companies? The author does not want to speculate how the situation would have evolved if this had happened to a small offshore IT provider. Would the company have ever found out that there was an attack at all?

■ The hackers were 21 years old.

How many years' experience do they have in this business? If the years in primary school and early teenage time are not fully counted, only a short period of experience remains. This means a talented individual can arrive in only a few years' autodidactic training at a level that makes it possible to hack virtually every network in the world.

■ It was difficult to find out who the hackers were.

The American police had to analyze resources at various ISPs to trace back the attack to these persons. This step requires a number of prerequisites:

– These resources must exist at all.

That is, the ISP must have such records. One reason can be that they are legally obliged to keep such records. The author is not sure which developing countries have mature enough legislation that the existence of such records can be taken for granted.

– The traces back to the attackers must still exist at the time the police are searching for them.

Modern networks have high speed, and one hour is a rather long time when speaking about networks. In this time an incredible amount of traffic might have passed the network. Thus, deciding which data is recorded on a permanent basis requires strict parsimony. The crucial detail that is later needed to identify the attackers might have already been deleted.

It is like finding a counterfeit bill in the cash desk of a large supermarket; it is virtually impossible to trace back who used this counterfeit bill for payment unless the teller notices that something is wrong immediately after receiving the money.

suspect an intruder in their networks. They might fear unwanted publicity regarding the safety of their systems. In other cases the police might discover other data on their networks that gets the company into trouble — e.g., regarding taxes.

■ It was difficult to bring an action against the attackers even after they were identified.

In this case the police applied the trick with the bogus company that allegedly asked for consultancy to lure the hackers into the United States — a method reminiscent of a James Bond movie. This time, the trick was successful. Meanwhile, however, other hackers have heard of the case and analyzed it and are carefully considering ways to forestall such police actions in the future.

■ Russian authorities complained about these practices.

The author is not a specialist in international crime investigations. However, this very fact indicates that the U.S. police might have worked at the borderline of international laws.

In the anecdote above, powerful U.S. authorities made substantial efforts to identify and prosecute the attackers. The situation was serious enough, and perhaps the police wanted to set a warning example, which acts as a deterrent for other hackers and destroys their confidence that they can crack any system they want without being caught. Finally, with a bit of good luck, the attackers were sentenced. In other cases, however, things have turned out less favorably, as the following anecdote shows.

An American citizen, let us call him "Mike," made a financial transaction worth $80,000 using the Internet. After a few days his bank reported another transaction that practically zeroed his investment. He complained at the bank that he never made this second transaction; he said he was sleeping at the time it was made. His statement sounded plausible; after all, why should he make a transaction that zeroed his investment? The bank, however, responded that the transaction was made using the correct password and was hence valid. Mike employed a consultant to look into the situation. The consultant found traces of so-called spyware — i.e., malignant code that can be used to hack passwords — on Mike's computer. It seems that Mike was right: an intruder had stolen his password and made a

system, without Bill knowing about it. This way the attacker remained unidentified and Mike not only lost his money but also had to pay for the consultant.

This case shows how difficult it might be to identify an attacker.

In many cases it is possible to trace back an attack while the attack is carried through. It requires the cooperation of the ISPs all the way back to the attacker; each ISP reports from where it obtained the malignant traffic. This way the forensic analysis works backwards towards the attacker and might finally identify that person.

It is also possible to trace back the attack after it has happened, although it is more difficult. This approach is most likely to be successful if the attacker uses a similar pattern again and again. It is like studying a rare bird; you saw the bird once on a certain tree. Then you install a camera near this tree hoping the bird will come again. Installing more and more cameras, you finally might find the bird's nest.

It is extremely difficult to trace back a past attack when the attacker uses the pattern only once (or very rarely). Back to the analogy of the rare bird; it is like studying its habits when the only evidence about the bird is some half-rotten fragments of an old nest.

Frequently, attackers use so-called "reflection sites" to "launder the connection." A reflection site is a vulnerable system that is not perfectly protected; in the anecdote, Bill's system was a reflection site. Usually, the owner of the reflection site does not know that his system is being abused and is also a victim. The attacker installs malignant software on the compromised reflection site and covers the traces of this action. Now the conquered system can be used to attack other sites, leaving very limited traces back to the attacker.

A reflection site is somewhat similar to a stolen car that has been used to commit a crime. The police might find the car and identify the owner. However, the legitimate owner will provide evidence of having nothing to do with the crime.

It is possible to trace back an attack even from a reflection site, although it is far from easy; it requires that an expert have access to that system. These experts usually ask fees of around $200 per hour. In addition, it implies getting permission from the compromised system's owner (in the anecdote, Bill's permission). Even in this case, the trace will lead most likely to another reflection site.

this specific computer in a Russian Internet café on a specific Thursday evening? An organization such as the U.S. Central Intelligence Agency (CIA) might know what is to be done in this case, but the author does not.

Even in the very lucky case that the attacker is identified, the evidence must be legally valid to be considered in court. We all know from our experience as TV viewers how it looks when the police arrive at a crime scene. A few hairs that they might find are sealed in plastic film and carefully labeled with a number. Later, the evidence is brought to a protected place, monitoring when and for what reasons access was granted to whom.

A police officer who knows his business also knows all this and thus will not make any mistakes in this regard. System administrators, however, rarely undergo training at institutions such as the Federal Bureau of Investigation (FBI). They know about versions of operating systems, network cables, and the like, not about evidence that may or may not be legally valid. Thus it is quite likely that the administrator might make mistakes that destroy the legal validity of the evidence.

The defending counsel will probably carefully analyze exactly what happened with the "evidence" in the minutes and hours after the incident; perhaps the computer was unsupervised for a few hours, or people had access to the computer without being supervised. Is the "evidence" still valid in this case? Perhaps the computer was switched off and on again. Notice that rebooting changes numerous files on the hard disk and changes the contents of the memory cells, which are also part of the evidence, of course.

In the anecdote above the counsel for the defense might say, "Well, it seems that Mike performed a very risky financial transaction. When he became aware of the stupid thing he had done he looked for a scapegoat to blame. So he installed some spyware on his own computer, pretending he has been hacked."

This is what the counsel might say after the attacker has been identified, captured, and charged. Notice that each of these steps constitutes a challenge in itself.

10.4 DEFENSE AGAINST ESPIONAGE

Careful preparation of lines of defense and tight monitoring of human resources can greatly improve the security of confidential material. Another important solution is severe punishment

AU7017_book.fm Page 247 Thursday, March 16, 2006 5:07 PM

10.4.1 Tight Screening of Human Resources

Many computer scientists are honest employees. They want to earn their money by developing quality software, not by stealing intellectual property. In addition, most of them do not maintain the necessary contacts to criminal circles to forward stolen intellectual property to its final destination. However, there are exceptions. To some extent it is possible to "guess" which employee constitutes a particular risk for the organization's security and which does not. Some guidelines may help:

- Employees who have stayed with the company for many years are rarely involved in disloyal actions. This is an additional reason for having a closer look at the vendor's retention rate — i.e., how high is the percentage of employees who have already worked for a long time within the company.
- Another risk emerging from high attrition of staff is the fact that even a short contact with confidential material can be long enough to steal it. The higher the attrition rate, the more people are in contact with the protected data.
- A particular risk comes from individuals who have a high need for money — e.g., because of alcohol addiction or other substance abuse. Such persons need far more money than can be earned by a usual job. They will look for other sources of income.
- Persons who express excessive dissatisfaction with their working condition in the organization may also present a high risk. They might think that the "real value" of their work is much higher than the "few bucks" they get. Perhaps they feel the "moral right" to compensate for the difference. Remarks such as "They owe me a lot" should be taken seriously, and their implications should be evaluated.
- There might be disgruntled employees in the company who feel they have reasons for revenge, whether justified or unjustified. Frequently, these individuals do not want to earn money by selling stolen intellectual property, but they want to cause damage. They can be even more dangerous than those who are stealing for financial reasons. Making confidential material public is a particularly good way to take revenge because it usually causes high damages.
- People who have a low degree of morality as far as the distinction

■ Frequently, people who steal intellectual property or engage in other disloyal actions avoid usual office hours and prefer to work at night or during weekends. This observation, however, is prone to debate; most people are very busy, and IT jobs are infamous for their long hours' work. If the project reaches a crisis, they have to work even at night or on weekends. Nevertheless, some employees seem to prefer working during the hours when the "office is less crowded."

All these listed items are mere hints that might justify further investigation. There can be quite a number of perfectly legitimate reasons why somebody would rather shift working hours from the normal schedule to the later part of the day. This person might have children to look after and does not have an option. In some cases, however, it might be justified to have a closer look at the situation. A (secret) transaction log of all accesses of that person to confidential material might be advisable. Another possibility could be to trace all activities within the network during the night, if such steps are compliant with the country's privacy laws.

10.4.2 Understanding of the Legal Systems

The case studies above have shown that it might turn out to be quite difficult to bring an action against an offender in developing countries. A situation where the offender cannot be sentenced even under the optimum conditions where the law enforcement authorities had all possible evidence does not act at all like a deterrent. On the contrary: it is an invitation to behave in a disloyal manner.

To some extent the problem comes from the underdeveloped legal system in developing countries. Another important reason, however, is the complicated legal situation of international business, where the very different legal systems of two or more countries are involved. If the offshore scenario wants to achieve a certain degree of security against espionage, the companies have to provide sufficient deterrence for spies. A well-known deterrence against all kind of criminal behavior is a high risk that the offender will be captured and a reliable legal ground for litigation will exist. For this reason, the responsible managers should consider the following steps:

- Analyze carefully whether the vendor should be allowed further subcontracting.
- The contract should make the offshore vendor responsible for the actions of its employees, freelancers, and subcontractors.
- The contract should include a choice of the controlling law, jurisdiction, and venue — if possible, the legal system in the industrialized country.
- Ensure that the vendor has enough assets in case the vendor has to pay indemnities. These assets have to be within the reach of the court that decides for the indemnities.

10.4.3 Analysis of the Risks

The customer has to analyze which risks its organization can afford and which risks it is willing to take. Not in all offshore scenarios will each of the risks explained above occur. Regulated industries like health care and financial services need higher protection of their data than, say, production of consumer cameras. It is important to be aware of all potential risks, of the available measures to be taken against these risks, and about the residual risks that cannot be avoided in the envisioned offshore scenario.

The risks and the costs for managing them have to be compared against the advantages of the offshore cooperation. The cost advantages might be so compelling that the partners decide to enter an offshore scenario despite significant risks. For example, the CAD producer in one of the case studies above decided to continue the offshore cooperation even though the company had almost lost its source code. However, there might be other scenarios where a careful analysis shows that the advantages of the offshore cooperation do not justify the risks. Military projects, for example, enjoy the highest degree of protection because of export regulation laws and because espionage in such projects endangers national security. Usually, such projects cannot be outsourced to developing countries.

11

TERMINATION OF THE OUTSOURCING RELATIONSHIP

ABSTRACT

Only a few outsourcing scenarios continue indefinitely. All others end sooner or later; they are limited to one or more projects, or they are designed for a certain period of cooperation. The customer should retain the ability to terminate the relationship with the vendor and continue its business with another provider or bring the services back in house. This step requires access to key personnel and to technical material such as source code and documentation. Contractual provisions are important, of course. Experience shows, however, that contractual provisions alone are not enough to meet the requirement of business continuity after finishing the outsourcing relationship. The exit plan must also include careful management of in-house know-how and practical business decisions, e.g., maintaining leadership in essential business relationships.

These conditions seem obvious; nevertheless, they cannot always be taken for granted in practice. In many outsourcing relationships, the customer's dependency on the vendor constantly grows until it reaches an extent where the customer cannot go on anymore without the vendor. In this case the customer cannot easily escape this binding relationship — even if it is not necessarily legally binding and the contract includes provisions for termination of the cooperation.

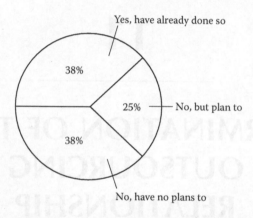

Figure 11.1 In May 2005, www.cio.com conducted a poll among its readership regarding services that have been brought back in house in the last year.

If the buyer is not really in a position to end the relationship, this vulnerability might turn to its disadvantage in time; the vendor might change its pricing strategy or decrease its service level.

A recent poll shows that it is anything but rare that IT services have to be brought back in house (see Figure 11.1).

11.1 CONTRACTUAL STIPULATIONS

Most contracts allow termination due to breach of material obligation. Termination for convenience allows the customer to end the contract without any reason whatsoever, paying a fee agreed upon in advance. Some contracts include other reasons for termination — e.g., in case of insolvency or if the vendor leaves the business. Contractual provisions are important if the customer wants to terminate the contract. Additional practical preparations, however, are necessary to provide business continuity.

11.1.1 Termination for Cause

Most outsourcing contracts stipulate the possibility of termination of the contract "for cause" — i.e., breach of material obligations:

■ *Persistent failure to meet critical service levels.* In most cases the

- *Payment failure.* Because the customer will have to put up with discomfort, risks, and high costs when switching to another vendor, restricting the vendor's rights regarding contractual termination is indicated. For example, termination might be allowed only in the case of sustained failure to pay agreed-on sums.

11.1.2 Termination for Convenience

If the customer outsources the entire IT department, the contract should include a provision regarding cancellation of the contract without legal motivation. In some situations this step might be necessary:

- The customer might be discontented with the provider's service level. However, it may want to avoid the bureaucratic process of filing a suit against the provider and bringing evidence to court to substantiate its accusations about its partner's failure to meet the required service level.
- New and unexpected situations may require much less or completely different IT services, which are better provided by another vendor.
- The client's company might merge with another organization, which may enlist the services of a different provider. The joint organization is faced with two outsourcers and so, for the sake of efficiency or for contractual reasons, it could be necessary to discontinue working with one of them.
- The customer might merge with an IT service provider that delivers the same quality and efficiency as the outsourcer. Why pay an external vendor?

These examples include cases where the contract was bound to be terminated even if the vendor was doing an excellent job. The customer usually has to pay a substantial fee to the vendor — the so-called "early termination fee" — when the contract is cancelled, as compensation for the investment the vendor has made in the outsourcing relationship.

In some cases the outsourcing relationship can become very unbalanced through the years, quite often to the advantage of the vendor. In other cases the relationship might have been unbalanced from the very beginning, but the customer only gradually becomes aware of this. In

of material obligations." This task can turn out to be difficult because vendors avoid breaching advantageous contracts. In practice, termination for convenience is frequently the only effective way out of the deal.

Hence, smart buyers pay attention to a carefully negotiated termination clause, especially to a reasonable early termination fee. Although vendors usually agree to "termination for convenience," the fee is a subject of hard negotiations. If the fee is very high, termination for convenience is strongly discouraged or even impossible.

In some scenarios the customer is charged with a fee equaling all the profits estimated for the whole remaining contractual period. Such is the case if the contract does not include a termination-for-convenience clause but the customer has to terminate the contract for strong reasons — e.g., changing business facts. Other cases of unduly high early termination fees occur in scenarios where the vendor had drafted the contract and the customer was not aware of the strategic importance of the termination-for-convenience clause.

A reasonable early termination fee could be calculated from the vendor's unamortized investment plus the pro rata profit — i.e., the service provider is offered as compensation a sum covering its costs and receives the profits for the time it worked, but the customer is not forced to pay the vendor's estimated lost profits. The vendor's investments for setting up the relationship are usually made in the beginning and are amortized over the entire term of the contract. For this reason, the early termination fee declines over the term.

11.1.3   Other Termination Conditions

The partners may consider additional provisions that permit early termination of the contract without paying any fee. These conditions include:

■ *Insolvency or bankruptcy.* If the solvency of the vendor's business is in serious danger, the customer might rightfully worry whether the service provision will have the necessary continuity. Unfortunately, it might be too late for a smooth transfer to another vendor when the current provider is already insolvent. For this reason some customers negotiate earlier indicators that allow termination for lack of business stability — e.g., deterioration in credit rating. Other contracts couple this termination clause with strong audit

insolvency or bankruptcy. Thus, the vendor finds itself in a vicious circle.

■ *Important changes in the control of the vendor's organization.* For example, the vendor leaves the business.
■ *War or disaster.* The author can hardly imagine how Indian vendors could ensure business continuity if India goes to war with Pakistan, for example.

Some customers negotiate a tailor-made exit clause for their specific business. Drafting such clauses, however, requires an experienced business attorney because they are unique, situation-adapted documents.

11.1.4 Importance of Contractual Provisions

Switching the IT services to another provider constitutes a complex business transaction that involves a number of challenging management tasks. The customer has to design the plan for exiting the contract years before this can actually happen — maybe even from the onset of the relationship. At this time, all assets that will be needed to put the plan into action have to be specified and included in the contract. This plan will be untried until the "emergency case" occurs — i.e., the termination of the contract. Some practitioners consider it unlikely that an untried plan for complex management tasks will be successful right away, especially if an important participant in the plan — the dismissed service provider — does its best to make the plan fail.

So far, few successful stories where a customer switched to another vendor have been published. A number of suggestions and sample contract clauses are available. Many of them, however, have not passed the acid test of practical application. The most frequent criterion for success in such situations is if the customer could switch to another IT provider without risking its entire business solvency. It is just as in sports; successful cases of athletes who can run very fast are publicized. However, when doctors speak about cancer operations they do not mention how fast the patient can run after the operation. It is already a big success if the patient survived. Starting the offshore scenario is like the sports event; terminating it is more like the cancer operation.

Given these risks, the contract should include a well-prepared exit plan. Without a well-drafted contract, the customer is lacking even the

11.2 VENDORS FORESTALL THE DEPARTURE OF A CUSTOMER

The vendor has good reasons to build up a strong position with the customer and thus increase the customer's dependency on its services:

- *The vendor wants to receive additional orders from that customer in the future.*
- *The vendor tries to keep the client away from potential competitors. During the time of the contract, the vendor will take measures so that the customer can switch to another provider after the contract is finished only with considerable difficulty.*
- *The outsourcer might want to increase the margins of the services provided for that customer. The buyer, on the other hand, faces a number of obstacles when it wants to switch from one vendor to a competitor. These obstacles help the provider consolidate its position with this client.*

11.2.1 An Introductory Case Study

A customer asked for an offer for a new software project that was of strategic importance for its organization. One vendor made a surprisingly cheap offer. Because everything seemed to be all right with this vendor, the customer accepted the offer. The customer's management had only superficial background know-how about software technology and no experience with software outsourcing. However, they knew that the source code and some technical documentation would be needed if another team had to continue the project. For this reason, the contract included the obligation that the vendor has to deliver these products.

The vendor did what it was asked for, and the project was finished successfully. However, even before the first version was installed, the customer discovered that major extensions would be needed; some functions had simply been forgotten. Other features had been deliberately delayed for later versions. So far the customer was satisfied with the vendor. For this

and the technical documentation was entirely useless. Consequently, they refused to offer assistance for the extensions. What
had gone wrong?

The promotional cheap price of the first version was not
cost-covering. From the very beginning, the vendor had foreseen that there would be extensions. The vendor expected to
make profits only with these extensions. The vendor's management knew that the customer could not simply cancel this
project of strategic importance. They only had to take care that
no other vendor could qualify as a competitor for the orders
regarding the extensions.

If a competitor wanted to continue the project, they would
need source code and technical documentation. The contract
stipulated that source code had to be delivered. However, other
important project files existed as well. From a purely legal point
of view, these other project files are not "source code." For this
reason, the vendor was not obliged to disclose them to the
customer. Nevertheless, they were of crucial importance for the
project. The source code alone, without these project files, was
of limited value. When the contract was signed, the customer
was not aware what deliveries must be specified in the contract.

In addition to the source code, the vendor had to deliver
some kind of "technical documentation." The specification of
these terms in the contract turned out to be rather ambiguous.
The vendor delivered some documentation that just met the
wording of the contract. From a technical point of view, the
documentation was completely useless. Note that it is difficult
to specify in legal terms what a "useful technical documentation"
actually means.

Finally, the customer found out that it would not be possible
to order the extensions for this strategic project from another
vendor. Their unfair vendor had prepared its position very well
before the contract ended. Thus, the customer could not avoid
cooperation with it. For future extensions, the vendor could set
a price of its choice. It did not have to consider competing
offers from other vendors.

This case study may show an extreme situation. However, it highlights

that was why they had to switch to another vendor irrespective of how much the transfer would cost. Other cases have been reported by large organizations where the customer had enough funding to afford the financial sacrifices caused by the transition. A customer who considers outsourcing must be aware of the challenges and risks that only become apparent when the collaboration is to be ended and consider such a possibility from the onset.

11.2.2 Practical Preparations for "Day X"

To some extent, the transition problem is similar if a company wants to outsource its internal IT department. There are important differences, however, which are outlined in the following list.

■ Careful preparation of a line of defense against competitors
   The vendor is fully aware that the contract will end sooner or later because the contract reaches its term or for other reasons. The provider will use the time of the contract and invest know-how as well as creativity to forestall the actual ending of business relationships after the contract is terminated.
   Permanently employed staff might occasionally consider the possibility of being laid off. However, an outsourcer's top management prepares carefully conceived plans to guard against being kicked out years before this could actually happen. Plans at this level and of this quality are unusual when permanent employees are concerned with the possibility of losing their jobs.

■ Influence on the technical staff
   The employees of an internal department have important obligations of loyalty toward their organization; they have legal obligations due to their employment contracts. In addition to this, many employees feel morally obliged to be loyal to their organization, at least to some extent. The vendor's IT staff, on the other hand, is employed by the service provider, a legally independent organization, and is loyal to the outsourcer's organization, of course. If it comes to a conflict of loyalty between vendor and customer, they are on the side of the vendor. They will make suggestions and technical decisions that are good for the vendor, not necessarily the very best for the customer. This is particularly true if the contract comes to its end and the vendor wants to be

are finally paid by the customer (i.e., the money comes via the invoices based on the outsourcing contract).

Transition Period

If an organization decides to outsource its internal IT department, it can try a strategy that has proven successful in quite a number of cases: the management offers money to those who are willing to train the new outsourcer's staff. This, however, works only if the IT staff is employed by the customer's company.

If the customer wants to switch from one outsourcer to a competitor it cannot use this strategy; in most countries it is illegal to offer money to the employees of another company (i.e., to the vendor's employees) for disclosing internal information. Even if the information is related to the customer's projects, from a purely legal point of view it might be considered "internal." This raises the question of how the customer can transfer know-how from one vendor to another in case it wants to switch to a competitor. Any means of doing it will turn out to be difficult, especially if the vendor resists losing that customer.

These reasons support the conclusion that, in general, it is not easier to change from one external vendor to another than to outsource an internal IT department.

Planning for Divorce

Many customers do not have a clear and realistic plan of how they will end the relationship with the vendor without having to cope with overwhelming losses. At the time when the outsourcing relationship starts, the customers frequently only bear in mind the prospects of getting good software at a cheap price. They do not carefully consider the possibility of terminating the outsourcing deal. In the rare cases when customers have a realistic plan of how they can end the relationship, they do not actually follow their plan. Most contracts between customer and vendor are designed for a limited time only — i.e., the contract includes some provisions for how the cooperation can be ended. Nevertheless, this type of contractual stipulation is often enough purely theoretical. In the day-to-day reality, the cooperation seems to have unlimited validity. In many cases, the customer has to pay a high price to put an end to the relationship with the vendor.

vendor. It is as if one analyzed the terms of a marriage in which one partner relies on the idea that the marriage will last forever but the other partner uses the time to carefully prepare for the process of divorcing. It is obvious how the divorce process will end.

11.3 ISSUES OF THE POSTTERMINATION TRANSITION

A customer who wants to switch from one vendor to another will encounter a transition problem that includes:

- *The necessary transfer of know-how from the old vendor's staff to the new vendor's staff*
- *Access to technical documentation, intellectual property, source code, and other deliverables*
- *Leadership in business relationships*
- *The posttermination assistance might turn out to be inefficient because the relationship is strained and the vendor is uncooperative.*

Access to Key Staff

In the context of posttermination assistance, usually one of the most important resources is the key staff that has been working on the customer's projects. For the customer, it would be ideal if the contract allows direct access to these workers (not via the vendor's office) and perhaps even the possibility of hiring them. This request has some implications.

Disjunctive Teams

The team working for various customers must be disjunctive; the engineers should not be working for different customers. Otherwise, the customer's posttermination access to key employees is difficult. Termination of the contract would perturb other projects for clients who wish to continue doing business with the same vendor because the remaining clients would lose key workers who have been working for both projects. Hence, in the context of nondisjunctive teams, the fee for direct access to the vendor's employees will be rather high, if the provider can agree at all to this provision.

cannot benefit from the flexibility that should be a characteristic feature
of outsourcing because the disjunctive team must be kept more-or-less
busy unless the customer is willing to pay for the periods of idleness
between projects.

Subcontractors

Freelance workers or subcontractors may have an important contribution
to the buyer's projects and consequently, the posttermination assistance
conditions should stipulate that the customer assumes the subcontracts
that have been used for providing the services.

Definition of "Key Employees"

An important issue of posttermination assistance is the question "who
exactly are these key employees?" Some employees will be assigned full
time to the projects of the departing customer; for them, the decision is
easy. However, quite a number of other colleagues will have worked only
part time or for certain periods on the projects of the departing customer.
The reasons include that some specialists (e.g., software architects) are
needed only in certain phases of the project. The question is which of
these employees fall under the conditions of the posttermination clause.
One possibility is that the clause is very general and states that all
employees who had any contribution to the projects of the departing
customer are included. In this case a large number of the vendor's staff
might be affected, including some top executives who have invested a
certain fraction of their working time in the relation with the customer.
For many vendors, such a general stipulation is not acceptable. The other
extreme is a very narrow inclusion under the posttermination clause of
the engineers who worked exclusively for the departing customer. In this
case, the customer may find itself in the unacceptable situation where the
"real key staff" is not covered because they did not work full time for the
projects.

Balance of Power

A posttermination clause that allows the customer almost unlimited access
to the vendor's key employees constitutes a huge danger to the vendor's
business continuity and even to the solvency of the vendor's entire

leave the marketplace before too long. Many vendors, however, have substantial experience in offshore deals and understand the dynamics of outsourced software projects better than most of their customers do. For this reason, the author is usually suspicious of an outsourcing contract that seems overly unbalanced to the advantage of the customer. The vendor might already have a well-prepared strategy to avoid the detrimental effects of the termination.

One possibility to establish the meaning of the term "key staff" could be lists of names. This practice avoids disputes around the question "who exactly is the key staff?" Usually, however, the customer cannot assess the practical importance of the listed engineers for the project. The list may include junior programmers who only do the routine work; the brains of the project might not appear on the list. Also, the list may only include representatives, and the "real work" is done in the back office. Anyway, the vendor will do its best to remove important staff from the "dangerous" list — dangerous for the vendor's business continuity.

Another reason why the vendor would sign such a potentially dangerous clause is that the vendor has strong reasons to trust the "key staff." Perhaps they own a part of the vendor's organization, or the so-called key staff and the entrepreneur are in fact relatives. In this case the key staff will teach the customer a lesson — on early termination and other advanced topics.

Fees for the Posttermination Assistance

Posttermination assistance is not cheap. Even in the easiest (and rarest) case, where the project of the departing customer is carried through by a separate department that does not have any overlap with other departments, the vendor has to sell a part of its organization — the department that worked for the departing customer. Although the department is not "sold" in a narrow legal sense, the effect is very close to selling it; the customer has access to the employees, takes control of the subcontracts, and gets the equipment, the software, and the intellectual property. There is not much left under the control of the vendor from this department. Selling parts of its organization might not be in line with the vendor's strategic plans. For this reason, the vendor may ask for a high fee if the customer insists on using its workers in the context of posttermination assistance.

Nondisclosed Technical Documents

In many scenarios, the "key staff" is of crucial importance. However, there might also be important technical documents besides the IT know-how that the IT staff provides. The vendor can attempt to refuse disclosing crucial technical documents once the contract has ended. This way the customer cannot continue developing the projects with another vendor without support from the old provider.

Because these documents have been written by the vendor's staff, the vendor is the legal owner of the documents. The vendor might have contractual obligations to deliver some of these documents to the customer. This, however, is different from the situation where the customer is the owner of the documents from the very beginning. For many customers, this difference is not obvious. Some customers might think that if the document has been written in the course of the project and they have paid for the hours during which the document was drafted, the document is their property. However, this is not always true. The customer gets nothing else but the documents that are specified in the contract. The vendor will probably not deliver any material that might be helpful for potential competitors unless it is forced to do so.

There can be a number of reasons why the customer finally does not receive all documents that are needed to continue work with another vendor; the customer might forget to specify crucial documents in the contract, perhaps because the customer might be unaware that certain material is important. Throughout the development of the project, some new, important, unstipulated information can emerge. If the customer does not employ qualified IT staff, it might not even be aware of the existence of these additional documents.

To sum up, at the beginning of the project, when the contract is signed, the customer has to foresee all kinds of technical information that will be needed for smoothly continuing with another vendor after the contract is ended. For customers who have little experience in outsourcing and have only superficial know-how in software technology, this task might be challenging. In such cases, the customer might not receive all the important technical documentation it needs to efficiently turn to another vendor.

Source Code

If the customer wants to continue a software project with another vendor,

However, it cannot make any changes. Even the smallest corrections and adaptations, let alone major extensions, require changes in the source code. To avoid this problem, most customers demand a provision in the contract stipulating that they will receive the source code that has been developed during the project. This rider, however, can turn out to be too vague and indefinite when it comes to a judicious analysis.

> A customer ordered new software in C++. The contract provided that the C++ source code had to be delivered. The vendor's software team used a tool named "yacc," which is widely applied for developing compilers for UNIX operating systems (see Figure 11.2). This tool is a so-called code generator: it takes a specification-file (in jargon, "yacc-file") as input and produces a C++ file as output. The produced C++ file is highly cryptic and not intended for human readers. Human readers are expected to work with the initial specification only — i.e., with the yacc-file. From a technical point of view, this yacc-file is in fact the real source code. The C++ file has only the role of an intermediate technological file. However, from the legal point of view of the contract, the C++ text was considered the complete source code. For this reason only the C++ has to be delivered. The vendor delivered the C++ code (i.e., yacc's output) but not the specification (the yacc-file). Thus, the wording of the contract was observed; the customer received C++ source code. Nevertheless, the customer did not stand a chance to go on with this project without access to the yacc-file. This file was available only to the vendor. For this reason, no competitors of the vendor could bid offers for extensions.

Intellectual Property

A more subtle technique is denying the customer access to the *full* source code: the outsourcing contract may provide that the customer receives the source code that has been developed exclusively for this customer. However, it does not receive source code for general libraries and similar programs. The legitimate motivation behind this provision might be that sometimes even the vendor does not have the source code for the general libraries because it bought them from other specialized providers. Another sound technical reason is that the vendor developed libraries that are

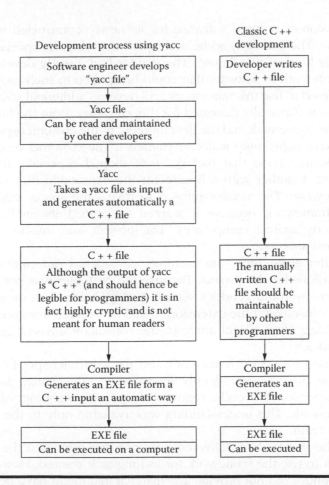

Figure 11.2   Software development process using "yacc" compared with the classical C++ development process. Using the yacc-process, it is not enough to deliver C++ source code. The new team also needs the yacc-file; otherwise, it cannot maintain the project. Notice, however, that in classical C++ development, delivering the C++ code is completely sufficient.

against access from competitors. For this reason, it is a widespread practice for the vendor not to disclose this material.

As long as the customer does not want to switch to another vendor, there are only advantages if the latter uses its own intellectual property in the customer's project. The problem appears, however, in case the

A customer ordered software for its newly constructed warehouse. The company addressed a provider who was specialized in this kind of warehouse. The vendor had already developed a framework of software that could be applied to such projects. It offered to use this framework and develop additional software that was especially designed for this customer. Both the license for the framework and the development of the customer-specific software constituted major investments. The customer received the source code that had been developed especially for its project, together with a license for the executable files of the framework. The vendor refused to reveal the source code of the framework because it wanted to protect its intellectual property against competitors. The project was finished with modest success.

After some time, the customer considered ordering some extensions for the project. Because the customer was not fully content with the vendor's service quality, it asked an independent consultant if the extensions could be ordered from another provider. After careful analysis, the consultant advised against this idea.

The proprietary framework and the customer-specific part of the project were deeply interwoven. Any change in the customer-specific code requires deep understanding of the framework. This understanding was available only to the vendor's team.

The vendor had delivered a license that permitted the customer to use the framework for as long as it wanted. However, the vendor did not provide any material that might have helped other software developers to use the framework and make changes to the customer's source code.

As if that was not enough, it became obvious that in time new hardware and new versions of operating systems would become available and consequently, adapting the vendor's framework to these new platforms would definitely require access to the framework's source code, which was available only to the owner of the framework — i.e., the vendor.

Finally, the customer had no choice but to either to go on with this vendor or to switch to another vendor and throw

AU7017_book copy.fm Page 267 Monday, March 27, 2006 4:23 PM

access to these materials. Even though the customer usually gets the rights to use the copyrighted material as long as it wants, this license is valid only for the current version. It might be necessary to change the framework or to adapt it to new versions of operating systems.

If the customer switches to another vendor, the old vendor is usually not obliged to deliver new versions of the library. The vendor is not even obliged to maintain the library at all anymore. A new vendor, on the other hand, has no access to the intellectual property of the old vendor. For this reason, the new vendor cannot maintain the library either.

Obfuscated Source Code

Even if the full source code is delivered, it is not at all certain that another vendor can continue developing the project because source code and documentation can be obfuscated. It is difficult to make specifications in the contract to forestall cloudy technical documentation and unclear source code.

> Technical documentation is something like a math book; a fictitious professor has a contract to write a book, say, on analysis. If the professor writing the math book does not want the readers to understand it, the readers will definitely not understand anything — without the professor breaking any provision of the contract. It might even come as a challenge to merely establish whether the formulas in the math book will help solve a certain problem at hand. Because this requires that someone understand the math book in depth by resorting to high skills as well as much time and effort, simply glancing through the book is definitely not enough.

Technical documentation is somewhat similar. Even if the vendor provides full source code and technical documentation according to the provisions of a contract, it is anything but certain that another vendor can cover the costs of continuing the project. The author has personally seen only very few software projects where a completely new team could cost-efficiently continue the project without the active support and the goodwill of the team that developed the project. The new team might be able to make small corrections or very limited changes. However, they will face serious difficulties when it comes to developing major new features. This

new colleagues in the project, let alone if they want to block out the new staff, as might be the case if a competitor wants to continue the project.

As a rule of thumb, it can be said that it takes more time to understand unclear written source code than to develop the same functionality from scratch. In most projects, this is a prohibitive barrier against competitors.

> A small vendor received an order from an attractive customer. The contract specified that source code had to be delivered. The delivered project was all right — i.e., it met the specified requirements at an acceptable quality. Closer investigation, however, showed that the source code was very unclear. There were even suspicions that the source code had been deliberately disguised. As a result, it was completely impossible for other vendors to continue the project.
>
> This raises the question of how the vendor was at all able to deliver a project of acceptable quality if the source code was a mess. Using informal channels of communication, the customer found out that the vendor's team had in fact a good (yet secret) version of the source code. However, they used a tool that deliberately obfuscated the source code — e.g., by deleting comments and changing names of variables that were crucial for understanding the program.

The Vendor Does Not Want to Continue

In most cases the outsourcing relationship is a profitable business for the vendor, and it is only natural for the provider to wish to continue the relationship. There are exceptions, however. In some cases, the vendor changes its policy and is not interested in the cooperation anymore.

> A small company's field of activity was providing consultation for transportation companies. Although software was not its main business, it had a small internal software department that was rather inefficient and poorly qualified in modern software technology. Superficial analysis of the economic situation showed that the software department had only a very limited contribution to the profits. To management, it seemed that this software department was more a kind of hobby than a serious source of income and they wanted to "dispose of this overval-

special training to continue the work of the internal team. Therefore, the management offered money to those who were willing to train the outsourcer's staff. Because the software engineers were rather disappointed by the unsatisfactory professional situation, they did not defend their jobs very vehemently; they took the money and did what they were asked to do. The shift of know-how to the vendor's team during the transition period went rather smoothly, and the outsourcing relationship started in a very promising way. After some time, however, the vendor shifted the focus of its business and lost interest in maintaining the rather specialized know-how about consultation of transporting companies. The rather small customer did not contribute much to the income of the vendor's large organization anyway, and so the provider dramatically decreased the quality of its services. The vendor's top management had already decided that they did not want to go on with this customer and that if the customer wanted to cancel the contract the vendor would not object.

It was only then that the customer's top management became aware that the software was of crucial importance to their business. The accounting numbers alone suggested only a marginal contribution to the results. However, other departments used the software as well, and for these other departments the software constituted a competitive advantage — i.e., the software was involved in crucial business processes that were important for the customer's success. This fact was not obvious from the financial data, and that was why the previous, superficial analysis had not revealed this relationship. The management had not been aware of the strategic importance of this rather small software department and saw only the costs of a rather inefficient team.

Unfortunately, the customer could not easily move the software business back in house. This kind of software requires detailed knowledge about mathematical transportation algorithms and the interaction of the software with the specific transport consulting business. This know-how had been lost for the company when the software production was outsourced. As a consequence, the customer experienced serious trouble

Other cases where the vendor does not want to continue are reported in the context of small offshore companies. In these companies, the owner is at the same time the general manager and the software lead — i.e., a one-person company. If the company has only a few projects, this person is doing most of the work alone. When the company has many orders, the individual may cooperate with some freelance software developers — classmates from a university, for example.

> A talented young software engineer in Russia started his own company. He found a partner in France from whom he obtained a constant ingress of orders for his one-person company. After a while, the Russian software developer received an attractive offer to go to the United States. However, the American head-hunter requested that he start working in the United States immediately. The Russian software developer did not finish the project that was in progress but left to go to the United States. Of course, the French customer did not pay for this last project. Nonetheless, this small amount of money was not important in comparison to the attractive new offer. For the French customer, however, the situation was rather frustrating because he had relied on the results from the project.

Companies of this kind can be attractive partners for small customers who have a limited volume of orders because such small companies are frequently cheaper than the larger providers. But even though the central person of the company may have rather good technical skills, such companies are lacking in stability and continuity. This means that there is a good chance that the entrepreneur will receive a more attractive offer from other offshore or onshore companies. In this case, the customer can consider itself lucky if the current project is completed and a total failure is avoided.

Leadership and Control

Involving an outsourcer has a number of strategic consequences on the organization that are particularly applicable if the entire IT department is outsourced to a single vendor that is an economically and legally independent organization.

The vendor might try to expand its influence to the customer's business relationships, and in extreme circumstances these relationships will evolve directly between the vendor and the customer's business partners and not between the customer and its partners as was the case before.

> An organization maintained a medical database. It obtained the raw data for its database from a scientific institute. Thus, the relationship was between the owner of the database and the scientific institute. The organization decided to outsource its software from an external provider. Software technology played only a small role in the relationship between the owner of the database (i.e., the customer) and the scientific institute; nevertheless, data formats needed to be discussed, and some other technical decisions were necessary as well. The vendor discussed these topics directly with the scientific institute. In time, the outsourcer started taking more and more of the responsibility for this relationship, becoming involved in discussing not only data formats but also schedules, deadlines, and other aspects. This process of growing responsibility continued for a while. In the end, the outsourcer was in fact the partner of the scientific institute, which resulted in all communication between the customer (the provider of the database) and the scientific institute passing the desk of the vendor.

This way, the outsourcer can become a surrogate for the customer in the customer's business relations; in fact, the vendor is maintaining those relationships. The customer's management plays only a walk-on part, receiving no more than copies of the e-mails. The reason behind the outsourcer's strategy is that the relationship with the customer's business partners might become a source for new orders. In addition, it will be extremely difficult for the customer to switch to another provider once the contract has ended. This brings the outsourcer into a position where it can improve its margins once it is well established and integrated in the customer's business processes.

Technical Decisions

The vendor will take an important role not only in business relations that

department is in house, this translation is the duty of internal IT managers. If the IT business is outsourced, this trusted organization is usually the vendor. The outsourcer, however, is a legally independent organization with its own top management and its own balance sheet. It has interests of its own that are not necessarily identical to the interests of the customer. Some of the customer's decisions might be more advantageous than other options for the vendor. For this reason, the suggestions might be biased and might only work to the advantage of the vendor — not necessarily optimizing the advantage of the customer.

The outsourcer has a lot of influence on the customer's decision. Even though a serious vendor will mention the pros and cons of a certain option, the vendor is free to decide to what extent it emphasizes the various chances and risks. Note that an experienced software engineer is able to give apparently plausible reasons for any kind of technical decision. No matter how the decision looks, it is always possible to give some explanations that sound reasonable, just as an experienced banker can explain the advantages of any given investment to a customer.

In most cases, the customer's management will agree to the decision suggested by the service provider and will sign the corresponding documents. Usually, this decision had been prepared in the vendor's office well in advance in a closed meeting in which the customer did not participate.

Risks of the Transition Period

Even under the most fortunate conditions, it is anything but certain that the transition phase will be smooth — if it is successful at all. The risks include:

- Early termination of the contract frequently occurs in a situation where the relationship is heavily strained or even damaged. The customer might be deeply dissatisfied with the vendor. The vendor is usually not much happier, and some providers have hard feelings about early termination. Under these tense circumstances, the vendor is unlikely to help the customer more than it is obligated to do according the contract's most narrow interpretation.
- Many vendors prefer to concentrate their resources on serving their continuing customers instead of their departing customers. The

AU7017_book copy.fm Page 273 Monday, March 27, 2006 4:23 PM

- The outsourcer's organization might be in a doubtful position. Even if the provider is not (yet) insolvent, it is not at all certain that the offshore vendor is still maintaining regular business activity. Anyway, the fact that the customer decides for the decisive step of early termination of the contract indicates that something might be going wrong with that vendor. Perhaps there is nobody left to provide posttermination assistance.

INDEX